The **Death** of the
American Death Penalty

The **Death** of the American Death Penalty

STATES <u>STILL</u> LEADING THE WAY

Larry W. Koch / Colin Wark / John F. Galliher

NORTHEASTERN UNIVERSITY PRESS Boston

NORTHEASTERN UNIVERSITY PRESS

An imprint of University Press of New England

www.upne.com

© 2012 Larry W. Koch, Colin Wark, and John F. Galliher

All rights reserved

Manufactured in the United States of America

Designed by Richard Hendel

Typeset in Scala and Fedra types by Tseng Information Systems, Inc.

University Press of New England is a member of the
Green Press Initiative. The paper used in this book meets
their minimum requirement for recycled paper.

For permission to reproduce any of the material in this book,
contact Permissions, University Press of New England, One Court Street,
Suite 250, Lebanon NH 03766; or visit www.upne.com

Library of Congress Cataloging-in-Publication Data

Koch, Larry Wayne, 1946–

The death of the American death penalty: states still leading the way
Larry W. Koch, Colin Wark, John F. Galliher.

    p. cm.

Includes bibliographical references and index.

ISBN 978-1-55553-780-7 (cloth: alk. paper) — ISBN 978-1-55553-781-4 (pbk.: alk.
paper) — ISBN 978-1-55553-782-1 (ebook)

1. Capital punishment — United States — States. I. Wark, Colin. II. Galliher,
John F. III. Title.

KF9227.C2K63 2012

364.660973 — dc23

5 4 3 2 1

To Professor David Protess

Contents

Introduction

A decade beyond the midpoint of the twentieth century, the death penalty appeared headed for the dustbins of history in Western Europe and North America. In 1981 France, under President Mitterrand, became the last European country to abolish the death penalty. The French last executed someone in 1977.[1] By 2011 European aversion to the death penalty had grown so strong that Britain and Germany banned the shipment of sodium thiopental to the United States. Both countries are urging the European Union to also forbid the exportation of the lethal injection drug.[2] Canada abolished its death penalty in 1976. Executions in the United States reflected the same tendency. Between 1930 and 1967, 3,859 executions took place in the United States. By the last decade of that period, the annual rate of execution had dropped to 31. Between 9 June 1967 and 17 January 1977, no executions occurred in the United States.[3] On 9 June 1972, the us Supreme Court ruled in Furman v. Georgia, a five-to-four decision, that all current federal and state death penalty statutes constituted "cruel and unusual punishment" and thus were unconstitutional.[4]

The conviction that the death penalty was no longer a legal or constitutionally allowable punishment in the United States was short-lived. By the end of the 1980s, thirty-eight states had enacted new statutes that met constitutionally acceptable guidelines specified by the us Supreme Court in 1976 in Gregg v. Georgia,[5] Jurek v. Texas,[6] and Proffitt v. Florida.[7] The populations on death rows across the United States expanded, and executions commenced again. Polls suggested that over 70 percent of the American public supported the death penalty.[8]

These international and national circumstances present puzzles concerning the persistence of the death penalty in the United States. Why does the United States continue using a punitive action that other Western democracies have rejected? And why do some us states proscribe the death penalty while others embrace it? The second question motivated us to undertake a fifteen-year research project that resulted in the 2002 publication of *America without the Death Penalty: States Leading the Way.* That book reviewed the social and legal histories of nine states (Michigan, Wisconsin, Maine, Minnesota, North Dakota, Alaska, Hawaii, Iowa, and West Virginia) that had eliminated their death statutes by legislative

U.S. DEATH ROW POPULATION BY YEAR, 1980–2010

Year	Population	Year	Population	Year	Population
1980	691	1991	2,482	2001	3,581
1981	856	1992	2,575	2002	3,557
1982	1,050	1993	2,716	2003	3,374
1983	1,209	1994	2,890	2004	3,315
1984	1,405	1995	3,054	2005	3,254
1985	1,591	1996	3,219	2006	3,228
1986	1,781	1997	3,335	2007	3,215
1987	1,984	1998	3,452	2008	3,207
1988	2,124	1999	3,527	2009	3,261
1989	2,250	2000	3,593	2010	3,242
1990	2,356				

Source: "Size of Death Row by Year (1968–present)," Death Penalty Information Center, 2011, www.deathpenaltyinfo.org/death-row-inmates-state-and-size-death-row-year.

action. Rhode Island, Vermont, and Massachusetts were important abolition states at that time, but they received less attention in our original analysis because their death penalty statutes were negated by nonlegislative processes. The significant post-*Furman* contributions to the US death penalty debate made by the people of Washington, D.C., moved us to treat the District of Columbia as a state. Thus, our previous book treated Washington, D.C., as a core abolition state.

Since the publication of *America without the Death Penalty*, significant changes have occurred in local and national politics. Much of that change—characterized by the election of George W. Bush to the presidency in 2000 and 2004—suggested that cultural sentiments in favor of the death penalty and conservative state institutions would accelerate the use of capital punishment.

With substantial numbers of death row inmates reaching the end of the appeal process, a return to pre-1960 execution levels was a real possibility. Additionally, with growing numbers of local conservative legislators, it seemed that states without capital punishment might reestablish their death statutes. Yet as we enter the second decade of the twenty-first century, the number of US executions is declining, and more and more states are seriously questioning the utility of capital punishment.

Chapter 1 examines recent death penalty debates in the traditional

Year	Executions	Year	Executions	Year	Executions
1976	0	1988	11	2000	85
1977	1	1989	16	2001	66
1978	0	1990	23	2002	71
1979	2	1991	14	2003	65
1980	0	1992	31	2004	59
1981	1	1993	38	2005	60
1982	2	1994	31	2006	53
1983	5	1995	56	2007	42
1984	21	1996	45	2008	37
1985	18	1997	74	2009	52
1986	18	1998	68	2010	46
1987	25	1999	98	2011	37

Source: "Executions by year since 1976," Death Penalty Information Center, 29 September 2011, www.deathpenaltyinfo.org/executions-year.

Note: 2011 executions as of 29 September.

abolition states reviewed in *America without the Death Penalty*. For the most part, however, this book will discuss past and current advances and defeats experienced by death penalty abolitionists outside these states. Chapter 2 reviews the problems confronted by New York legislators as they attempted to draft a bias free, or fair death bill. Ultimately, capital punishment was abolished in that state. Chapter 3 discusses the 2007 abolition of the death penalty in New Jersey. Chapter 4 considers the 2009 abolition in New Mexico. Chapter 5 covers the 2011 abolition of capital punishment in Illinois. These states became the first to legislatively abolish capital punishment after the *Furman* decision in 1972. Chapter 6 examines post-*Furman* death penalty struggles in Kansas. Chapters 7 and 8 take a historical view of abolitionist efforts that fell just short of success. Chapter 9 looks at those states that have retained their death statutes but seldom execute anyone. Chapter 10 goes to the stronghold of the death penalty, the US South. There we find both strong resistance to change and significant potential for abolition. Chapter 11 attempts to make theoretical sense of these data and offer practical information for those actively involved in attempts to abolish the death penalty. As in our earlier book, we used legislative floor debates and

xi

committee hearings, newspaper reports of the various legal actions, and interviews with those involved on all sides of the debate.

ACKNOWLEDGMENTS

Thanks are due to Hugo Adam Bedau, Michael Radelet, James M. Galliher, Fr. Fred Thayer, James Acker, Victor Streib, Richard Dieter, Herbert Haines, Lorry Post, Gail Chasey, Viki Elkey, Raymond Lesniak, James Galliher, Celeste Fitzgerald, Abraham J. Bonowitz, Tim Lydon, and Allen Sanchez for their assistance with various phases of this research. We also gratefully acknowledge the use of sections of two previously published articles. In chapter 2 we used much of an article originally written by James and John Galliher that appeared in the *Journal of Criminal Law and Criminology* in 2002. In chapter 6 much of the material we used was from another article by the Gallihers, published by *Social Problems* in 1997.

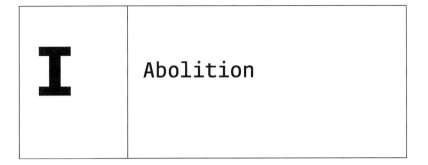

I Abolition

1

Death Penalty Debates in Traditional Abolitionist Jurisdictions

Efforts to reinstate capital punishment in traditional abolition jurisdictions is an ongoing legislative phenomenon. A successful citizens' advisory petition in Wisconsin to reinstate the death penalty and the tendency of federal prosecutors appointed by President George W. Bush to seek death sentences in abolition states presented the greatest threat to abolition in traditional anti–death penalty states during the first decade of the twenty-first century.

MICHIGAN

Records show that a relatively small number of official executions took place in Michigan before 1847, when the state abolished the death penalty. Thus, Michigan abolitionists did not confront strong legal and cultural traditions supportive of executions. Popular support for capital punishment was also eroded in the mid-nineteenth century by at least two problematic executions. Many early Michigan settlers also brought with them an aversion for the death penalty that was first cultivated in Europe and later reinforced in New York. Finally, in the 1800s the state's minority groups (African Americans and Native Americans) were not large enough to be viewed as a threat.

It is considerably more difficult to explain the maintenance of death penalty abolition in urban, demographically diverse, industrial and post-industrial Michigan in the twentieth and twenty-first centuries. The nature of the legal proscription against executions and the state's cultural identity are key ingredients. First, in 1962 death penalty abolition became part of the Michigan Constitution. Thus, it requires a constitutional amendment to reinstate the punishment, which can only become law after a majority popular vote and a two-thirds super majority vote in both houses of the legislature—and winning such popular and legislative support for the death penalty is next to impossible in Michigan.

Second, death penalty abolition is a core component of Michigan's

3

cultural identity. The state's newspapers consistently remind residents of their moral leadership and, using numerous Southern examples, the perils of regressive public policy. Roman Catholic clergy in Michigan often supported executions during the 1940s and 1950s. However, after Roe v. Wade in 1973, the church developed the pro-life position as a "seamless garment" and since then has never advocated executions. The rare legislative supporters of the death penalty are marginalized in the press.[1]

Little changed as Michigan moved into the twenty-first century. Records show that there were five legislative efforts to resurrect Michigan's death penalty over the past decade. In 1999 nearly identical joint resolutions were introduced in the House (HJR H) and Senate (SJR F)[2] by marginalized politicians. Although passage of HJR H was somewhat questionable, the Republican Senate majority leader predicted SJR F would pass by the necessary two-thirds margin required to amend the Michigan Constitution.[3] A *Detroit Free Press* article used the term "nastiness" to describe the interactions that occurred between "an unmistakably pro–death penalty House committee" and those giving testimony during the public hearing on HJR H.[4] If interactions were problematic at the House hearing, they were horrendous at the first of two Senate committee hearings on SJR F. There the bill's spokesperson accused Sister Helen Prejean of "'insulting' Michigan voters by opposing a voter referendum."[5] Another *Detroit Free Press* article reported that 75 percent of those present opposed putting the death penalty to a popular vote, while a *Michigan Citizen* article reported that 500 people had gathered in the Oakland County Commission chambers to tell Republican members of the Senate Judiciary Committee to end their effort to put the death penalty reinstatement on the November 2000 ballot.[6] Nevertheless, both resolutions were voted out of committee. Following a heated and often incoherent floor debate, the House voted on HJR H, which received fewer than half the votes needed for passage.[7]

On 19 February 2004, days after the killing of two Detroit police officers, the prime sponsor of the 1999 House effort introduced HJR W, legislation to amend the Michigan Constitution to allow the death penalty. The bill cleared committee on a six-to-four vote, but it fell eighteen votes short in the full House (fifty-five in favor, fifty-two opposed) of the two-thirds margin necessary. However, the 2004 death penalty debate did not end in the House. The family of one of the slain officers continued trying to gather the 317,000 signatures necessary to put death penalty reinstatement on the November ballot. But the eventual outcome was indicated by a sign at the location of the initiative petition's kickoff, a Knights of Columbus hall in suburban Detroit: 'The Knights of Columbus does not support abortion or the death penalty."[8] The petitioners were unable to procure the necessary number of signatures by the 25 July 2004 deadline.

Following the murder of two teenagers and a four-month-old baby, who was hit by a bullet while he slept, the president of the Detroit City Council concluded that Michigan needed the death penalty for those convicted of killing children. A *Detroit Free Press* editorial was quick to respond, noting that capital punishment was "a morally repugnant act the state of Michigan has resisted for more than a century," is racially and economically unfair, results in the execution of innocent persons, and would further cheapen life. The president's outburst, according to the editorial, "reflects a stunning lack of understanding of the practical implications of capital punishment, and the trend away from eye-for-an-eye justice that is sweeping other states."[9] So ended Michigan's death penalty debate for the first decade of the twenty-first century.

WISCONSIN

In 1853 Wisconsin became the second state to abolish the death penalty. Circumstances that led to abolition in Wisconsin were somewhat similar to those in Michigan. According to existing evidence, legal executions in Wisconsin were rare. The botched execution of John Mc-Caffary in 1850 provided the triggering event for the demise of capital punishment.

Republican State Senator Alan Lasee, author of numerous death penalty reinstatement bills, grew increasingly optimistic about the passage of a bill when the 1991 arrest of the serial killer Jeffrey Dahmer sparked nearly two decades of death penalty debate in Wisconsin. As was the case in Michigan, however, newspapers in Wisconsin did not support the return of capital punishment. In the words of Senator Lasee: "The media always portrays sympathy and empathy towards death row inmates and tries to scare the public into believing that an innocent individual may be put to death. To the contrary, you never hear about the victim that this murderer has raped, tortured, and killed."[10] On 27 April 2006 the Assembly Committee on Criminal Justice and Homeland Security held a public hearing on SJR 5, Senator Lasee's latest effort to seek an advisory referendum on the death penalty. Testimony at the hearings overwhelmingly opposed the referendum. Even after Lasee "reminded speakers that the referendum would not be binding, committee members were still flooded by hours of opposing testimony."[11] The representatives of churches and other religious organizations and human rights groups opposed to the death penalty dominated the hearing. Lasee told witnesses that the real issue was not the death penalty but democracy: "Why not allow the citizens of the state to have a say in this very important issue?"[12]

Lasee's moment came on 7 March 2006 when the Senate, by a twenty to thirteen vote, passed his referendum bill. On 4 May the Assembly voted forty-seven to forty-five in favor of SJR 5. The wording on the Senate-passed bill, however, was amended. The Assembly version asked the voters if they supported capital punishment for first-degree murder when a conviction was supported by specified physical evidence. Twelve days later, on 16 May, the Senate approved the Assembly's amended version, eighteen to fifteen.[13] As expected, the votes in both chambers followed party lines closely, with only two Republicans voting no and one Democrat voting yes. The following November, the general election ballot asked Wisconsin voters if they favored reestablishing the death penalty for first-degree murder when the conviction was supported by DNA evidence.[14] On 7 November 2006, Wisconsin voters approved reestablishing the death penalty by 55 to 45 percent.[15] The bill's author proclaimed: "The citizens have spoken very clearly, and the solid support indicates that our citizens are ready to reinstate the death penalty."[16]

With the news that SJR 5 had passed came reports that Republicans no longer controlled both legislative state houses. Democrats took control of the Senate, the Republican majority in the Assembly was reduced to five seats, and Jim Doyle, a Democrat strongly opposed to the death penalty, was reelected governor. Senator Lasee realized that there was no chance of passing a death penalty bill in the near future.[17] Indeed, his 2007 death bill (Senate Bill 115) restored a long anti–death penalty tradition in the Wisconsin State Legislature when it died in committee.

MAINE

Maine abolished its death penalty in 1876, reinstated it in 1883, and abolished it again in 1887. Although only nine people were executed after Maine achieved statehood in 1820, racial bias, wrongful convictions, and the brutality of those hangings were the triggering events for the initial abolition and subsequent reabolition of the state's death penalty. In the 1970s, Republican Representative Stanley "Tuffy" Laffin began to sponsor reinstatement bills, none of which succeeded. Maine's

political, religious, and media leaders agreed that the death penalty is racist, inhumane, and associated with the Deep South, characterizations often reflected in Maine's history of executions.[18]

Over the last two decades, six death penalty bills have been introduced in Maine's Legislature (in 1991, 1993, 1997, 1999, 2001, and 2005).

Twenty people testified before the Committee on the Judiciary considering the 1991 senate death bill (SB 1238). Only four of them—the bill's two sponsors, a constituent of one of the sponsors who appeared by request, and a Baptist minister—favored reinstatement. Testifying against the bill was the Lewiston police chief, the son of Sam Shepard, attorneys, and representatives of Amnesty International, the National Lawyers Guild, and Mainers against the Death Penalty, among others. The Committee on the Judiciary voted unanimously that the bill "ought not to pass."[19] The 1993 bill (LD 42) had a similar welcome. Of the sixteen people testifying, only one (the bill's sponsor) spoke in favor of the legislation. Those testifying against reinstatement were much like those who had appeared two years earlier. The committee responded with a ten to one vote that the bill "ought not to pass."[20] Evidence suggests that support in the Legislature and among community organizations has changed little since Representative Laffin's time.

The 1997 public hearing was relatively balanced, with eleven witnesses in favor of and thirteen opposed to reinstatement. The relative increase in support came from four of the bill's cosponsors and five citizens testifying before the committee. Pro–death penalty forces had not gained institutional support. Judiciary records on LD 1524 imply that the cost of the death penalty concerned legislators. In addition to an official estimate of the cost of implementing capital punishment in Maine, the records included a *Rocky Mountain News* article discussing the high annual cost ($1.8 million for the 1994–95 fiscal year) of Colorado's death penalty,[21] a *Reno Gazette-Journal* article discussing the hundreds of thousands of dollars necessary to prosecute capital cases,[22] and the abstracts of nine studies that identified the costs or projected costs of executions in various states. Committee members voted eleven to two against LD 1524.[23]

Records of people testifying in favor of the 1999 death bill returned to pre-1997 ratios, with six favoring the bill—four of whom were its sponsors—and twenty-five in opposition. As was the case with earlier bills, the committee voted that this one "ought not to pass."[24] In that session, the state's House of Representatives voted 103 to 44 to accept the committee's "ought not to pass" recommendation.[25]

The 2001 House bill, which limited those to be executed to people convicted of the first-degree murder of children, met the same fate, with the House voting 111 to 29 to accept the "ought not to pass" recommendation.[26] The extensive fiscal notes that accompanied the 2005 bill (LD 1501) to the Committee on the Judiciary facilitated its demise. A death row unit would cost the state $2,400,000 to construct and approximately $750,000 annually to operate. This was in addition to "significant costs" related to the employment of court-appointed attorneys, fees for expert witnesses, and other expenses associated with "complex trial activity."[27] Maine's death penalty debate was put on hold. Even the charging of a man and woman with the murder of one woman and the attempted murder of a second woman in Lincoln County did not trigger reinstatement legislation.[28]

MINNESOTA

Minnesota abolished capital punishment in 1911, after a history of executions that was considerably more complex than in each of the states examined above. Between 1680 and 1911, sixty-six executions occurred in Minnesota, including the mass execution of thirty-eight Santee Sioux by federal authorities on December 26, 1862. To gain the political and institutional support necessary to end executions in the state, advocates of abolishing the death penalty had to wait until Native Americans ceased to be a political, economic, or social issue in Minnesota. The triggering event occurred in 1906, when a man being hanged for the murder of a mother and child met a gruesome end. The convicted prisoner's weight caused the rope to stretch so that his toes touched the ground, and it took fifteen minutes for him to die of strangulation. Reporters defied laws prohibiting the publication of executions' details, and accounts of the execution became public knowledge. The governor stated that he would resign rather than preside over another execution. After two unsuccessful tries, the death penalty was abolished. Journalists credited a speech by Republican Representative George McKenzie, in which he referred to capital punishment as vengeance and judicial murder, for moving House members to vote ninety-five to nineteen in favor of abolishing the death penalty. Efforts to reinstate capital punishment were made in 1913, 1915, and 1919. The 1913 House bill was twice defeated by a floor vote. The 1915 and 1919 bills were not released from committee. In 1920, a mob in Duluth lynched three black men accused of raping a young white female. Some claimed that without the death penalty, lynching could not be controlled. The recently elected governor did not agree and called out the state's National Guard to restore order and arrest those involved in the lynching.

Death bills have been introduced in the four legislative sessions between 1997 and 2004, with the most significant effort occurring in 2004 with the introduction of House (HF 1602) and Senate (SF 1860) bills. Republican Governor Tim Pawlenty asked the state Legislature to reinstate the death penalty for the worst offenders, including "those with multiple victims, those involving sexual assault or those considered 'heinous, atrocious, or cruel.'"[29] His idea was to ask the Legislature to endorse putting the issue before the voters in the form of a constitutional amendment.[30] The House Judiciary Committee and the Senate Crime Prevention and Public Safety Committee held the first public hearings on reinstating the death penalty since 1989. The bill's author pegged the cost of an execution at $3.7 million.[31] The Senate committee rejected the referendum bill by an eight-to-two margin, and the House Judiciary Committee chair reported that his committee would not hold additional hearings or vote on the death bill. The bill was effectively dead.[32]

The Senate hearing differed little from the House hearing. Witnesses in the Senate hearing who opposed reinstatement included "parents of . . . murder victims, an exonerated death row inmate, a prosecutor and religious leaders headlined by Archbishop Harry Flynn of the Archdiocese of St. Paul and Minneapolis." Archbishop Flynn "stressed his Church's consistently pro-life message that 'every single life is sacred from conception to natural death.'"[33] Senator Mady Reiter, sponsor of the death bill and a Roman Catholic, attempted to use her catechism to support executions: "Traditional teaching of the church does not preclude recourse to the death penalty. . . . We've got to get rid of these predators among us."[34] She admitted that the cost of an execution was $2.3 to $3.2 million, 50 percent higher than life in prison without the possibility of parole. The Senate Crime Prevention and Public Safety Committee voted eight to two against a referendum on the death penalty. Two Republicans voted with the majority.[35] Minnesota's death penalty debate has been on hold since that time.

NORTH DAKOTA

North Dakota abolished capital punishment in 1915, during the Progressive Era. Sixteen people were lynched in the area now known as North Dakota between 1882 and 1930, but only eight legal executions occurred there, with the last occurring in 1894. Death penalty abolition was facilitated by a small and homogeneous agrarian population, with an extremely low percentage of nonwhites and a homicide rate considerably lower than the national average. Thus, people in North Dakota felt that if an execution were to be held in the state, the unlucky party would be "one of us."

The North Dakota Legislative Assembly has not considered a death bill since 1995, when SB 2097 failed in the Senate on a vote of fourteen to thirty-three and was never considered in the House.[36] The 2003 kidnapping and murder of a University of North Dakota student and the conviction and sentencing of the offender, Alfonso Rodriguez Jr., generated some discussion about reestablishing North Dakota's death statute. Rodriguez was tried in federal court in Fargo and sentenced to death by a North Dakota federal jury for his offenses in 2006. The state's attorney general, Wayne Stenehjem, reasoned that the Rodriguez case in conjunction with the recent murder of a Valley City State University student might increase popular support for the death penalty. North Dakota's governor expressed support in the press for reestablishing capital punishment.[37] His statements might be taken to mean that members of North Dakota's political elite were poised to seriously consider restoring the death penalty. However, legislative records and a review of articles from the *Bismarck Tribune* suggest that the death penalty was, once again, dead in North Dakota. In an *Associated Press* article, Stenehjem raised questions of the cost and consequences of capital punishment. Death penalty cases face long appellate reviews, often going to the US Supreme Court. The Legislative Assembly could spend a significant amount of time and money "on something that might not make a lot of sense for the state."[38]

HAWAII

Death penalty abolition is the easiest to understand in Hawaii and Alaska. In the former state, capital punishment played a key role in maintaining the colonial economic and political power of white planters between 1826 and 1947. Not surprisingly, only West Virginia experienced a higher number of pre-abolition executions: Hawaii had eighty-two, with the last occurring in 1944. The planters believed that the workers had to be controlled. Recipients of that control varied over time, beginning with Hawaiian natives, who were succeeded in turn by Chinese, Japanese, Filipinos, and African Americans. With the emergence of universal suffrage toward the midpoint of the twentieth century, these groups received access to the ballot. In 1957, two years before Hawaii became a state, its citizens abolished capital punishment.[39]

During the first decade of the twenty-first century, Hawaiian law-makers have introduced eight reinstatement bills. Although the number of these bills suggests that abolition was vulnerable, nothing is further from the truth. None of the bills were formally considered by the relevant committee.[40] A search of the *Honolulu Star-Advertiser* identified no major discussions of reinstatement efforts. In 2003, a state senator called for the reinstatement of capital punishment for those who kill children. However, this proposal was greeted with widespread opposition and got nowhere. The racist history of Hawaiian executions and the potential cost of capital punishment are clear to legislators and the voters,[41] many of whom are members of minority groups negatively affected by Hawaii's death penalty history.

Consistent with that history, the potential application of federal death statutes has met with resistance in the state Legislature and the popular press. House Resolution 52 and House Concurrent Resolution 49, introduced in the 2000 Legislature by seven legislators, asked "members of Hawaii's [federal] congressional delegation to seek the amendment of federal capital punishment laws to exempt Hawaii and the other states that have abolished the death penalty from the coverage of those laws."[42] On 2 November 2003, the *Honolulu Star-Bulletin* published an editorial titled "Opposition to Justice Department: Hawaii Should Not Be an Accomplice." And on 12 August 2005, the *Honolulu Star-Advertiser* published a similar editorial, "Death Penalty Not Welcome in Hawaii." In summary, barring a dramatic increase in extremely violent crimes, death penalty abolition is safe in Hawaii.

ALASKA

Under us law, the death penalty was used in Alaska only twelve times between 1911 and 1957. Yet three of those executed were Native Alaskans, and two were African Americans. Many Alaskans recall that white Alaskans typically received a prison sentence, rather than execution, for murder. Native Alaskans led a quasicolonial existence under Russian rule. After the United States gained political control of the territory in 1867, both white and Native Alaskans viewed federal criminal sanctions as colonial law and, by definition, overly harsh. Increasing access to the ballot and a strong resentment of colonial rule among white Alaskans facilitated the abolition of capital punishment in 1957, two years before statehood.

The first death penalty reinstatement bill that received a degree of legislative support was Senate Bill 60 (sb 60), introduced in the 1997–

98 Legislature. That bill sought to place a nonbinding advisory death penalty referendum on the November 1998 general election ballot. Death penalty proponents reasoned that it would be difficult for opponents to go against a positive vote of the electorate. Hearings were held by the Senate Judiciary Committee and the Senate Finance Committee before the vote. The testimony was strongly opposed to passage, mentioning morality, racial and ethnic bias, the chance of executing innocent people, and cost. Nonetheless, the Senate passed SB 60, thirteen to six.[43]

The House Judiciary Committee also held hearings on SB 60. As was the case in the Senate, testimony was strongly opposed to reinstatement of the death penalty. The House committee amended the proposed referendum text so that it would inform voters that each execution would cost the state $4,065,000, while a life sentence without the possibility of parole would cost $1,700,000.[44] The bill was forwarded to the House Finance Committee, where yet another public hearing was held with witnesses who derided the idea of reestablishing the death penalty. Sister Helen Prejean, the author of *Dead Men Walking*, was among those who testified.[45] The members of that committee voted to "hold [the bill] for further consideration," thereby killing it. An attempt to forcibly remove the bill from that committee by the whole House action failed, thirty votes against to one in favor.[46]

House Speaker Mitch Chenault, the cosponsor of a 2009 death bill (HB 9), stated that he would have been surprised if the Legislature reestablished capital punishment that year. The speaker simply wanted to restart the debate and move on from there.[47] And start it he did. Three public hearings were held. Most of the testimony pointed to the penalty's lack of deterrence; moral issues; racial, ethnic, and class bias in executions; the potential of executing innocent persons; and the cost of capital punishment.[48] Chenault did nothing to lessen fears of racial bias when he met with members of Juneau's Native Alaskan community. Freda Westman, President of the Alaska Native Sisterhood Glacier Valley Camp 70, referred to Chenault's lack of knowledge about discrimination in the criminal justice system as "irresponsible."[49] In the end, the costs associated with capital punishment defeated Alaska's latest death effort, as had happened with earlier death bills.[50]

IOWA

Harold Hughes, a well-known Progressive with pro–labor union sentiments who was totally opposed to capital punishment, defeated his

Republican opponent in the race for governor in a landslide in 1964. Democrats had gained control of both houses of the Iowa General Assembly for the first time since the Great Depression. Significant margins in both houses—101 to 23 in the House, and 34 to 25 in the Senate—facilitated the state's abolition of the death penalty in 1965.

The General Assembly came closest to reinstatement in 1995. A bill that the governor had endorsed was passed by the House but soundly defeated by the Senate. That vote became a significant part of numerous Republican campaigns.[51] Ten years later, during the 2005 and 2006 legislative sessions, reinstatement efforts—triggered by the kidnapping, rape, and murder of a ten-year-old-girl by a convicted sex offender and by a *Des Moines Register and Tribune* Company poll showing that two-thirds of Iowans favored reinstatement—once again seemed likely to succeed. The Senate Democratic leader, Michael Gronstal, whose party made up 50 percent of the Senate, threatened to block debate "if Republicans try to attach a capital punishment proposal to a high-priority bill [then being considered] that would lengthen prison sentences and require more treatment and supervision for sex offenders."[52] Republican Senator Jeff Angelo admitted that reinstating the death penalty was a political issue that would be talked about as Iowans moved toward the fall elections: "But when people call this political grandstanding, it minimizes the fact that there are legislators who wholeheartedly believe that this is an option a jury should have."[53] A House committee passed a 2006 bill that would have allowed the death penalty in cases where a child is kidnapped, sexually assaulted, and murdered. The House Speaker noted that he would not allow a full House debate if the Senate would not consider the issue. Gronstal said he would block debate there,[54] so Senate Democratic leaders ended that Republican attempt to reinstate the death penalty.

Support for death penalty abolition remained strong in the editorial pages of the *Des Moines Register*, the most prestigious paper in the state. An editorial on 28 December 2006 titled "Rise above Barbarism of Capital Punishment" argued: "'Eye for an eye' punishments are barbaric and unacceptable in contemporary society. Juries do not order rapists to be raped. Judges don't steal from thieves or order those guilty of assault to be beaten. Civilized societies don't mete out equal retaliation because they realize they're supposed to rise above the level of criminals." Another editorial, on 15 December 2008, reminded Iowans that operating a death row and carrying out executions were expensive propositions.[55]

From the *Register*'s perspective, a "silver lining" of the country's economic problems was a fourteen-year low in the number of executions across the country.

In 2005 the death penalty was imposed in federal court in Sioux City, Iowa—the state's first death sentence in forty years. The defendants, Dustin Honken and Angela Johnson, were convicted of killing two girls, ages six and ten, along with their mother.[56] Death sentences will probably be handed down in other Iowa cases tried in federal court. Additionally, over the past two decades the death penalty has played a significant role in state politics. Although numerous state Republican politicians support abolition, the political power associated with reinstatement could move significant numbers of Republicans and some Democrats to endorse capital punishment. Death penalty abolition, with its relatively abbreviated history in Iowa culture and politics, has a tenuous hold in the state.

WEST VIRGINIA

West Virginia, like Iowa, abolished its death penalty during the progressive 1960s. Two noteworthy factors separate West Virginia from other abolitionist states: a southeastern location, and a high number of pre-abolition executions—a whopping 155. Research suggests that the combination of a quasicolonial economy based on coal mining, low crime rates, the symbolic appeal of opposition to the death penalty, the support of key religious figures, and the unwavering support of the state's most prestigious newspaper, the progressive and pro-union *Charleston Gazette*, largely explain the 1965 decision to abolish capital punishment. A strong legislative committee system chaired by opponents of the death penalty, the lack of a mechanism for citizen initiative petitions, and a newspaper editor willing to vilify the death penalty and marginalize the small number of legislators willing to sponsor capital punishment bills largely accounts for its maintenance.[57] Moreover, data presented here suggest that West Virginia's death penalty debate remains largely unchanged.

Delegate John Overington has introduced death bills or resolutions in every session of the West Virginia Legislature since 1986, involving at least twenty-three distinct pieces of legislation. Only five additional pro death statutes have been introduced by other legislators.[58] *Charleston Gazette* polls find that 80 percent of West Virginians support the death penalty, yet the state has not restored it. Overington and Bob Holliday, a key actor in West Virginia's 1965 successful abolition effort, agree with the polls' conclusions. Capital punishment bills are killed by judiciary committee chairs and "never see the light of day on the floor."[59]

At times Overington and other death penalty advocates have attempted to remove legislation from committees or attach capital punishment to other legislation. In an attempt to wrest power from legislators opposed to the death penalty, Republicans made reinstatement of capital punishment part of their 2004 West Virginia Party Platform.[60] So far, none of these efforts has been successful. The *Charleston Gazette*'s reporting and editorializing remain as central to the failure of reinstatement efforts as they were in the demise of the death penalty in 1965. The paper remains an unapologetic supporter of abolition.[61]

RHODE ISLAND

In 1852 the Rhode Island legislature abolished the death penalty for everyone except those who murdered prison guards. The action was motivated, in part, by the ongoing outrage expressed in the states' large Irish immigrant community concerning the 1845 execution of John Gordon, an Irish immigrant, for murdering an infamous Protestant businessman. The legislature reinstated capital punishment in 1973 for prison inmates who commit murder, but in 1979 the state's Supreme Court ruled the law unconstitutional.[62] The statute has never been applied. Efforts to reinstate Rhode Island's capital punishment law were probably weakened by the passage of a "life without the possibility of parole" statute the same year that the state's Supreme Court ruled the death penalty unconstitutional. Nevertheless, death penalty bills have been routinely introduced in Rhode Island's General Assembly. In 1994, the House approved reinstatement legislation, but the Senate failed to act.[63] Over the past twenty years, legislative committees have heard public testimony on a number of death penalty reinstatement bills.

Records of committee hearings in 1989, 1996, and 2001 confirm that witnesses who opposed the death penalty were well organized and two to three times more numerous than witnesses who wanted it restored.[64] A witness in favor of the death penalty at the 1989 hearing reported that the few witnesses favoring the bill "were outnumbered by clergy and others."[65] A reporter observing 1996 testimony on the desirability of a death penalty referendum noted that the bill's sponsors were "in a distinct minority at yesterday's lengthy State House hearing."[66] Descriptions of the 2001 hearing suggest that numbers of witnesses on the two sides were more equal. However, the nature of the testimony offered by witnesses was nearly identical to that at the earlier hearings.

Those in favor of restoring the death penalty tended to offer horrific personal experiences along with their sentiments about executions. People testifying against reinstatement tended to represent religious, professional, or human rights groups and to defend their sentiments with religious, moral, economic, or deterrence arguments. Speaking about the effects of religious testimony, a long-time supporter of reinstatement complained: "The reason we don't have one [a capital punishment law] is because the religious leadership has been so effective in the debates. . . . I've got an uphill battle with legislative leadership and I think everybody knows that."[67]

In 2005, Rhode Island State Representative Raymond E. Gallison proposed the establishment of a legislative commission to study the advisability of the state's use of capital punishment for people who committed heinous crimes—like the recent killing of a Providence, Rhode Island, police detective and the murder of a nine-year-old Florida girl by an alleged sex offender.[68] Gallison stated: "Someone who takes another person's life intentionally and is proven guilty, they're not innocent and they shouldn't be living."[69] The bill was sent to the House Judiciary Committee for consideration. It died there.

As of 2010, no reinstatement bill has reached the governor's office. The importance that activists place on Roman Catholic involvement in retaining abolition in Rhode Island became clear in 1997, when the Massachusetts House and Senate narrowly approved different versions of a death bill. Abolitionists asked if the death penalty were resurrected in a highly Catholic state with nearly the same demographics as Rhode Island, would Rhode Island not follow suit? Fortunately, the Massachusetts legislature did not produce a bill that both houses could support, and thus the answer to that question remains speculative.[70]

VERMONT

In 1972, the US Supreme Court ruled in Furman v. Georgia[71] that existing death statutes were unconstitutional. Among the fatalities of that decision was Vermont's death penalty statute. In 1987, the state's Legislature reinforced that decision by removing death as a possible punishment for murder.[72] As is the case with some other abolitionist states, Vermont retained the punishment of the yet-to-be-used death penalty for the crimes of treason and terrorism when the United States is "at war or threatened with war."[73] A Vermont Law School professor defined the untested treason statute as "short, succinct and unconstitutional."[74] A review of newspapers found no discussion of the terrorist

16

component of the statute. There is no evidence that executions were ever central to Vermont's culture. Although executions were legal from the early seventeenth century until the 1972 *Furman* decision, only twenty-six people were executed between 1630 and 1970. Since 1900, only eight prisoners have been killed by the state of Vermont.[75] A search of legislative records found that eight reinstatement bills have been introduced in the Vermont Legislature since 1987, but only two since 2000, and the last in 2004. There is no evidence that any of these bills was seriously considered by the relevant committee or house of the Legislature.[76]

A *Rutland Herald* article linked the 2001 House bill to the December 2000 drug-related killings of three Rutland County residents, including the "unfathomable murder of Teresa King."[77] Commenting on the likelihood that these murders would move legislators to approve a death bill, a Vermont Press Bureau reporter noted that "most lawmakers have consistently blocked attempts to reinstate it [the death penalty]. Proposals were floated in . . . the early 1990s after the grisly murder of a Richmond girl" without success.[78] The bill died in committee. The 2004 Senate bill, which called for death as a punishment option in cases involving aggravated murder or the killing of a police officer, was no more successful. Before the bill was formally introduced, the Senate Secretary gave it little chance of success.[79] In fact, it had none.

A search of Vermont newspapers from 1990 to 2010 suggests that support for reinstating the death penalty was not any stronger in the executive branch. In 2007, a spokesman for Governor James Douglas told reporters that the governor was not "unalterably opposed to the death penalty, but he doesn't have any plans to introduce it."[80] During his term in office (1991–2003), Governor Howard Dean said that he would not introduce a death bill, but neither would he veto one that reached his desk.[81]

With the benefit of hindsight, it seems clear that the December 2000 murder of Teresa King, and the subsequent trial of Donald Fell in federal court, dominated Vermont's death penalty debate for a decade. Since the case involved kidnapping and transportation across state lines, federal prosecutors were free to try Fell in federal court and seek the death penalty. For the first time in fifty years, a Vermont jury was asked to consider death as a potential criminal sanction.[82] The debate became more intense in 2005, when Fell was convicted and sentenced to death. Some people, including King's family, were pleased with the federal intervention, but many resented outside forces for imposing their will on the citizens of Vermont. Those opposed to capital punishment feared that the ongoing application of federal death statues in Vermont might well move the state toward reestablishing its own death statute. As they feared, in 2009 federal prosecutors announced that they intended to seek the death penalty in the case of Michael Jacques, accused of killing his twelve-year-old niece.[83] US District Court Judge William Sessions III has rejected Jacques's request to have his trial moved out of Vermont and ruled that US attorneys can seek the death penalty and use Jacques's past conviction as a sex offender as evidence in the punishment phase of the trial.[84] As of 7 September 2011, no trial date had been set.[85] Abolition appears healthy, but the full consequences of federal intervention remain to be seen.

MASSACHUSETTS

According to existing records, the first execution in Massachusetts occurred in 1630. When the last execution occurred, on May 9, 1947, Massachusetts had executed 345 people[86]—twenty-six of whom were executed for witchcraft, including twenty who were victims of the infamous Salem witch trials.[87] From 1947 to the 1972 *Furman* decision, courts continued to sentence people to death, but Massachusetts governors simply commuted the sentences to life imprisonment.[88]

Massachusetts legislators struggled to write and pass a post-*Furman* death bill. Two confrontations between the Supreme Judicial Court and legislators left the state unable to pass a constitutionally acceptable death bill.[89] To bridge that gap, a referendum asking the electorate to amend the Massachusetts Constitution to specify that no part of that document could be construed to ban punishment by death was placed on the November 1982 ballot. The referendum was approved by 60 percent to 40 percent.[90] The legislature rewrote its death statute one more time. Since the revised bill specified that a death sentence must be preceded by a jury trial, the Supreme Judicial Court ruled that it coerced people charged with a capital offense to plea bargain, so they could escape execution. Thus, the court ruled the bill unconstitutional.[91] By the time the legislature received this news, Michael Dukakis, a strong opponent of capital punishment, had become governor. Thus began a death penalty hiatus that lasted until the election of a series of governors supportive of reinstating the death penalty.

Motivated by a series of heinous crimes in the state, Massachusetts came closer to reestablishing the death penalty on November 7, 1997, than on any other occasion. Earlier, both the House and Senate had passed different versions of death penalty legislation. Nine days after approving the House's initial death penalty bill, Representative John R. Slattery refused to accept a compromise bill that allowed fifteen categories of first-degree murder. The resulting eighty-to-eighty tie killed the measure and prevented it from being reconsidered during 1997–98 legislative session. Representative Slattery stated that fear of executing an innocent person, limited protection for juveniles, and potential racial bias had motivated him to change his vote.[92] Death penalty legislation resurfaced in 1999, but that bill was rejected after six hours of passionate debate, by a vote of eighty-three to seventy-three. In an attempt to save the 1999 bill, Republicans offered a number of amendments that would narrow its scope and reduce the chance that an innocent person would be executed—but to no avail.[93] The margin of defeat for the 2001 bill was ninety-two to sixty, a substantial gain for opponents of the death penalty.[94]

Four death bills were introduced in the 2003–4 legislative session. The legislature held a six-hour public hearing on the issue. Approximately 100 people attended, and not a single person testified in favor of the legislation: "Those testifying said capital punishment is too costly, is applied unfairly, and there is too much room for error."[95] In 2005, Governor Mitt Romney offered a death penalty bill, the product of a blue ribbon panel. Confirming growing opposition to capital punishment among legislators, it was defeated 100 to 53.[96] These data indicate that death penalty abolition is noticeably more secure in Massachusetts than it was a decade ago.

WASHINGTON, D.C.

The District of Columbia was governed by a territorial legislature from 1871 to 1874. After that government was abolished in 1874, it was replaced by a "temporary commission form of government," and in 1878 the District of Columbia was given a permanent three-person Board of Commissioners, appointed by the president of the United States. That form of government lasted nearly a century. It was replaced in 1967 by a mayor-commissioner appointed by the president. Residents of the District were not given the power to elect their local leaders until 1974.[97] Judges serving in the District's Appeals and Superior Courts continue to be nominated by the president of the United States and confirmed by the US Senate.[98]

Between 1853 and 1957, 118 people were executed in the District of Columbia.[99] The District's elected council repealed its post-*Furman* death penalty statute in 1981.[100] Movements to reestablish capital pun-

19

ishment in the District have not been grounded in local politics. On the contrary, federal legislators—using their economic control over the District—have attempted to coerce the District Council to reestablish the death penalty. That coercion is consistently interpreted by the predominantly African American residents of the District as racism.[101]

The issue came to a boil in 1992, following the Capitol Hill killing of an aide to Senator Richard Shelby, a Democrat from Alabama. Congress passed a measure that required D.C. officials to place on the November general election ballot a referendum asking the electorate if they favored the reestablishment of the death penalty in the District.[102] A coalition of civil rights and local religious groups mobilized to fend off this effort. On November 3, 1992, the electorate rejected the return of capital punishment by a two-to-one ratio. Although the measure failed to pass in both white and African American neighborhoods, the ratio was three-to-one in black communities: "Voters cited a variety of reasons for blocking the measure. Many said they feared that it would be applied unfairly against Blacks; others said they were angered by Congress's interference."[103]

Following the failure of the referendum, federal interference in the District's death penalty debate was less direct. During the first decade of the twenty-first century, the local federal prosecutor increasingly sought the death penalty in the US District Court located in the District. This interference in traditional local matters motivated the Council of the District of Columbia to pass two "Sense of the Council" bills, asking the US attorney general to cease the practice.[104] A January 8, 2007, letter from D.C. Representative Eleanor Holmes Norton to the US attorney for the District of Columbia also asked for an end to death penalty prosecutions that "show neither a wise use of scarce resources nor a sensitivity to the needs of the communities of the victims."[105]

The outcome of two extremely violent death cases heard in US District Court suggests that juries composed of District residents are unlikely to order the death penalty. In 2005, a jury failed to recommend death for two professional killers.[106] Two years later, a defendant convicted of multiple murders was sentenced to life in prison, which marked the third time in recent years that the Bush administration failed to persuade a Washington jury to impose the death penalty on a convicted D.C. murderer. James G. Connell III, one of the defense attorneys said the murders were not the most heinous even though the defendant killed three people.[107] In reference to these events, Representative Norton concluded: "It's entirely predictable, and it's time for the U.S. Attorney to stop wasting taxpayers' money trying to get the death penalty in a jurisdiction that has shown over and over again it will not give the death penalty."[108] Barring extremely repressive federal action, abolition of the death penalty is safe in the District of Columbia.

| 2 | The New York State Death Penalty Debate |

On January 24, 2004, New York joined the ranks of abolitionist states. The journey from the US Supreme Court's rejection of New York's pre-*Furman* death statute through legislative reestablishment of the death penalty in 1995 to the ruling by the New York Court of Appeals that the reestablished statute was unconstitutional demonstrates that the issue was highly contested along the way. Franklin Zimring and Gordon Hawkins have observed that "a history of frequent executions . . . serves as a kind of precedent, reassuring political actors that their own participation is neither inhumane nor immoral . . . on the grounds that, historically, executions do not violate local community morality."[1] Thus, after the US Supreme Court cleared the way for the resumption of legal executions in 1976, it wasn't only southern states that rushed to enact new death penalty laws. According to the ESPY file on executions,[2] New York ranked second among American states in the number of legal executions prior to *Furman*, with 1,130 people executed between 1641 and 1963. Correspondingly, polls of New York state legislators in the 1980s and 1990s indicated that a majority supported capital punishment.[3] As a consequence, post-*Furman* death penalty debates were held in the New York State Senate and Assembly for nineteen consecutive legislative sessions, covering nineteen years.

From 1977 to 1994, the Assembly and Senate passed death penalty bills by large margins, only to have the bills vetoed by two Democratic governors: Hugh Carey, 1975–83; and Mario Cuomo, 1983–94. During some sessions, the Senate was successful in overriding the governor's veto, but the Assembly's efforts always fell short by a few votes. George Pataki, elected governor in 1994, fulfilled a campaign promise when he signed a death penalty bill into law on 7 March 1995,[4] making New York the thirty-eighth state to have restored capital punishment.

The nineteen-year debate preceding the successful 1995 bill testifies to the strength of pro–death penalty narratives in one Northeastern state, while providing a natural laboratory that helps us to understand why the United States is the only Western industrialized democracy to retain capital punishment statutes. As Zimring has observed, "the ongoing debate in New York was the most visible and sustained at any level of government in the United States since 1980."[5] With a population of approximately nineteen million, New York is among the most populous of US states, and its cities have the same problems of urban decay, poverty, and crime found in other states.[6] Thus, there is no basis for suggesting that the factors underlying the legislative strength of capital punishment in New York would not appear elsewhere in the United States.

BACKGROUND TO THE POST-*FURMAN* DEATH PENALTY DEBATE

Executions increased dramatically in New York after the introduction of the electric chair in 1890, with 644 people electrocuted between 1900 and 1963. These executions peaked in the 1930s and dramatically declined after the 1940s.[7] The reduced use of the death penalty accompanied legislative efforts to abolish it.[8] Between 1950 and 1963, at least one abolition bill was introduced in the Legislature every session. On July 1, 1963, New York became the last state in the country to abolish mandatory death for murder, although death remained the mandatory punishment for treason.[9] In 1965, the Temporary Commission on Revision of the Penal Law and Criminal Code (also known as the Bartlett Commission) recommended that the death penalty be abolished in the state.[10] The legislature enacted a new statute, effective June 1, 1965, that "so narrowed the class of capital offenses that de facto abolition of capital punishment had almost been accomplished."[11] The sanction remained a possible punishment for "deliberate and premeditated" murder of an on-duty police officer, or a murder committed while an offender was serving life in prison or attempting to escape from serving a life prison sentence.[12]

In spite of the narrow coverage of New York's death penalty statute, in 1973 the New York Court of Appeals ruled in *People v. Fitzpatrick* that it allowed the jury too much discretion.[13] In response, the Legislature enacted a statute in 1974 making death the mandatory punishment for the intentional killing of a police officer or a correctional officer, and for a killing committed by a life-term inmate, a statute very similar to the state's 1965 discretionary death penalty law.[14] In 1976, the US Supreme Court rejected mandatory death penalty statutes for murder and approved the "guided discretion" capital punishment statutes of Georgia, Florida, and Texas.[15] Such was the legal situation when the Legislature met in January 1977 to consider another bill to reinstate the death penalty.

By the mid-1970s, when the Legislature began to debate the reinstatement of the death penalty, the number and rate of homicides had risen dramatically. In 1965, there were 836 cases of murder and non-negligent manslaughter reported in the state, a rate of 4.6 per 100,000 state inhabitants during the year.[16] At its peak in 1990, the number of murder and nonnegligent manslaughter cases jumped 210 percent to 2,605, a rate of 14.5 per 100,000 state inhabitants.[17] In 1991, New York's homicide rate began to decrease, and soon thereafter the same pattern emerged for the entire United States.[18] By 1995, when New York reinstated the death penalty, the state's homicide rate had declined more than 40 percent compared to the 1990 level, but it was still 85 percent higher than in 1965.[19]

PRESENTING THE DETERRENCE ARGUMENT IN SUPPORT OF CAPITAL PUNISHMENT

From the opening of the 1977 legislative session to the enactment of the capital punishment law in 1995, deterrence was the principal issue driving the legislative debate. Early on, Assemblyman Christopher Mega argued: "Deterrence, we spoke about whether or not capital punishment is a deterrent and the Supreme Court mentioned that the question of deterrence is something that each individual state should consider when they consider a capital punishment bill."[20] Similarly, the bill's annual senate sponsor, Senator Dale Volker, cautioned: "We are going to get into all sorts of arguments. . . . We are debating several issues. One is certainly the issue of the death penalty itself, and the issue of it as a deterrent."[21] Assemblyman Andrew Hevesi insisted: "The deterrent effect. That is the main argument for the advocates of the death penalty and if it is not, ladies and gentlemen, say so on this floor."[22] Senator Eliot Bernstein asserted: "I've been through [the debate] like everybody else for years and years. We hear the same things, the same arguments. What is the purpose of the proposed death penalty if not as a deterrent?"[23] Assemblyman Chris Ortloff summarized the situation: "It has been said here, as it is every year, that the issue in this matter is whether capital punishment deters."[24] Even toward the end of the debates, the question remained: "Is this [the death penalty] a deterrent? You know that's the great question of our day."[25]

Deterrence Works: Dead Men Don't Commit Crimes

Death penalty proponents buttressed their deterrence arguments by including the incapacitation of convicted offenders. According to Assemblyman Alexander Gromack: "Too often we have seen convicted murderers get out for good behavior only to kill and murder again."[26] Various estimates were provided. Assemblyman Joseph Robach said: "I think that number [of recidivist murderers] is at least 200 a year across this state, if not higher."[27] Assemblyman Stephen Kauffman argued: "Do you know that 850 people last year who were convicted of murder got out of jail [and] committed murder again? . . . But, I tell you, if you had the death penalty, 850 people would not have been out to kill again."[28] After asking what punishment other than death should be given to prevent incarcerated murders from killing again, Assemblyman Stephen Saland continued: "What are we going to do when he kills the next time? Take away his conjugal visits? That is really good. Maybe we can take away his library privileges, or tell him he cannot pump iron two hours a day."[29]

Although the imposition of the death penalty would result in no additional crimes being committed by the person who was executed, this represents the incapacitative rather than the deterrent effect of capital punishment.[30] Assemblyman Eric Vitaliano referred to this as the "incapacitative deterrent" effect.[31] Assemblyman David Skidman claimed: "All I know is that if that murderer is given the death penalty, he will murder never again, and that is deterrent enough for me."[32] Senator Hugh Farley agreed that "there's [deterrence] studies on both sides, but . . . it would be a deterrent to that person that has killed several times. He won't kill again."[33] And Assemblyman James Tedisco summarized the argument: "I suggest to you that it is irrefutably a deterrent. . . . And for all those individuals who have been given the death penalty and are no longer in existence, you cannot stand up and tell me they will murder again. They will not only never murder again, they will never steal your car or rape your wife or your daughter."[34]

Yet Hugo Bedau, dean of death penalty researchers, has noted that it is impossible to measure the effects of incapacitation because most people convicted of homicide do not kill again, thus making it impossible to know which convicted murderers will become recidivists.[35] Whatever the empirical merits of the death penalty proponents' position, the confluence of incapacitation and deterrence appears to have made their commitment to deterrence much stronger.

Increased Homicides and the Perceived
Need for Capital Punishment

An undisputed fact that death penalty proponents seized on throughout the debate was that homicides in the state had increased dramatically since the mid-1960s—at about the same time when executions ceased in New York. In opening the 1977 debate, the bill's sponsor in the lower house, Assemblyman Vincent Graber argued: "I am not saying the only reason for this increase [in homicides] was because the death penalty has declined . . . [but it is true that] homicides have increased at the same time that capital punishment has declined."[36] Senator Martin Knorr was more explicit: "We all know in 1965 they abolished capital punishment. Prior to the abolishment . . . there [were] . . . approximately 400 innocent victims of murder. But as soon as the capital punishment was abolished within a period of three years the numbers of innocent victims of murder arose to around 1,500 per year."[37]

Senator Volker calculated that "since 1965, 41,667 people have been murdered as opposed to the previous 23 years, when only 11,513 were murdered. And last year we set a record."[38] Later, he said: "More people have been murdered on the streets of New York than were killed in the entire Vietnam War."[39] Assemblyman George Pataki voiced the same concern: "I believe the cause and effect is clear: the absence of a death penalty has led to a massive increase in the instances of rational [sic] murder."[40] And Assemblyman Graber asserted: "I would not be proposing this [death penalty] bill, incidentally, if our murder rate was as low as it was in [other] nations."[41]

THE PREDICTED EFFECTIVENESS OF
A REINSTATED DEATH PENALTY

If the premise that the absence of a death penalty resulted in increased homicides was true, according to Senator Volker, it was reasonable to conclude that reinstating the death penalty would result in decreased homicides: "If we had the death penalty in this state, we would not have as much murder."[42] Senator Knorr argued: "I am voting here today to save the lives of several hundred innocent victims annually in the near future."[43] Assemblyman George Friedman asserted that "capital punishment would deter a significant part of them and the percentages would be greater than simply saving 10 percent, it would be a very large percentage of the intentional killings."[44] Assemblyman Pat Hickey echoed this sentiment: "I agree that the restitution of the death penalty will significantly drive down the murder rate in this state."[45] Assemblyman Anthony Seminerio even referred to reducing all criminal activity: "I am begging you to vote for the death penalty if you want to stop crime."[46] All of these comments reflect the overconfidence that Richard Nisbett and Lee Ross say is typical of the lay observer.[47] All the quotes in this subsection could be construed as referring to the incapacitative powers of capital punishment, as well as to deterrence.

Although supporters of capital punishment often referred to the deterrence argument in relationship to previous and future homicides, there was little mention of research supporting the death penalty's deterrent effect. The notable exception was the work of Isaac Ehrlich,[48] which was periodically referred to: Professor Ehrlich "offered his evidence that the death penalty has a . . . remarkable deterrent effect. I have since encountered no valid study to rebut his position."[49] This limited reliance on scientific literature was not an oversight by death penalty supporters; there simply was very little published research that showed the death penalty was a deterrent. Clearly, these legislators' attitudes toward capital punishment influenced how they interpreted evidence of the deterrent effect of capital punishment.

THE OPPOSITION'S CHALLENGE TO THE DETERRENCE ARGUMENT

Opponents of the death penalty could not deny that homicides in New York had increased since its de facto abolition in 1965. Nonetheless, they did not accept this as evidence of the deterrent effect of capital punishment. Senator Bernstein argued: "You have not established in your argument that the abolition of the death penalty in 1965 is the causal factor for the increase in homicides. . . . The increase is national, and . . . caused not by the abolition of the death penalty [in New York]."[50] Instead, the opponents argued that the burden of proof regarding the deterrent value of capital punishment is "on those who are for it."[51] They insisted on scientific evidence. Senator Ray Goodman asked: "Who says that the death penalty deters? Where is the evidence? Produce it forthwith. Now is the time we need it to evaluate this measure."[52] And Senator Franz Leichter lamented: "I don't think that the absence of proof can be overcome by parroting over and over again the phrase 'The death penalty will be a deterrent.' . . . All we have is the claim, we don't have the proof."[53]

If death penalty supporters seldom relied on scientific studies, the opposition devoted most of its attention to the results of social science research to argue that the death penalty in New York would not deter homicide. Early in the annual debates, Assemblyman Jim McCabe an-

nounced: "As some people have already said, the death penalty is a deterrent to the crime of murder, I have searched all the literature I could
find, and I can find no objective evidence that proves that such is the
case. . . . [T]he deterrent argument appears to be without merit."[54] Believing that death penalty opponents had met their responsibility in
presenting research evidence against deterrence, Assemblyman Scott
Stringer asked rhetorically: "So, how many studies and statistics do you
need . . . to figure out that as far as deterrence goes, the death penalty
is an abysmal failure?"[55] And Assemblyman Hevesi concluded: "So, you
have evidence, you have citations, you have academic studies and you
have numbers."[56]

Some death penalty opponents argued that the penalty actually had
a "brutalizing" effect and resulted in increased homicides. Such claims
were supported by the research of William Bowers and Glenn Pierce,
who found that in New York from 1907 to 1963, approximately two
additional homicides occurred the month after an execution.[57] Possibly
drawing on this study, Senator Catherine Nolan explained: "Executions
spread violence by signaling that it is acceptable to kill."[58]

In addition to this criticism, in 1994 Senator Leichter noted a change
in local crime rates: "In fact, in New York State in the last two years, the
homicide rate has gone down. So, so much for that argument."[59] A year
later, Senator Emanuel Gold observed the same trend: "In the *New York
Post* today . . . [it was reported] here that from last year to this year, the
murder rate . . . is down 36 percent."[60] By this time, however, the state
had a new governor, George Pataki, who favored the death penalty, and
these patterns didn't matter. Caught up in the continuing and strident
debate, death penalty opponents argued that no evidence existed to support the claim that capital punishment was a deterrent. It would have
been more precise for them to have said that there is little scientific evidence that capital punishment is a more effective deterrent than long-
term imprisonment.

DEFENDING THE DETERRENCE
ARGUMENT AGAINST CHALLENGES

Given the evidence presented against the deterrent effect of the death
penalty, proponents of capital punishment reacted by challenging the research literature. Their response was three-fold: (1) they questioned the
objectivity and honesty of deterrence researchers and, thus, the validity
and relevance of the deterrence literature; (2) they presented other, non-

scientific evidence of deterrence; and (3) they argued that the burden of proof rested with the opposition to disprove deterrence.

The Reported Research Evidence Is Flawed

From the beginning, supporters of the death penalty questioned the validity and relevance of published research challenging claims that it was a deterrent. Not only did the research contradict commonsense theories of crime and punishment, but death penalty proponents also questioned the motives and qualifications of social science researchers. Senator Volker argued: "Almost all of the deterrence studies that have found that the death penalty has no deterrence [value were] done by people who started out opposing the death penalty and wanted to find out how in effect they could find out how to oppose it through the deterrence argument."[61] Senator Israel Ruiz agreed: "All the so-called studies that have been done by the so-called liberal experts [claim] that there is really no deterrence if there's a death penalty."[62] Assemblyman Saland remarked: "I heard a lot of talk of studies. . . . These studies basically are the work of criminologists, of social scientists; and why they are called scientists, I don't know."[63] Saland later observed: "None of your social scientists, and I use the word rather loosely, none of them have the ability to measure this type of conduct."[64] In referring to this academic research, Senator Volker concluded: "We have looked at all the so-called deterrence studies, and what we determined is they are all phonies."[65]

Assemblyman Graber asserted: "I would surmise that . . . we are going to hear about statistical studies that seem to show capital punishment is not a deterrent. . . . I would like to indicate I am not impressed by [the] Sellin [study showing no differences in murder rates among death penalty and abolition states]."[66] The debate also was punctuated with frequent negative characterizations of deterrence research and empirical studies. Assemblyman Vincent Nicolosi claimed that "we can play the statistics game. . . . The statistics are unclear, sure they are. Because figures don't lie, but liars figure."[67] And Assemblyman Daniel Frisa observed: "We have heard a lot of arguments in opposition to this measure. Most of them have tended to rely on statistics and studies and logic that is not very logical and sense that is not very common."[68] Senator Volker sarcastically added: "So the anti-death penalty people that did those wonderful studies back in the '60s, after they decided that they were opposed to the death penalty, they did studies to prove why they were right. . . . It's unbelievable. . . . [Father Theodore] Hesburgh . . . now president of [the University of] Notre Dame, the celebrated death penalty opponent, did a study which I think a third grader could probably tear apart on the issue of deterrence."[69]

The next year, Volker said: "There are some people in this country who are so opposed to things that they will manufacture facts." Then, referring to the testimony of Professors Hugo Bedau and Michael Radelet before the Committee on the Judiciary, Volker added: "They manufactured facts and, if they did it here, I'm sure they did it in other places across this country."[70]

As to a possible brutalization effect documented in the research literature, this was even harder for death penalty proponents to take seriously. Assemblyman David VanVarnick remarked: "I reject that possibility [that one more person would be murdered due to the death penalty and its brutalization effect]."[71] And Assemblyman Arnold Proskin claimed that the deterrent effect was not inconsistent with increasing murder rates: "The figures shown to us that . . . where there is a[n] execution, that the rate of killings may rise. That doesn't say that the death penalty is not a deterrent."[72] Assemblyman Friedman explained: "[P]erhaps the murder rate in those states [with the death penalty] would be twice what it is today if they didn't have capital punishment."[73]

Thus, the reported research and empirical evidence presented by death penalty opponents showing either no measurable deterrent effect of capital punishment or a "brutalization effect" were simply dismissed. Assemblyman Friedman stated: "Capital punishment is a deterrent, there is no question about it, and the findings of any studies notwithstanding."[74] A similar view was presented by Assemblyman Arthur Kremer: "I don't work with charts . . . I am in the real world."[75] This was reiterated by Assemblyman Philip Healey: "Don't give me statistics . . . what we are living [with] in New York State is a condition that is out of control."[76]

Others suggested sardonically that if severe punishments did not deter criminals, then the criminal sanctions needed revision—to make them less severe. Assemblyman Friedman argued: "A compilation of statistics and charts that are aimed at proving that a more severe penalty does not result in less crime. . . . I [suppose] what he is really saying is that the less severe the penalty the less crime we will have."[77] And Assemblyman Tedisco said: "The logical conclusion tells me that when those states go to a death penalty, they seem to increase the amount of murders. . . . So, the logic to that is we take them [the murderers] to dinner, buy them a drink, we treat them nice and say, 'Don't do it anymore,' and that will solve all the problems."[78] This sarcasm reflects both a strong belief in punishment and an inability to alter opinions based on disconfirming evidence. Politicizing the research of social scientists makes this intransigence possible.

In the end, there would be little agreement on any of these issues by the contending parties—a legislator's position on deterrence and the death penalty was typically consistent. Senator Fred Eckert remarked to an opponent of the death penalty: "You are not opposed to capital punishment because you don't think it's a deterrent. You don't think it's a deterrent because you're opposed to it."[79] The same could be said of those in favor of the sanction. This theme was repeated by Senator Manfred Ohrenstein: "I think . . . that nobody is going to convince anyone on either side as to whether capital punishment deters or doesn't deter."[80]

Other Evidence in Support of Deterrence

Although proponents could advance little scientific research in support of their assertions about the deterrent effect of capital punishment, they did rely on other more personal and direct forms of evidence. Assemblyman Steve Greenberg announced: "It is true I haven't any statistics . . . in fact, I doubt if anything I say can be documented, but I offer you the benefit of the instinct and knowledge I have acquired while dealing with the criminal element. . . . Instinct and experience tells me the threat of execution is a deterrent to murder."[81] This position was also presented by Assemblyman Raymond Kisor: "I would like to speak in favor of this bill, and I don't speak from some academic study. . . . I speak from 25 years of experience with the New York State police."[82] Senator Ruiz referred to his constituents: "I think it [the death penalty] truly is a deterrent and it's not because I've made this determination by myself. It's because I've walked my district, I've talked to hundreds of . . . people in my district and they tell me, 99 percent of them, that if there is a death penalty they would . . . think twice before they killed anyone."[83]

Assemblyman Harry Smoler mentioned other evidence: "I want to cite, finally, the experts. The experts are killers who are under a death sentence and being marched before the firing squad, and they say, 'There is only one way to stop added killings, and that is to have capital punishment.'"[84] In a similar fashion, Michael Davis has concluded that since death is generally the most feared punishment, commonsense tells us that it must be the most effective deterrent.[85] The comments in this subsection reflect the lay person's reliance on a small number of cases, belief in punishment, reliance on myth, and considerable overconfidence.

The Burden of Proof: Show That Sanctions Don't Deter

Death penalty proponents argued that the deterrence provided by the death penalty was no different from the deterrence provided by other legal sanctions. Senator Eckert claimed early in the debate: "The argument that we cannot conclusively prove that capital punishment deters begs the question. All of our law is based on the presumption that there is a relationship between the penalty imposed and the likelihood of the occurrence of crime."[86] And given this underlying principle upon which American corrections is based, Assemblyman Vitaliano asserted: "I submit the burden is on the opponents to establish the exception, not on us to prove the rule . . . it is on the opponents to establish the deviation from the norm, the deviation from the bedrock principles which undergird our criminal justice system and the common sense understanding of the desire to avoid death."[87] As Bedau observes, capital punishment opponents have left themselves vulnerable to such criticism because "abolitionists look like fools if they insist (as they often do) that 'the death penalty is no deterrent to murder' since this flies in the face of what passes for common sense."[88]

Assemblyman Mega testified: "My belief is [that] nothing is feared more than death, and I believe it is a deterrent."[89] Assemblyman James Fremming concurred: "It simply defies all common sense and my knowledge of human nature to argue that a penalty of death does not act as a deterrent."[90] Senator Serphin Maltese concluded: "Common sense and the fact that just about every responsible law enforcement group has come out in favor of the death penalty indicates that it is a deterrent."[91] Assemblyman Gerald Solomon shared this conviction: "There is no question in your minds, and there is no question in mine that this is a deterrent."[92] Senator Steve Bloom argued: "There is no more effective deterrent than the condemning to death for taking the life of another fellow citizen."[93] And finally, Assemblyman Clark Wemple stated his belief in the deterrent effect of a capital punishment law, even if it is never used, because of the message that it sends to potential offenders: "I think the death penalty is a deterrent. Whether it's ever used or not, it's a deterrent because it will be on the books of the State of New York."[94] Only in this last instance is it clear that the speaker was referring to deterrence as opposed to incapacitation.

THE DEATH PENALTY RESURRECTED

Legislators supporting the death penalty tended to favor three central arguments favoring the deterrence proposition that could not be contested readily and that, when taken together, constituted an effective commonsense theory of punishment and crime.

First, some legislators relied on the "dead men don't commit crimes" conception of deterrence, referred to—as noted above—by Assembly-man Vitaliano as "incapacitative deterrence." Although criminologists might argue that this term makes no theoretical sense (because those who have been executed cannot refrain from committing new crimes due to fear of additional legal punishment), the commonsense logic of this notion was to combine incapacitation and specific deterrence and make the deterrence argument (capital punishment as a means of crime prevention) much stronger. Moreover, to the extent that proponents of the death penalty claimed that first-time killers were responsible for vast numbers of subsequent homicides (either in prison or after their release) the argument became even more compelling. Indeed, a series of studies suggests that incapacitation may be more important in people's thinking than previously imagined.[95]

Second, without a death penalty as the ultimate punishment, homicides would increase. Homicide rates had increased dramatically since the 1960s, the time when executions had stopped and death penalty laws had been abolished. These rates were presented as evidence in favor of the deterrent effect of capital punishment, along with the logically consistent prediction that a reinstated death penalty would result in fewer homicides. Had these rates remained fairly constant after the ban on the death penalty in 1965, the chances of reinstating a death penalty might have been greatly reduced. Proponents of capital punishment implied that the increase in homicide rates was partly due to killings carried out by convicted murderers. Death penalty opponents' evidence that homicides had in fact increased in Florida and Texas after those states reinstated the death penalty and began executing inmates was countered by the untestable proposition that these states' homicide rates might have been even higher without the restoration of capital punishment.

The third argument was that the death penalty was similar to other penalties in at least one respect: it was imposed by the state with the legislative intent of deterrence. Harsher penalties had received widespread support in New York's recent past for offenses ranging from the sale of illicit drugs and drunk driving to spousal abuse.[96] Proponents further argued that deterrence underlies American jurisprudence and corrections, and to require proof of the law's effectiveness would impose an unnecessary burden on legislators. Such proof had not been demanded of other sanctions, so why was it now being required for capital punishment? Moreover, this demand might set a precedent, requiring uncontested evidence in the form of published research about the deterrent effect of other legal sanctions. Thus, to argue against the deterrent effect of the death penalty and, by implication, legal penalties in general was to argue against the philosophical foundations of American jurisprudence: (1) legal penalties of some sort are necessary to deter potential offenders; (2) harsher penalties deter more effectively than less severe penalties; and (3) the death penalty is the most severe of all sanctions.

This commonsense theory of crime and punishment allowed legislators to support the deterrence proposition regardless of empirical evidence against it. Research showing no deterrent effect of capital punishment was routinely criticized as biased and untruthful. The commonsense theory made sense to its proponents: its assertions were logically consistent; others tended to agree with it; it was parsimonious; it was broadly applicable; and it had clear implications for public policy. Given this theory, even the most rigorous and value-neutral research could be dismissed by death penalty proponents with little confidence in social science and statistics as a way of obtaining knowledge. When published research is faulted on methodological grounds, whether deservedly so or not, and its authors' political motives and scientific status are questioned, then the purported evidence can easily be dismissed. The scientific evidence then takes on the epistemological status of opinion, nothing more than the personal views of those who are attempting to undermine the legal system and the institutionalized worldview on which it is based. Ideology thus becomes authoritative, and science becomes ideological.

At the end of these debates, very few minds had been changed regarding the deterrent effect of capital punishment. Assemblyman John Behan lamented: "I feel like I've been here 2,000 years debating this bill . . . you're not going to change my mind at all. I haven't even changed my socks since Christmas. I'm certainly not going to change my vote on this bill from sixteen years ago."[97] Thus, New York's nineteen-year-long legislative debate suggests that supporters of reestablishing the death penalty developed and retained a commonsense theory of capital punishment that was strongly and widely held even though it was based on very little empirical research and instead relied on unreliable and idiosyncratic sources, leading to capricious inferences about the control of human behavior.[98] A "mistrust of the criminal justice process is inherent in public advocacy for punitiveness. It is reflected in a cultural common

34

sense that holds that courts do not punish severely or effectively enough, that prisons release incarcerated offenders 'far too soon.'"[99]

Even though the preponderance of published research did not support the deterrence argument, that research was often assumed to have been conducted by liberal social scientists opposed to capital punishment, and thus the published evidence could be dismissed as invalid, inconclusive, or ideological. Some proponents of capital punishment shared a disdain or even contempt for social scientists and criminologists, much like that displayed by one conservative newspaper columnist: "Unlike the victimized, our Advanced Thinkers argue that the problem isn't crime, but the jail [or punishment]. The trouble . . . isn't the criminals, but that too many are being locked up. To borrow a line from George Orwell, you have to be an intellectual to believe that sort of thing; ordinary folks have too much sense."[100]

The same skepticism was found regarding evidence of the brutalization effect of the death penalty; it was contrary to the claims advanced by proponents of deterrence, counterintuitive, and based on suspect evidence. In its place, other published research[101] or nonstatistical evidence in the form of "expert" testimony from selected law-enforcement officials, potential perpetrators, or convicted murderers was introduced, along with legislators' own claims of the deterrent effect, supported by instinct, or ordinary knowledge based on personal experience with crime and criminals. When faced with contradictory evidence, legislative advocates of capital punishment focused on critiques of research and researchers who opposed capital punishment. The fundamental issue of the morality of capital punishment was only infrequently debated — perhaps because unlike the empirical issue of deterrence, the basic moral principles of legislators do not lend themselves to floor debate. Unlike these legislators' opinions that seemed invariable for nearly two decades, Ellsworth and Gross found increasing levels of support among the general public for capital punishment as retribution during the 1970s and 1980s.[102] Perhaps one reason for the relative stability of legislators' justifications for their support of capital punishment is that, unlike those surveyed in polls, many legislators went on public record with their positions early in the debates or in their legislative careers. As a result, in 1995, the New York Legislature passed a "revised and expanded death penalty statute which was signed into law by Governor Pataki. The law authorized the death penalty for thirteen categories of intentional murder, including murders committed in furtherance of other crime like robbery, rape or burglary."[103] It is clear that majorities in both houses of the Legislature wanted a capital punishment law that would be broadly applicable. This was not symbolic legislation. Not surprisingly, after two decades of debate in which the preponderance of scientific evidence presented did not support the deterrence argument, the 1995 New York death penalty debate concluded by noting that: "The enactment of the death penalty will . . . send a strong deterrent message to persons who might be inclined to commit such crimes."[104]

THE NEW YORK COURT OF APPEALS RESPONDS

Less than a decade later, the highest court in New York overturned the state's death penalty by a vote of four to three, declaring that it violated the state's constitution. The successful legal challenge to the statute was made by a man who had confessed to the rape and murder by stabbing of a female jogger. The court's majority ruled that in sentencing, "no other death penalty scheme in the country requires judges to instruct jurors that if they cannot unanimously agree between two choices, the judge will sentence the defendant to a third, more lenient choice."[105] Jurors tend to underestimate how long murderers stay in prison, and "thus, jurors might impose the death penalty on a defendant whom they believed did not deserve it simply because they fear that the defendant would not serve a life sentence."[106] New York Attorney General Andrew Cuomo strongly opposed the death penalty and thus did not appeal this ruling.

Legislators' initial reaction to the ruling was determination to restore the death penalty in a modified form. Three New York Assembly committees (the Committees on Codes, Judiciary, and Correction) initiated the process within two days of public hearings. Later three more days were added to accommodate the large number of people and organizations wishing to testify. In the end, testimony was heard between December 15, 2004, and February 11, 2005. One hundred and forty-six people testified in person, and twenty-four people and groups added written testimony, totaling 1,500 transcribed pages and 2,500 written pages submitted to the committees.

Ironically, an attempt to revitalize New York's death penalty debate largely ended that debate: the testimony was devastating to the interests of death penalty advocates. Of the 170 people giving oral or written testimony, only nine argued in favor of the death penalty; 148 testified against it. Individuals from every major religious organization, death penalty scholars with national reputations, lawyers (both prosecutors and defense attorneys), relatives of murder victims, people wrongfully convicted and sentenced to death, and criminal justice professionals were among those who spoke. Claims of retribution and deterrence, issues that had dominated post-*Furman* legislative debates, were quickly refuted by academics and people of faith. It was generally concluded that capital punishment, as a deterrent to murder, was no more effective than life without the possibility of parole. The cost of capital punishment was thoroughly discussed. Witnesses often noted that less than a decade of capital punishment had cost New Yorkers $170 million, with a total of seven death sentences imposed. The small number of witnesses who supported the deterrence and retribution arguments and who dismissed economic concerns were representatives of law enforcement and prosecutors' organizations. The records suggest that the lone academic testifying in favor of executions was a professor from New York Law School. Two organizations representing African American police officers (the National Black Police Association and the Grand Council of Guardians) argued against the death penalty, citing racial bias.

Racial and economic bias, the danger of executing innocent people, the morality of executing mentally ill people, and the effect that executions have on the families of victims became core issues over the course of the hearings. Only one of the numerous religious leaders and a small proportion of victims' family members testified in support of capital punishment. Professor William Bowers informed the committee members that a study conducted by the "Capital Jury Project" found "racial bias in capital sentencing determinations" in fourteen states.[107] Barry Scheck, codirector of the Innocence Project at Cardozo Law School, reminded committee members "that since 1995, 153 people in the United States, including fourteen men under sentences of death, have been exonerated by post-conviction DNA testing."[108] In New York, legislative activity on the part of death penalty proponents has all but ended. Although Andrew Cuomo's father, Mario, lost his reelection bid in 1994 by supporting abolition, on 2 November 2010, the younger Cuomo easily won election as governor of New York.[109] As of 2011, abolition appears secure in New York State.

3

The Abolition of Capital Punishment in New Jersey

New Jersey was the first state since 1965 to legislatively abolish the death penalty.[1] On December 10, 2007, the New Jersey Senate voted to abolish capital punishment. Three days later, the New Jersey Assembly followed the Senate's lead. Voting in both legislative houses did not totally reflect party affiliation. Three Assembly Republicans and forty-one of fifty Assembly Democrats voted in favor of the bill. And four Senate Republicans joined seventeen Senate Democrats to cast the twenty-one votes necessary to secure passage in that chamber.[2] Immediately after the Legislature passed the bill, Governor Jon Corzine signed it into law.[3] "In a contemplative and at times emotional speech," the governor called this an end to "'state endorsed killing' [adding that capital punishment] 'undermines our commitment to the sanctity of life.'" When signing the bill, the Protestant governor recognized the New Jersey Catholic Conference for creating a "fundamental grassroots groundswell that put pressure on those of us in public service to stand up and do the right thing."[4] The demise of capital punishment was also motivated by a very practical consideration. In the words of Republican Senator James J. McCullough, "we spend hundreds of thousands, maybe millions of dollars in the appeals process for people on death row. . . . And the fact is, on death row people die of old age."[5]

In 1992, voters supported an amendment to the New Jersey Constitution that would have removed a legal barrier to executions. This vote suggests that public support for capital punishment in New Jersey was similar to that in other states. National opinion data for the first decade of the twenty-first century indicates that 64 to 70 percent of Americans favored the death penalty for people convicted of murder,[6] with 68 percent of whites, 40 percent of African Americans, and 47 percent of Hispanics in favor. Support for the death penalty was highest (at 74 percent) among evangelical Protestants, while white non-Hispanic Catholics who attended church regularly were the least supportive (at 61 percent).[7] Roman Catholics comprise 42 percent of New Jersey's population, which makes the state the second most Catholic—behind Rhode Island and just ahead of Massachusetts, Connecticut, New York, and California. The question was, were there enough Roman Catholics in New Jersey to help turn the state away from the death penalty? The League of Women Voters points to polls conducted in 2002 and 2005 by the Eagleton Institute of Politics at Rutgers University (sponsored by New Jerseyans for Alternatives to the Death Penalty) as evidence of declining support for capital punishment among New Jerseyans. When offered the choice between life in prison without the possibility of parole and execution for people convicted of first degree murder, these polls reported that approximately 48 percent of New Jerseyans favored life, while only 36 percent favored execution.[8]

LETHAL VIOLENCE IN NEW JERSEY

New Jersey has been no stranger to executions, having put 361 prisoners to death between the seventeenth century and 1963.[9] Moreover, the relationship between race and capital punishment in New Jersey is consistent with the execution histories of other abolitionist states.[10] At least 116 of the people executed in New Jersey were African American, and at least 209 were white.[11] With the exception of twelve African Americans who were burned to death, people executed between 1690 and 1906 were hanged; thereafter, the condemned were electrocuted.[12] The first hundred legally prescribed executions, carried out between 1690 and 1844, reflect a distinctively Southern composition: at least forty-four of those executed were African American, and at least thirty-seven were white.[13]

The volume and racial composition of executions changed little as the state moved into the twentieth century. Hugo Bedau found that between 1907 and 1960 alone the state executed sixty-eight prisoners,[14] and the overrepresentation of African Americans among those executed remained. Of the last fifty people executed in New Jersey, twenty-four (48 percent) were white and twenty-two (44 percent) were African American.[15] Throughout the twentieth century, African Americans comprised between 3.5 and 13.4 percent of state's population.[16] When the death penalty was abolished, approximately 61 percent of New Jersey's population was white, and 14.5 percent African American.[17] The state carried out its last execution in 1963.[18] Franklin Zimring and Gordon Hawkins have ranked New Jersey twenty-third out of thirty-seven death penalty states in terms of its number of executions.[19]

Between 1960 and 2007, New Jersey's murder rate moved between a low of 2.5 per 100,000 residents in 1961 to a high of 7.4 in 1973; since 1982, it has been below 6.0.[20] In 1990, twenty-seven states and the District of Columbia recorded higher murder rates than New Jersey.[21] When New Jersey abolished the death penalty, twenty-six other states and the District of Columbia recorded higher murder rates.[22] Thus, the successful 2007 death penalty debate was buttressed, as was the case in most states that had abolished the sanction, by nearly a half-century of tacit abolition and relatively low murder rates, factors conducive to abolition.[23]

THE LEGAL CULTURE IN NEW JERSEY

The process of reinstating capital punishment in New Jersey after Gregg v. Georgia[24] in 1976 was delayed until 1982 by Governor Brendan Byrne's veto of two death penalty bills in 1978.[25] Byrne explained his actions by arguing that the death penalty was arbitrarily imposed: "I spent almost nine years as the prosecutor of Essex County. . . . It was me who decided which cases should be exposed to the death penalty. And I think that that's shocking. . . . I remember one case where I withdrew a recommendation for the death penalty because the attorney for the defendant was having a nervous breakdown."[26] New Jersey's 1982—post-*Furman*—death penalty statute allowed the execution of a defendant who "purposely or knowingly causes death, or serious bodily injury resulting in death, and (2) commits the homicidal act by his own conduct, or contracts for the murder. Also eligible for the death penalty are the following defendants: A defendant who, as a leader of a narcotics trafficking network, commanded or solicited a murder, and (2) a defendant who committed a murder during the commission of the crime of terrorism."[27] Those convicted of "felony murder" and juveniles "tried as adults" were ineligible for the death penalty.[28]

Although the New Jersey Supreme Court declared the bill to be constitutional,[29] it blocked the execution of the first twenty-eight people sentenced to death.[30] In reaction to a number of state court decisions vacating death sentences on constitutional grounds, the voters approved an amendment to the state Constitution, which read: "It is not cruel and unusual punishment to impose the death penalty on a person who has purposely or knowingly caused death or purposely or knowingly caused serious bodily injury resulting in death, if he committed the act himself or paid another to do it."[31]

The first death sentence upheld by the New Jersey Supreme Court involved a wealthy white male defendant.[32] However, a complete review of all the court's death penalty decisions since 1982 reveals that little changed over the years: the court failed to uphold death sentences in forty-four of sixty cases. Reflecting frustration over these events, Representative Gordon Johnson, a death penalty advocate, noted during a New Jersey Assembly debate that the state's death penalty had been in place since 1982, yet no one had been executed. Edward DeFazio, a New Jersey prosecutor, elaborated: "Since the enactment of the death penalty in 1982 there have been 228 capital murder trials. Juries returned a death sentence in 60 and we have only 9 defendants on death row."[33]

After nearly a decade of such state Supreme Court decisions, a *New York Times* article asked: "Is Court Killing Death Penalty in New Jersey?"[34] The state's attorney general argued that "the court appeared intent on preventing executions in New Jersey under any circumstances."[35] In November 1992, there was an unsuccessful move in the New Jersey Legislature to change the situation by altering the constitution so that justices of State Supreme Court Justices would be elected.[36] That move was not successful.

Tension between New Jersey's death penalty statute and the state's appellate court system continued into the twenty-first century. When New Jerseyans for a Death Penalty Moratorium filed suit against the state Department of Corrections, the Superior Court of New Jersey Appellate Division unanimously ruled to stop all executions until the department could present evidence that it had the "medical expertise" necessary to reverse the effects of a lethal drug if a condemned person should receive a last-minute stay of execution after being injected, or else show that "appropriate lethal drugs [existed] whose effects might be reversible;" and demonstrate that "institutional safety and security" necessitated the Department's "blanket" proscriptions against filming executions, permitting any contact between condemned people and "members of the news media," and public viewing of executions before the person is strapped to the gurney.[37] The court reasoned that New Jerseyans might better judge the ethics of capital punishment by observing its real-world application, if "the inmate can be given the choice of whether he wishes to speak to the press or have the execution filmed or have it witnessed by the media at some point prior to being strapped to the gurney and [having] the intravenous lines connected."[38]

Later in the same year, on 2 June 2004, the New Jersey Supreme Court added yet another obstacle to the state's death statute in State v. Marcus Toliver and Ryshaone Thomas. The court ruled that any prosecutor seeking a capital indictment must present to the grand jury the aggravating factors that "he or she intends to rely on in seeking the death penalty."[39] In short, the decision required prosecutors seeking a capital conviction to provide evidence of aggravating and mitigating factors to grand jury members.[40] This ruling, however, did not affect people already sentenced to die. With some New Jersey death row inmates having exhausted the appeal process, the outcome of death penalty debates in the Legislature became even more timely and significant.

GRASS-ROOTS ORGANIZATION

Lorry Post's early experiences as an activist against the death penalty are informative. Although Post is not a Roman Catholic, he recalled that his friend "Jack Callahan is, and Jack guided me around the State House in the early days, having once worked for the State Senate, and interestingly enough, sought out those legislators he knew to be Catholic for us to speak to. At the beginning we had only two Assemblymen in our corner, including Assemblyman Caraballo. . . . It was a question of winning others over, one by one."[41] In 2005, Sister Helen Prejean visited New Jersey to lobby against capital punishment in the Legislature and at a Catholic high school.[42] By 2007, she had made dozens of trips to the state to urge repeal of the death penalty.[43] Celeste Fitzgerald, a Roman Catholic who was head of New Jerseyans for Alternatives to the Death Penalty, managed to increase her organization's budget to $600,000 with the help of approximately 200 sponsoring groups. This budget allowed her to hire staff and open an office near the state capitol.[44] Fitzgerald's abolitionist efforts began in 1999, and in 2008, she received an award from the Diocese of Metuchen for her long-term service.[45] Over eight years, with the assistance of priests, nuns, and bishops, the coalition of abolitionists conducted hundreds of events in New Jersey churches. One of those won over was Roman Catholic Senator Raymond Lesniak, a primary cosponsor of the 2007 abolition bill.[46]

THE ABOLITION DEBATE MOVES TO THE LEGISLATURE

In 2003, the New Jersey Legislature passed a bill—which had been introduced on 21 February 2002—that suggested the legislators shared the state's appellate judges' aversion toward implementing the death penalty. Assembly Bill No. 1913 sought to create a study commission to examine: (1) if capital punishment has a deterrence value or other "legitimate penological intent;" (2) if the cost of capital punishment from "indictment to execution" is "significantly" more than the cost of life without parole; (3) whether capital punishment is consistent with "evolving standards of decency"; (4) if any "variability in the sentencing phase" or the selection of capital defendants is "arbitrary, unfair, or discriminatory"; (5) if there exists a "significant difference" between the crimes of those who receive the death penalty and those who are sentenced to life; (6) whether the possibility of executing an innocent person is justified by any potential value of capital punishment; and (7) if there are acceptable alternatives to the death penalty.[47] To gain the legislative support necessary to pass the bill, an addition was passed that included a "recommendation that no execution should be carried out until the commission has completed its report."[48] However, James E. McGreevey, the Democrat who was governor at that time, vetoed the effort.

Two years later the Legislature, with near-total Democratic and mixed Republican support, was able to pass a bill similar to the 2003 effort with a moratorium on executions intact. The bill was sponsored by two members of the Assembly, Democrat Reed Gusciora and Republican Christopher Bateman. Signed by acting Governor Richard J. Codey on January 12, 2006, it was the first moratorium on executions imposed by any state legislature in the country.[49] Celeste Fitzgerald, chair of New Jerseyans for Alternatives to the Death Penalty, told a National Public Radio journalist that "the turning point came on Good Friday of last year when the U.S. Conference of Catholic Bishops called for an end to capital punishment. Not only did that boost church involvement, but it influenced some of New Jersey's Catholic legislators."[50]

To carry out its charge, the resulting New Jersey Death Penalty Study Commission "held a total of five public hearings during which the members heard from numerous witnesses including: family members of murder victims, persons wrongfully convicted, and members of the general public. Invitations to speak were extended to leading academic experts on the subject of capital punishment, both opposed and in favor of the death penalty; victims' rights advocates; and public officials from the Judiciary, the office of the Public Defender, and the Department of Corrections."[51] Witnesses' accounts and sentiments expressed in the commission's hearings closely paralleled testimony at the public hearings held by the New York State Legislature following the 2004 decision by that state's Court of Appeals that abolished the death penalty in New York (see chapter 2). For example, Barry Scheck, codirector of the Innocence Project at Cardozo Law School, reminded members of the New Jersey commission "that 182 individuals in the United States have been exonerated with post-conviction DNA testing, 14 of whom had been sentenced to death."[52] Expressing the views of the religious community, Rev. John M. Smith, bishop of the Catholic Diocese of Trenton, reminded commission members that the Catholic bishops of New Jersey believed the death penalty to be inconsistent with "evolving standards of decency."[53] Few witnesses spoke in favor of retaining the death penalty. Even fewer cited credible legal, ethical, economic, or deterrence justifications for executions. Given the dearth of evidence that capital punishment is a deterrent, one committee member who favored executions stated: "I have never attempted to justify the death penalty on an empirical deterrence argument because it cannot be done. . . . I have long suspected that the death penalty may be a deterrent for certain murders for hire and terrorism, but it cannot be proved. It also cannot be definitively disproved that the death penalty is a deterrent."[54] In the end, given the numerous problems with implementing the death penalty discussed during the course of five hearings, the suspicion of deterrence was not enough. Twelve members of the New Jersey Death Penalty Study Commission concluded that "the death penalty in New Jersey [should] be abolished and replaced with life imprisonment without the possibility of parole, to be served in a maximum security facility."[55]

Republican Senator John Russo—a former Democrat who had been president of the state Senate and sponsor of Senate Bill 112, which had reestablished capital punishment in 1982—was the lone dissenter to the commission's conclusions. In its report's "Minority View," he claimed that his position on capital punishment was not motivated by "the death of [his] father who was killed in his home during a robbery."[56] He blamed the failure of capital punishment in New Jersey on "liberal judges . . . who have consistently disregarded the legislative will and refused to enforce the law as written."[57]

However, the New Jersey Legislature tended to accept the analysis of the other twelve commission members, and it began the process of abolishing capital punishment. Four months later, the Senate Judiciary Committee voted eight to two in favor of a death penalty abolition bill cosponsored by Senator Lesniak. He gave the bill a fifty-fifty chance of succeeding on the Senate floor. Public testimony on the bill was largely supportive. Two groups who were generally in favor of capital punishment nonetheless testified in favor of abolition: a representative of the state prosecutor's association reasoned that abolition "would lead to swift and sure punishment"; and forty-two relatives of murder victims signed a petition supporting "life without the possibility of parole as a way of providing finality in their grieving."[58]

By the last two months of 2007, the momentum to abolish the death penalty had peaked. Conservative Republican Senator Gerald Cardinale held a news conference with death penalty advocate Professor Robert Blecker of the New York Law School to argue against fast-tracking the abolition bill. Blecker argued that "there is no emergency here. As everybody knows, New Jersey hasn't executed anybody in decades."[59] However, Senator Cardinale's statements strengthened the legislators' determination to abolish capital punishment before the end of the year. The Democratic leaders in the Legislature, the Corzine administration, and Republicans favoring abolition reasoned that the "opportunity for victory" was greatest in the lame-duck legislature. "'We wanted to win,' said Senator Robert Martin, a Republican who helped secure votes in his party. 'So you try to pick your game plan and you go for it.'"[60]

THE SENATE'S FINAL WORDS

Consistent with earlier hearings, the testimony heard by the Senate Budget and Appropriations Committee was largely opposed to the death penalty. Edward DeFazio, a prosecutor and ex officio member of the New Jersey Death Penalty Study Commission, called the state's death penalty "a cruel hoax on the families of the victims." Vicki Schieber, a board member of the national organization called Murder Victims for Human Rights, noted that capital punishment gave victims' families no closure. Kathleen Garcia, another witness, agreed, stating that she had worked "on the Death Penalty Study Commission with prosecutors DeFazio and Kelaher [and learned about murder survivors'] trauma and grief with every new trial and appeal." She argued that "what survivors of crime victims need most is certainty in sentencing."[61]

Roman Catholic Bishop John Smith testified that "over many decades the Catholic Bishops of New Jersey have called for the abolishment of the death penalty. . . . The death penalty takes human life and should be abolished. . . . We cannot teach respect for life by taking a life." To illustrate the effectiveness of that effort, Thomas Kelaher, a prosecutor, noted that "to pick a jury we went through almost 200 people before we were able to seat 14 people . . . who would vote for the death penalty. . . . People released from the jury were concerned with the position of the Church: [and thus the death penalty was] 'an exercise in futility.'"[62]

Yet some opponents of abolition in New Jersey emphasized their Catholicism. Senator Russo noted that he had been a student at the University of Notre Dame and had great respect for Bishop Smith, but he also observed that "I'm a practicing Catholic and have always been pro life" and opposed to abortion, but not to capital punishment. Another opponent of abolition, John Tomicki, noted that he had been educated by "the Jesuits at Fordham [University]," and they had emphasized that executions were approved by the Bible.[63] In the end, members of the Senate Budget and Appropriations Committee voted eight to four in favor of releasing the bill for consideration by the full Senate.

One week later, the Senate passed the measure, twenty-one to sixteen. Republican Senator Leonard Lance noted: "The Senate Republican Caucus has chosen not to take a position on the issue and each Republican member of the senate will be voting his or her conscience on the issue." With few exceptions, however, legislators' comments during the debate before the vote had a partisan character. Democrats tended to argue that New Jersey's failure to carry out a single execution after the *Furman* decision indicated that the state's penal policy was a failure that could be corrected only by abolishing capital punishment. Conservative Republicans instead recommended simply reforming the existing law. Democratic Senator Lesniak argued: "We shouldn't have the death penalty unless we're going to use it. And we shouldn't use it." Senator Richard Codey concurred, noting that since the state had reinstated the death penalty, only nine people had received a death sentence and no one had been executed: "How could I intelligently argue for the deterrent aspect of the death penalty when we have never used it?"[64]

On the other hand, Republican Senator Leonard Lance was confident, since New Jersey prosecutors and judges were appointed by the state's governor with "the advice and consent of the Senate [instead of being elected], that there's no question as to the guilt of the nine persons who have been sentenced to capital punishment in New Jersey." Senator Cardinale added: "Common sense tells us that penalties deter crime. [But] we haven't used the death penalty in New Jersey." Senator Ronald Rice agreed, noting that the courts had prevented executions from taking place: "We need to fix the system. In order for deterrent mechanisms to be there punishment must be swift and certain."[65]

The Assembly's Final Words

The Assembly Law and Public Safety Committee heard testimony in favor of abolition from Assemblyman Wilfredo Caraballo, who said that "this is not a Democratic bill, this is not a Republican bill; this is a bill about the people in the state." But a Protestant clergyman, Rev. Douglas Batchelder from the Fellowship Church of Phillipsburg, stated: "By removing the death penalty you would be communicating the fact that justice in New Jersey is diminished in regard to the value of human life."[66]

Republican Assemblyman Chris Bateman noted the special harm that capital punishment does to victim's families: "The death penalty despite necessary precautions and attempts to make it work remains deeply flawed causing nothing but delays and pain. . . . The commission heard from dozens of family members and victims' advocates who said that the death penalty had harmed them." Charles Bennett agreed, noting that his daughter and two grandchildren had been murdered and that he had been a police officer and US Marine during the Vietnam War. He stated: "I can assure you that I am not testifying in favor of ending the death penalty because of any sympathy for murderers. I am here because my law enforcement experience has shown me that the death penalty has been a colossal failure. It is not a deterrent [and] has only served to hurt victims' families and distract from justice."[67]

Marilyn Zabinsky, a New Jersey citizen who challenged the integrity of pro-abolition witnesses, asked that the testimony of the New Jersey prosecutors DeFazio and Kelaher (both abolitionists and members of the New Jersey Death Penalty Study Commission) be taken with a grain of salt. She noted that during the legislative sessions and commission meetings, they were waiting for the governor to reappoint them to their positions. In any case, the committee released the bill to the full Assembly for consideration.[68]

The Assembly had a somewhat shorter debate before voting forty-four to thirty-six to abolish the death penalty. Chris Bateman shared with his fellow legislators the details of his first meeting with longtime New Jersey abolitionist Lorry Post, the father of a murder victim: "In 2001 Lorry Post walked into my legislative office and told me that he had lost his only daughter to murder [and that] the death penalty fails victims' families and exacerbates their pain."[69] Assembly Majority Leader Bonnie Watson Coleman read a letter from a constituent: "As the son of a woman who was murdered and whose killer received life without parole, I can tell you that your vote to repeal the death penalty will save countless families the unnecessary suffering that death penalty processes by their nature entail."[70]

Assemblyman Caraballo reported: "Sister Helen Prejean, the author of *Dead Man Walking* was here in New Jersey a couple of weeks ago at a statehouse press conference where she said that New Jersey is going to be a beacon on the hill. The Death Penalty Study Commission found a system that lacks closure. . . . Our death penalty is fatally flawed. It creates a false sense of security for those who want to see justice done and it is hurtful to the families of murdered ones who only want to see justice done." Assemblyman Michael Doherty disagreed. He summed up his position: "The reason the death penalty has not been a deterrent in New Jersey is that we haven't used it."[71]

REFLECTIONS OF THE PARTICIPANTS

Key legislative leaders in the successful effort to abolish the death penalty were Richard Codey, president of the Senate; Assemblyman Gordon Johnson, a former police officer; and Senator Lesniak, sponsor of the abolition bill. The irony of this coalition is hard to overstate. Codey was part of the alliance that reestablished New Jersey's death penalty in 1982. Johnson confessed to spending most of his life as a proponent of the "eye for an eye" approach. And Lesniak voted in favor on the 1982 reinstatement bill.[72] Before Governor Corzine's remarks at the bill signing, Lesniak spoke as a former death penalty supporter: "Today I'd like to thank some folks who helped correct that mistake. The support of the New Jersey Bishops lead [sic] by Archbishop Smith and the Catholic Conference was of particular significance to me. . . . My struggles with the faith of my baptism and their support strengthened my beliefs. Pope John Paul II would be proud. . . . And I want to thank Governor Corzine for not listening to me when I tried to convince him to change his position against the death penalty when he first ran for the U.S. Senate more than seven years ago."[73]

Only death penalty supporters emphasized that they were pro-life by being opposed to abortion. Those Catholics who testified on behalf of the abolition of capital punishment had no need to assert their faith since they stood with the hierarchy of the Catholic Church. The irony is that vigorous Catholic opposition to the death penalty occurred simultaneously with aggressive Catholic opposition to the US Supreme Court's Roe v. Wade decision[74] and women's new right to freedom of choice. In fact, neither side of the abolition debate adopted a "seamless garment" position consistent with the teachings of the Catholic Church. Assemblyman James Holzapfel asked his colleagues: "What would we do if we caught someone similar to Osama Bin Laden tomorrow?"—contending that only killing such an individual would be appropriate. Assemblyman Michael Patrick Carroll agreed: "The Left concerns itself very little with the preservation of innocent life except for innocent whales and harp seals. Many of these same folks who shed tears over the fate [of those on death row] can locate not the slightest mode of compassion for the innocent unborn." Yet it was left to Assemblywoman Marcia Karrow to speak in the strongest terms: "The eight monsters that are on death row are monsters. We shouldn't even call them men or humans."[75] Their stridency suggests that they knew they were losing the debate on capital punishment.

<table>
<tr><td>**4**</td><td>The Abolition of
Capital Punishment
in New Mexico</td></tr>
</table>

Just over a year after New Jersey's historic change, New Mexico abolished its death penalty law,[1] becoming the second state to legislatively abandon capital punishment since 1965. On 11 February 2009, the New Mexico House voted forty to twenty-eight to repeal capital punishment, and on 13 March, the Senate concurred, with a vote of twenty-four to eighteen. Legislators, death penalty activists, and other interested parties were not sure, given his previous campaign statements, if Governor Bill Richardson would sign or veto the repeal bill. In fact, the governor was unsure himself, and he set up a hotline and invited the state's citizens to share their opinions on the subject with him. On 17 March, he "released details of more than 9,400 calls, E-mails and walk-ins he's received on the issue," with 7,169 people for and 2,244 against the repeal of New Mexico's death penalty.[2] After much indecision, the Hispanic Roman Catholic governor signed House Bill 285 on 18 March 2009.[3] Governor Richardson cited three factors that moved him to reverse his "lifelong" support for capital punishment and sign the repeal bill: (1) the danger of executing an innocent person; (2) the overrepresentation of members of racial and ethnic minority groups in prisons and on death rows; and (3) changing international standards for human rights.[4] He said:

> If the State is going to undertake this awesome responsibility [capital punishment], the system to impose this ultimate penalty must be perfect and can never be wrong. But the reality is the system is not perfect—far from it. . . . DNA testing has proven that. Innocent people have been put on death row all across the country. . . . And it bothers me greatly that minorities are overrepresented in the prison population and on death row. . . . From an international human rights perspective, there is no reason the United States should be behind the rest of the world on this issue. Many of the countries that continue

to support and use the death penalty are also the most repressive nations in the world. That's not something to be proud of.[5]

The governor recognized Representative Gail Chasey, sponsor of House Bill 285, for her long-term efforts to repeal New Mexico's death penalty statute and for replacing death with a "true life without the possibility of parole—a sentence that ensures violent criminals are locked away from society forever."[6]

As was the case in New Jersey, in New Mexico, popular support for the death penalty depends on how you measure it. New Mexico is the seventh most Roman Catholic state, with Catholics making up 33 percent of its population.[7] Does the relatively high proportion of Catholics significantly alter public opinion about the death penalty? In 2002, 66 percent of a "New Mexico likely voter" sample backed capital punishment.[8] In 2005, Brian Sanderoff—a long-term Albuquerque pollster—stated that support for the death penalty remained high in New Mexico: "Catholics, Hispanics, women, Democrats and people who live in north-central New Mexico are less supportive . . . , but even among these groups, a majority or plurality still supports it."[9] However, in December 2008, when a random sample of likely New Mexican voters was asked by Sanderoff's polling firm, "Would you support or oppose replacing the death penalty with a sentence of life without possibility of parole for people convicted of murder, plus restitution to the victim's family, meaning the prisoner would work in prison to pay compensation to the family of the murder victim?," 64 percent indicated that they would support such a bill.[10] When likely voters were simply asked if they would support the substitution of a life sentence without the possibility of parole for the execution of convicted murders, 53 percent said they would, but the share of those opposed increased to 37 percent, while the proportion of people who did not know or would not answer increased to 10 percent.[11]

LETHAL VIOLENCE AND POPULATION SHIFTS IN NEW MEXICO

New Mexico executed seventy-three people prior to 1976 and one in 2001. Sixty-five condemned individuals were hanged between 1851 and 1923. Between 1933 and 1956, seven people were electrocuted. One individual was killed by gas in 1960, and one person died of lethal injection in 2001. At least forty-two of those seventy-three people persons were

Hispanic, as were thirty-four of the last fifty people executed in New Mexico.[12]

The Census Bureau did not distinguish between the categories of "White, not Hispanic" and "White Hispanic" until 1970. However, data since then suggest a significant interaction between race and executions in New Mexico. A 1970 sample of 15 percent of New Mexicans who responded to the decennial census of that year indicated that 37.4 percent of the state's population was Hispanic, while 53.8 percent were white, not Hispanic.[13] During the rest of the twentieth century, the gap in size between the two groups narrowed.

The population of New Mexico grew from an estimated 195,310 people in 1900 to 2,009,671 in 2009.[14] According to Don Albrecht, "in 1980 the population of New Mexico was 53 percent White, 37 percent Hispanic. . . . During the ensuing two decades, the White population increased by 18 percent, while the Hispanic population increased by 60.5 percent. . . . As a consequence, by 2000, the New Mexico population was less than 50 percent (45.5) White and . . . 42.8 percent Hispanic."[15] The state has become more diverse in recent years: by 2009, 45.6 percent of New Mexicans were of Hispanic or Latino origin, and only 40.9 percent were non-Hispanic whites.[16] A 2009 Pew Hispanic Center report indicates that New Mexico had a higher proportion of Hispanics in its population than any other state.[17] Thus, the ethnic category that is overrepresented on the state's execution record has become New Mexico's dominant group. The Pew Forum on Religious and Public Life has found that support for capital punishment is related to race: support for the death penalty is 68 percent among white Americans, 48 percent among Hispanics, and 40 percent among African Americans.[18]

Between 1960 and 2009, New Mexico's recorded rate of murder and nonnegligent manslaughter ranged from a low of 5.4 per 100,000 residents in 2001 to a high of 13.3 in 1975. Ironically, New Mexico held its only post-*Furman* execution during the same year that the state was enjoying its lowest murder rate since 1960. The state's highest murder rate over the past two decades was 11.5, in 1996. Only five states and the District of Columbia recorded a higher average murder rate than New Mexico for the period 1990–2009. In 2009, New Mexico's reported murder rate was 8.7. Against historical odds, New Mexico abolished the death penalty during a year when only one state, Louisiana, was recording a higher murder rate per 100,000 residents.[19]

A recent article in the *New Mexico Law Review* reflects New Mexico's legal culture: From the reinstatement of the death penalty in July 1979 through 2007, 211 capital cases were filed. Nearly half of these went to trial, but of those cases, only fifteen defendants were sentenced to death by juries. One of the fifteen was executed, and two remain on the state's death row. Death penalty cases have increased in only one of the state's thirteen judicial districts.[20] House debate on the abolition bill picks up on this reluctance: Representative Gail Chasey noted that the number of death penalty cases filed in New Mexico had decreased since the death penalty was reinstated in 1979. She pointed out that only 7 percent of death penalty cases drew a death sentence, 68 percent of which were overturned—giving New Mexico the highest reversal rate in the country. Chasey stated: "We have executed 1 person since 1961, in 48 years. In 48 years we've spent several million dollars a year for this one execution. That's not much of a return."[21] She also noted that 310 black people were murdered in New Mexico between 1980 and 2000, yet prosecutors asked for the death penalty in only one of these cases.[22] Representative Eleanor Chavez added that 135 prison inmates had been shown to be innocent and released during the past thirty-five years.[23] The picture that emerges from the administration of the death penalty in New Mexico is one of reluctance, incompetence, and racism. That picture is enhanced by reviewing the individual and political dynamics involved in New Mexico's only post-*Furman* execution.

When Governor Toney Anaya left office in 1986, he emptied New Mexico's death row by reducing the sentences of five inmates to life in prison. He would have reduced six sentences had the judge who accepted Terry Clark's guilty plea not delayed his sentencing until after Anaya had left office. Thus, New Mexico, once again, had a death row inmate. Clark's sentence was overturned in 1995 but reinstated the following year. Enter New Mexico's new "tough on crime," pro–capital punishment governor, Gary Johnson, in 1994. During his first term, Johnson failed in his attempt to expand the categories of those eligible for execution to include juveniles as young as thirteen, and to put a two-year limit on death row appeals. However, he was successful in expanding New Mexico's death penalty statute to apply to "child killers, [those who commit] multiple murders, and drive-by killers."[24] On 9 December 2000, Johnson summarized his death penalty sentiments: "If you have committed murder, I happen to believe that you should pay for that with your own life."[25] New Mexico's legislators appeared to agree. On 9 February 2001, the Senate rejected a death penalty repeal bill (SB 165) sponsored by the Democratic Senate Majority Leader, Manny Aragon, by a vote of twenty-one to twenty.[26]

As Terry Clark's execution grew closer and apparently became unavoidable unless Johnson intervened, the governor's execution rhetoric softened. He admitted that racial and economic discrimination affected the application of the death penalty, and that even though New Mexico's capital appeals process is "too long," if the system were not in place, innocent people might be executed.[27] The governor stated that he was open to a debate on capital punishment and that, "given the reality of the sentence today," abolition "may prove to be better public policy."[28] However, Johnson did not intervene in Clark's execution. Two correctional officers from Texas's death row in Huntsville were hired to carry out the killing. After the execution, Johnson again hinted that he might be ready to sign a bill repealing the death penalty.[29] And in 2009 there was little ambiguity in the former governor's sentiments: he now opposed capital punishment, referring to it as "flawed public policy" and stating that "I unequivocally believe that innocent people have been executed in this country and there will continue to be innocent people executed."[30] Not surprisingly, efforts to repeal New Mexico's death penalty gained momentum and strength at this point.

GRASS-ROOTS ORGANIZATION

In 1997, the New Mexico Coalition to Repeal the Death Penalty was organized and held its first legislative interim committee meeting. At this meeting, Gail Chasey, an Episcopalian and a newly elected representative, volunteered to lead the legislative effort to repeal the death penalty. She introduced legislation in 1999, 2001, 2003, 2005, and 2007,[31] typically failing by a close vote in committee or on the Senate floor. According to the coalition's executive director, Viki Elkey, the group had more than 3,800 individual members around the state, including members of trade unions, and more than 140 organization members, including the New Mexico Catholic Conference and Murder Victims' Families for Reconciliation.[32] The coalition's financial backer was the New Mexico Conference of Churches.[33]

In 2005, the coalition's efforts focused on how the needs of violent crime victims were not being met because of the death penalty, with a campaign called "Victims' Families First."[34] The 2009 repeal effort was further strengthened by the increasing number of innocent people being released from death rows across the country.[35] Juan Melendez, freed in 2002 after spending almost eighteen years on Florida's death row, spoke to numerous New Mexico legislators and the governor about prosecutorial misconduct, lying witnesses, and the poor defense he had received, all of which had helped land him on death row. Commenting on the successful 2009 abolition effort, Viki Elkey declared: "I will never forget the look on Governor Richardson's face as he listened to Juan just two days before he signed the legislation—he was disgusted by the way Juan was railroaded onto death row."[36]

Although Governor Richardson had supported the death penalty while campaigning for president, he asked state senators to give the 2009 repeal bill a fair committee hearing and floor consideration.[37] This helped get the bill through the Senate Judiciary Committee where it had stalled in the previous two sessions.[38] Elkey also praised the Roman Catholic clergy, observing that the "Catholic Church was wonderful here in New Mexico and literally got us the votes we needed. Our archbishop had several dinners with our governor to help convince him that abolition was the best thing to do."[39] Elkey recalled that Allen Sanchez, director of the New Mexico Conference of Catholic Bishops, told her that Governor Richardson had told him that prior to his meetings with the New Mexico Archbishop he would have vetoed the bill.[40]

A LEGISLATIVE MORAL ENTREPRENEUR

Representative Gail Chasey formally entered New Mexico's death penalty debate in 1999 when she introduced House Bill 305, which would have abolished the death penalty replacing it with life imprisonment without the possibility of parole.[41] The core abolitionist figure in the New Mexico Legislature, Chasey had her first major success in the campaign against the death penalty in 2005. Her abolition bill of that year, HB 576, won thirty-four cosponsors, was approved by two House committees, passed the full House by thirty-eight votes to thirty-one, and was approved by the Senate Rules Committee before being defeated in the Senate Judiciary Committee by a vote of five to four.[42] Chasey's 2007 bill, HB 190, enjoyed similar initial success and also faltered in the Senate Judiciary Committee.[43]

Evidence suggests that the Victims' Families First campaign, official estimates of execution costs, and ever-increasing concern about executing innocent people[44] all played key roles in the increasing success that Chasey's bills enjoyed over time. From 1999 on, every death penalty repeal bill that she introduced was accompanied by bills to benefit crime victims or murder victims' families. In 2005 and 2007 she sponsored two bills (HB 578 and HB 193, respectively) that were designed to give crime victims paid or unpaid leave from their jobs so that they could attend legal proceedings without fear of losing their jobs and to financially reimburse employers for granting paid leave and victims who had to take unpaid leave.[45] During those same legislative sessions, Chasey sponsored bills that would grant college tuition assistance to family members of murder victims.[46] The successful repeal bill (HB 285) continued that effort, by allotting a portion of the money saved from repealing executions to provide expanded services to the families of murder victims, while a separate bill (HB 211) again sought job protection for crime victims who took leave to attend court hearings and trials.[47] Thus it was difficult to paint Chasey or her associates at the New Mexico Coalition to Repeal the Death Penalty as uncaring or callous toward victims.

The "Fiscal Impact Report" attached to Chasey's 2005 abolition bill began to seriously reevaluate execution costs. Earlier impact reports tended to minimize judicial and corrections costs. For example, the 2001 Fiscal Impact Report said: "The cost of a life sentence without parole could be ten times the cost of imposing the death penalty."[48] The 2005 Fiscal Impact Report, while remaining silent on corrections' costs, reported significant increases in judicial expenditures as a potential problem with executions: "An estimate of what a death penalty case cost for the jury and witness fee fund is approximately $20,000–$25,000. In contrast, a non–death penalty murder case cost approximately $7,000–$8,000."[49] If the 2005 report suggested that criminal justice expenditures in New Mexico were escalating, the estimates of costs in the 2007 and 2009 Fiscal Impact Reports were chilling. Taking full advantage of the 2004 report published by the State Bar Task Force to Study the Administration of the Death Penalty in New Mexico, along with other data and studies, the 2007 and 2009 reports concluded that the cost of an execution in New Mexico could equal North Carolina's cost of $2.16 million. Moreover, the chance that a multimillion dollar death penalty prosecution in New Mexico would end in the execution of a defendant was approximately 4.5 percent. The New Mexico Public Defender Department contended that repealing the death penalty would save the state millions.[50] These figures, in some form, were discussed during every subsequent legislative debate and public hearing reviewed by the authors of this book. Elkey commented: "While our supporters [members of the New Mexico Coalition to Repeal the Death Penalty] did not speak about the cost argument when they stood in support of repeal, they all wanted us to give them the information so they could study and learn why the death penalty costs so much. By educating [supporters] about the costs, we were able to combat any opposition on this issue among legislators."[51]

THE HOUSE'S FINAL WORDS

On 29 January 2009, the New Mexico House Consumer and Public Affairs Committee—consistent with its past support for bills to abolish the death penalty—voted five to two to release Chasey's abolition bill of that year, HB 285, from committee with a "Do Pass" recommendation. The vote was along strict party lines, with five Democrats voting for the bill and two Republicans opposing it.[52] Earlier, in a quavering voice, a woman had told committee members that the 2008 Texas execution of her son had caused her marriage to fall apart, and that she had had to be hospitalized several times during his appeals. She said: "I am the survivor of a murder victim. . . . When Texas murdered [her son] . . . it altered my life. . . . My family, my friends, my community all have been damaged. It was because of his execution."[53] Another witness testified about the 1999 murder of her husband, a lawyer, who had been killed while traveling to the Santa Fe courthouse. Allen Sanchez, director of the New Mexico Conference of Catholic Bishops, also testified.[54]

The next stop for HB 285 was the House Judiciary Committee. That committee voted eight to five to send the legislation to the House floor with a "recommendation that it do pass."[55] All of the eight members in favor were Democrats; one Democrat joined the four Republican members in opposing the bill.[56] Before the vote, a number of people had addressed the committee. Michelle Giger, a founder of Murder Victims' Families for Reconciliation and the daughter of a murder victim, argued that victims' families needed help, not executions. She said that the money saved from repealing capital punishment could be used to expand services for the families. Her message was: "'Let's put victims' families first."[57] Democratic Representative Antonio Maestas argued that capital punishment was the least effective law on the books.[58]

Some opponents of the bill contended that there was no way of guaranteeing that a convicted capital murderer would not get out of jail. Republican Representative Paul Bandy stated that the two people then on New Mexico's death row had been sent there by citizens of his county, and he could not "say they were wrong in that."[59] Republican Representative Dennis J. Kintigh disputed the idea that repealing capital punishment would save money, and in any case "the issue here is justice. . . . I beg this committee not to repeal the death penalty."[60]

57

The issues discussed during the House floor debate on HB 285 were largely the same as those addressed in testimonies delivered during earlier committee hearings. Representative Chasey stressed the death penalty's lack of deterrence, along with the irrationality and racism reflected in the courts. In the United States, she pointed out, both the highest murder rates and the highest levels of execution (83 percent of the country's executions in 2006) are found in southern states. White people and the wealthy are largely excluded from death row, where 53 percent of the people are Hispanic or African American. Furthermore, 85 percent of the victims of those on death row were white. Representative Eleanor Chavez agreed that the death penalty was "racially biased and unfair," noting that capital punishment is primarily reserved for the poor and people of color. She also noted that the majority of people facing the death penalty are unable to afford a lawyer, and that those who are executed are denied the right to due process because they are unable to benefit from new evidence.[61]

Representative Chasey quoted Sam Millsap, a former prosecutor from San Antonio, Texas, who she said believes that he was responsible for having an innocent man executed. Although he had placed a number of people on death row, he decided to change jobs when he discovered that this particular person was probably innocent.[62] On the other hand, Representative Kintigh spoke of his special standing as a law enforcement official who "had strived to put men on death row." He stated that he was required to protect people from "predators" even though, at times, members of his profession did not receive the respect that they deserved.[63]

Representative Antonio Maestas, a former prosecutor, and Gail Chasey expressed concern over the economic cost of the death penalty, compared to its benefits in controlling crime. Chasey lamented that New Mexico had spent millions of dollars on capital punishment, yet the state had executed only one person since 1960 and currently had only two on death row. Representative Maestas argued that New Mexico needed to scrutinize its expenditures very carefully in a time of scarcity.[64]

During the House debate, the special standing of certain witnesses was mentioned by the bill's sponsor, Representative Chasey, who shared the stories of an Albuquerque police officer whose daughter-in-law was kidnapped, raped, and murdered while walking her dog and a woman whose son was murdered. Both survivors stated that the execution of the murderer would not relieve their pain. Chasey also spoke of a woman whose brother was killed in the terrorist attacks of 11 September 2001 who said that the deaths of the attackers was no consolation to her, and she did not feel that justice had been done. Representative Sandra Jeff offered similar arguments against the death penalty. She quoted a woman who had lost two of her family members to murder and would not want to make someone else have the same experience. The victimized woman had stated: "Executing someone through use of the death penalty is simply murder. And putting someone to death will not bring my family members back." Jeff noted that this woman is "Catholic and a Native American and believes in the sanctity of life no matter what that life is."[65] Another representative said that a cousin of hers had been murdered, and another cousin had murdered her own husband. In both cases the victims' family members did not ask for revenge. Representative Chavez summed up the others' comments: "The death penalty does not deter crime. Killing people to show that killing people is wrong is not justice, it's revenge." Chavez further noted that the United States is the only Western nation that still upholds the death penalty and said: "I support this bill and I oppose the death penalty."[66]

The Roman Catholic Church made a prominent appearance in the New Mexico House debate. Representative Chasey pointed out that the church approves of the death penalty only when there is no other way to protect society from a dangerous person. With modern prisons, she noted, such situations no longer exist. Chasey quoted Pope John Paul II, who said: "If a person is incarcerated it is unethical to put him or her to death."[67] Chasey continued: "If you stop the attack, you no longer have the right to kill."[68] Representative Roger Madalena spoke of his background in the pueblo, how his people "embraced Roman Catholic beliefs" and native spirituality, and how the "Creator determines how much time people spend on earth, not people."[69] In the end New Mexico House members voted forty-one to twenty-eight to repeal the death penalty. Consistent with history, the vote was largely along party lines. Four Republicans voted with the Democratic majority, while seven Democrats sided with the Republican minority.

THE SENATE'S FINAL WORDS

The difference between success and failure in the Senate Judiciary Committee was the same as in 2007, except this time the one-vote margin was in favor of the repeal bill—which passed six to five. Voting in favor were six Democrats; one Democrat and four Republicans were opposed. Preceding the vote, the committee heard testimony from interested citizens and fellow lawmakers. Millsap told the committee that he was haunted by a decision he had made to prosecute an individual who might have been wrongly executed in 1993. He had decided to seek the death penalty on the basis of eyewitness identification, but the witness later recanted, claiming that the police had pressured him to make the identification.[70]

A number of the bill's opponents argued that the death penalty is a deterrent. The Senate Republican whip reasoned that police and corrections officers are best protected by capital punishment. Lemuel Martinez, a New Mexico prosecutor, stated that it was a deterrent and that people who said otherwise were wrong. Proponents of the bill cited a 1974 case in which four bikers were convicted of a "gruesome murder" and sent to death row, until they were exonerated when the real killer confessed.[71]

The last legislative hurdle for HB 285 was the full Senate. There, senators debated the merits of the bill for nearly three hours before voting. Numerous accounts of murders, often involving children, were presented to support the argument that capital punishment was just and necessary. Republican Senator Rod Adair reasoned that the death penalty is a deterrent because "six thousand years of recorded history confirms that it is and over 400 years of American Judeo-Christian traditions suggest that it is."[72] Senator Jerry Ortiz y Pino, an opponent of the death penalty, countered that New Mexico was striving to join states and countries that represent an "evolution . . . of our moral conscience." Responding to Adair's comment, Ortiz y Pino said that "during those six thousand years we have. . . . improved. We shouldn't be responding with the lizard part of our brain the way we did six thousand years ago."[73] The Senate majority leader reminded his colleagues that no one has been executed in New Mexico for killing a law enforcement officer in nearly a hundred years, and thus the death penalty was not a deterrent.[74]

Senator Michael Sanchez recounted the story of a rape victim in North Carolina who identified her attacker in a courtroom. The woman pointed to the person who "without a doubt" had attacked her. The person she accused went to prison for eleven years but was later exonerated based on DNA evidence. Sanchez stated: "It turned this young lady's life around to the point where to this day . . . this woman [and the man she accused] go around the country talking about eyewitness identifications and how they can be misleading."[75] Sanchez also noted that two psychologists—one from the University of California at Irvine, the other from Iowa State University—discussed how police can unintentionally persuade victims to identify a suspect. When they showed one police officer how this happened, he was surprised to learn that his witness identification procedures were suggestive.[76]

Sanchez also informed her fellow senators that a group representing family members of murder victims supported HB 285. The group had stated that the lengthy appeals process was difficult for victims' families, whereas a life sentence without parole could bring closure.[77] According to one account of the debate, it contained "repeated biblical references, leading one Senate wit to crack that he felt like he was somewhere other than the state Capitol."[78] After the debate, the Senate concurred with the House and voted to repeal New Mexico's death penalty by twenty-four to eighteen. All those who voted for repeal were Democrats. Three Democrats joined fifteen Republicans in opposing the bill. Governor Richardson signed the bill, and New Mexico joined the ranks of states leading the way.

REFLECTIONS OF KEY PARTICIPANTS

On 15 April 2009, an Albuquerque television station reported that Governor Richardson, Archbishop Michael Sheehan of Santa Fe, and representatives of the New Mexico Coalition to Repeal the Death Penalty, the Catholic lay organization that had spearheaded the effort to repeal capital punishment, were visiting Rome. To celebrate Governor Richardson's role in repealing New Mexico's death penalty, he was given "a warm welcome . . . as he met with Pope Benedict XVI."[79] When a condemned individual receives a stay of execution, or a state or country abolishes the death penalty, Roman officials turn the lights shining on the ancient Colosseum from white to gold, which happened when New Mexico abolished capital punishment in March 2009. To honor their efforts, the abolition group from New Mexico was treated to a repeat performance of the ceremony. In a news conference organized by Sant'Egidio (an international organization of lay Catholics opposed to the death penalty), Governor Richardson said his views on capital punishment were "softening" and that conversations with Archbishop Sheehan had influenced his sentiments.[80] Representative Chasey explained her success in moving HB 285 through the Senate Judiciary Committee and the full Senate with simple arithmetic, because the 2008 general election had added three Democrats to the Senate. Similarly, Lem Martinez referred to the outcome as "Obama's coattails."[81]

<table>
<tr><td>

5

</td><td>

The Abolition of Capital Punishment in Illinois

</td></tr>
</table>

A BROKEN DEATH PENALTY SYSTEM
AND GOVERNOR GEORGE RYAN

Prior to 1976, Illinois executed 348 prisoners, 81 of whom were black.[1] Since 1976, Illinois had fifteen prisoners on death row and had executed twelve prisoners. In 2000, the *Nation* reported that 49 percent of the death sentences imposed in Illinois had been reversed by the state's Supreme Court, pending retrial or resentencing. These reversals were in response to judicial errors, incompetent defense attorneys, and prosecutorial misconduct.[2] In response to a string of wrongful convictions in 1999, the *Chicago Tribune* investigated the 285 capital cases handled by the Illinois criminal justice system since the state's death penalty statute went into effect in 1977 and published a five-part series titled "Failure of the Death Penalty in Illinois."[3] The newspaper found that nearly half of the state's capital convictions had been overturned on appeal. Moreover, in 46 cases, important testimony had come from jailed informants often in exchange for lighter sentences. Investigators also noted that in 33 Illinois capital cases, defense lawyers assigned by the state "had been disbarred or suspended—sanctions reserved for conduct so incompetent, unethical or even criminal the lawyer's license is taken away."[4] Additional problems included misconduct by prosecutors and police, flaws in forensic evidence, and the deliberate exclusion of African Americans from jury duty.[5] In 35 cases, the *Tribune* reported, black defendants were sentenced to death by all-white juries. The *Tribune* findings were widely reported across the United States. At hearings in Springfield and Chicago, defense attorneys argued that the system has wrongly sent at least thirteen men to death row.[6]

After Illinois released thirteen prisoners from death row, Governor George Ryan put a halt to executions in the state for eighteen months. Some of the men who had received death sentences were shown to be innocent, while others had not received fair trials.[7] And the governor was considering whether to follow up his moratorium by commuting the sentences of all Illinois death-row inmates.[8] By executive order on 9 March 2000, Ryan formed the Illinois Governor's Commission on Capital Punishment—a body evenly divided between death penalty supporters and abolitionists—to study the issue. The commission recommended reforms that would significantly restrict the conditions under which a death sentence could be imposed—although even these changes might not prevent innocent people from being executed. The Governor's Commission on Capital Punishment issued its final report on 15 April 2002.[9]

The Northwestern University School of Journalism was centrally involved in the process. As of 2004, thirteen Illinois death row prisoners had been exonerated with the help of Northwestern's Medill Innocence Project—essentially David Protess, a professor at the school, and his students. Yet since Gregg v. Georgia, Illinois had executed twelve people. Ryan said of his state's death penalty: "'It's like flipping a coin'—that is, a 50–50 game of chance with someone's life at stake."[10] In a letter to the *Chicago Daily Herald*, a reader named Bill Ryan noted that 260 Illinois prisoners had been condemned and that 13 exonerated prisoners had spent "a combined total of 115 years surviving the horrors of death row for crimes they did not commit." He observed that the overturned convictions were due to the efforts of "journalism students, lawyers and in many cases [they were a result of] plain luck"—had the system had run its course, the 13 innocent people would have been killed as well.[11]

In 2002 Glenn Pierce and Michael Radelet reported on a study they had conducted of Illinois death sentencing, which was funded by the Governor's Commission on Capital Punishment. The authors found significant racial discrepancies in sentencing.[12] First, Pierce and Radelet noted that sentencing someone to death was an extremely rare event in Illinois. From 1977 to 1980, only 1 percent of homicides resulted in a death sentence. And from 1977 to 2002, whites comprised over 75 percent of the total population of the state, but less than 35 percent of those sentenced to death. Only 4 of the 101 whites sentenced to death had been convicted of killing an African American. Nearly 60 percent of those sentenced to death—regardless of their race—had been convicted of killing whites. The result was that in 2002, 63 percent of the 173 people on death row in Illinois were African Americans. Blacks were four times more likely to have been victims of homicide; yet in first-degree murder cases that resulted in a death sentence, nearly four times more cases involved a white victim than a black victim.

A 2003 *USA Today* editorial supported Governor Ryan's decision to clear death row, stating that the money used to maintain it could instead pay for "roads, schools and even more prisons." The editorial noted that postconviction proceedings waste tens of million of dollars, and that two-thirds of the state's capital convictions were reversed. Moreover, in cases where the defendant was retried, she or he most often received a sentence other than death.[13]

A GROWING LIST OF ABOLITION ALLIES

Along with the Northwestern University Medill School of Journalism, the Illinois political establishment joined the abolition cause. In backing Governor Ryan's moratorium, Richard Daley—a former Cook County capital prosecutor and then Democratic mayor of Chicago—stated that the defense lawyers he encountered were often incompetent and underfunded and thus provided ineffective counsel.[14] The University of Chicago Law School added its name to the growing list of abolition supporters. The law school's Macarthur Justice Center estimated that the state of Illinois spent $2 million per death sentence and $18 million per execution. In contrast, imprisoning someone for fifty years costs about $800,000, or far less than half the cost of imposing a death sentence.[15]

The University of Illinois's student newspaper also joined the cause. In 2010, the editors of the *Daily Illini* stated: "We join anti-death penalty advocates in calling for an end to this barbaric practice." The newspaper pointed to racism in the criminal justice system and systematic problems that led to wrongful convictions. It noted that capital punishment is "significantly" more expensive than life without parole. Part of the additional cost is the appeals process, but in addition both the state of Illinois and the city of Chicago are paying millions of dollars to those who were wrongly convicted and sentenced to death. The newspaper quoted a former Cook County judge as saying: "The state of Illinois is in deep trouble, and we should not be squandering money on the death penalty when there's such great need with the elderly, with children, for health care, and for education."[16] Just before leaving office in January 2003, Governor Ryan commuted the sentences of 167 inmates on death row. Four other inmates were pardoned, and the Governor was nominated for a Nobel Peace Prize.[17]

THE MONEY INVOLVED

In 2003, Illinois incurred over $700,000 in trial costs while placing two men on the state's death row.[18] The state Treasurer's Office estimated that the cost of defending a death penalty case could range from $500,000 to $700,000.[19] Bill Ryan had noted in his 2001 letter to the editor that since the death penalty was reinstated twenty-two years earlier, Illinois taxpayers had sent 260 men and women to death row, spending $800 million more than what it would have cost to sentence each of them to life without parole. The $800 million figure did not include the more than $40 million paid to settle lawsuits by people wrongly sentenced to death.[20] And a reporter noted that the price of each capital case exceeds $1 million, meaning that using the death penalty "translates to hundreds of millions of taxpayer dollars."[21]

The reporter said that Illinois's capital punishment system did not benefit the state's citizens because nobody was being executed. This system, she argued, provides "no deterrence. No closure for the victims' families. No retribution. No benefits beyond those that are provided by the far less expensive option of life without parole."[22] Another reporter noted in 2004 that fewer death sentences were being imposed, following a shift in public opinion after a string of commutations and overturned convictions.[23] Some state residents were worried about the impact of the death penalty on the state's budget; others disliked the Republican gubernatorial candidate's support for executions.[24] The level of attention given to this issue in Illinois far surpassed that found in other states.

THE RECENT LEGISLATIVE ABOLITION PROCESS

On 28 October 2010, the Illinois Capital Punishment Reform Study Committee issued its sixth and final report. The committee, which had been established in the General Assembly's 2003 session, was one of the Governor's Commission on Capital Punishment's recommendations for death penalty reform. The study committee's charge was to evaluate the effects of reforms implemented by the Illinois General Assembly on capital punishment. The study committee was headed by Thomas P. Sullivan, a Catholic attorney from Chicago. A core finding in the committee's final report was that Illinois had spent more than $100 million to prosecute death cases since 2000.[25] Prior to the 2010 state elections, Bill Brady, the Republican candidate for governor, voiced support for the death penalty and said that he would consider ending the moratorium on capital punishment established in 2000 by George Ryan, the former Republican governor.[26] But the newly elected Democratic Governor Pat Quinn, a former attorney general, supported the moratorium. And Nathan Fields of Chicago, who had been wrongfully convicted and spent eleven years on death row, was suing the city for $360 million. At the beginning of January 2011, a reporter wrote that the state faced a budget crisis of $13 billion, putting Illinois in a tie with California for the lowest state credit rating in the nation.[27] Even so, the state's prosecutors were gearing up to oppose legislation that would abolish the death penalty.

Just prior to the January 2011 session of the Illinois General Assembly, thirty-five relatives of murder victims wrote a public letter to the legislators: "To be meaningful, justice should be swift and sure. The death penalty is neither. . . . Only a handful of arbitrarily selected murderers are sentenced to death. In 2008 there were 790 murders in Illinois and 3 death sentences. . . . At the same time, eliminating the death penalty would save scarce funds."[28]

An abolition bill (SB 3539) was sponsored in the Senate by Democratic Senator Kwame Raoul, who recalled his Catholic upbringing and stated that his children attended Catholic school "because of its value-based education." He said: "I want to thank the Illinois Catholic Conference and Francis Cardinal George for the letter sent in support of abolition." Democratic Senator William R. Haine quickly challenged the claim of that the Catholic Church opposed capital punishment.[29]

The bill's House sponsor was Democratic Representative Karen A. Yarbrough, who noted that Illinois had put twenty innocent men on death row, and that the state trailed only Florida in such a miscarriage of justice. She commented: "Those 20 men spent about 250 years on death row." She called the death penalty "extremely wasteful [since] . . . we spent. . . . over $100 million in seven years, and not one person has been executed." Democratic Representative Barbara Flynn Currie agreed: "Pursuing capital cases costs millions and millions of dollars and yet we get no deterrence since defendants don't know if their state has the death penalty or not." Democratic Representative Lou Land summed up his position succinctly: "One of the 10 Commandments says, 'Thou shalt not kill.'"[30] While simultaneously condemning abortion, the Archdiocese of Chicago declared: "Capital punishment is no longer required to protect Illinois's citizens" since life without parole is now an option. And "there can be no guarantee that the death penalty would not again be imposed on an innocent person."[31]

The abolition bill passed both houses of the state legislature in January 2011. Floor debate in the Senate took place on 11 January 2011, and the vote was thirty-two to twenty-five. The House floor debate took place five days earlier; the vote in that chamber was sixty to fifty-four. Although neither vote was veto-proof, the bill was sent to the governor for his consideration.[32]

GOVERNOR QUINN SIGNS THE BILL

In January 2011, Governor Quinn signed a bill legalizing gay civil unions.[33] "Quinn signed the bill "to roars of cheers and applause" on what he called "a day of history," stating: "'We believe in civil rights and we believe in civil unions.'"[34] The Roman Catholic bishop of Springfield, Illinois, had claimed that if Quinn signed the bill, he would not be a good Catholic. Quinn had merely shrugged in reply.[35] Having established himself as a progressive, Quinn soon agreed to sign a temporary 67 percent hike in the state's income tax rates. Quinn said that he did this because "the state was careening to bankruptcy, to fiscal insolvency."[36] With these new funds, he agreed to spend $250 million more per year on education. The Republican governor of New Jersey called Quinn a "disaster" for his spendthrift ways.[37]

Thus it was probably not much of a surprise that—on March 9, Ash Wednesday—Catholic Governor Quinn signed the Illinois abolition bill and commuted the sentences of the fifteen inmates on the state's death row to life in prison without parole.[38] The bill directs funds formerly used on the death penalty to law enforcement and victims' families.[39] The day before, the US Roman Catholic bishops had urged Quinn to sign, saying that it would help build a "culture of life in our country."[40] In commuting the sentences of the prisoners on death row, Quinn said: "I believe if we abolish the death penalty in Illinois, we should abolish it for everyone." As he signed the bill Quinn called his decision to do so "the most difficult that I've made as governor."[41] Yet the decision seems to have been a foregone conclusion, since he had consulted with Anglican Archbishop Desmond Tutu of South Africa and Sister Helen Prejean before announcing his decision. Elsewhere the governor explained his decision: "We found over and over again: Mistakes have been made. Innocent people have been freed. It's not possible to create a perfect, mistake-free death penalty system."[42] Mike Farrell, former star of the television series *Mash* and now an activist in California against the death penalty, applauded the governor's action, as did the head of the Texas Coalition to Abolish the Death Penalty, who proclaimed that it creates a "national momentum towards repealing the death penalty."[43]

SUMMARY

In 2000, more than 3.8 million Roman Catholics were Illinois citizens, making the state the fourth most Catholic in the nation—behind California, New York, and Texas.[44] This Catholic connection was apparent in the legislative debate on the abolition bill, the faith of the head of the Illinois Capital Punishment Reform Study Committee, public pronouncements made by church officials on the issue, and ultimately the decision of the Catholic governor. The continuing efforts of Professor David Protess—founder and leader of the Northwestern's Medill Innocence Project—and of his students had a unique and profound impact on executions in Illinois. And without a doubt, the 2002 study by Pierce and Radelet that used Illinois government information strengthened the belief among legislators and citizens that the administration of the death penalty retained its racist character.

POSTSCRIPT: THE OTHER SHOE FALLS

In a shocking turn of events, Protess was forced to resign from Northwestern University, as the *New York Times* reported in June 2011.[45] Protess had spent three decades successfully defending innocent people, including five on Illinois's death row. The press secretary for former Governor Ryan acknowledged that Protess's efforts were of great significance in shutting down the state's death row. The *Times* article also noted that his former students had nothing but praise for him, but some of them admitted that he had a tendency to confront authority. A former dean referred to him as a zealot. The situation began to unravel in 2009, when an Illinois prosecutor asked to see e-mail messages from Northwestern's Medill Innocence Project. Protess demanded journalistic privilege under the state's shield law. But this law was neutralized by indications that those working as journalists were not wholly independent and were in fact collaborating with defense attorneys. The dean of the Journalism School withdrew his support for the project and demanded that Protess leave Northwestern. One explanation for these events, not mentioned by the *New York Times*, is that this was retaliation for the success of abolition in Illinois, so dear to David Protess's heart.

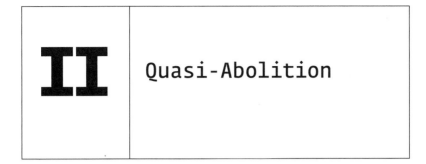

II Quasi-Abolition

6	The Recurring Life and Death of Death Penalty Legislation in Kansas

Previous chapters have considered the process of abolition in New York, New Jersey, New Mexico, and Illinois. This chapter examines the unanticipated reestablishment and maintenance of the death penalty in Kansas, a state with a lengthy abolition tradition. Between 1872 and 1907, the state's death penalty statute stipulated that anyone condemned to death should first be confined at hard labor for one year, after which time the governor would sign a death warrant. No governor authorized a hanging during this period. On 30 January 1907, Governor Edward Hoch signed into law a bill abolishing capital punishment. Republican Governor Alf Landon's 1935 signature on House Bill 10 reinstated the death penalty.[1] This law remained in effect until 1972, when the US Supreme Court ruled all existing state death penalty statutes unconstitutional in Furman v. Georgia. Thus, Kansas history is punctuated with long periods of de jure and de facto death penalty abolition.

Although most states rushed to reintroduce death penalty statutes after *Furman*, the legislative debate about capital punishment in Kansas began in 1973 and continued until 1994, when a new death penalty statute was finally passed. In 2004, the Kansas Supreme Court declared that statute unconstitutional by a vote of four to three. According to the majority opinion, when aggravating circumstances and mitigating circumstances are equally balanced, the death penalty should not be imposed.[2] The Kansas attorney general appealed this decision to the US Supreme Court, which upheld the Kansas death statute on 26 June 2006, by a vote of five to four. Writing for the majority, Justice Clarence Thomas noted: "Our precedents establish that a state enjoys a range of discretion in imposing the death penalty."[3] In 2008, the Kansas Supreme Court ruled that the state statute did not violate the Kansas Bill of Rights, and thus it was constitutional.[4]

PUBLIC OPINION AND THE LEGISLATURE

While the Legislature debated reestablishing the death penalty after *Furman*, informal polls and more systematic surveys showed that in Kansas, as in other states, a large majority of the population favored capital punishment.[5] During the 1994 debate on reestablishment, the Republican chair of the Senate Judiciary Committee stated that "public pressure probably encouraged legislators" to continue introducing death penalty legislation.[6] When asked why most House members favored a bill to reinstate the death penalty in the 1994 session, a Democratic representative replied: "I attribute it to public opinion polls." And a Republican representative asserted that a death bill had passed the House with a larger number of votes than expected because "a great deal of the margin is legislators responding to how their constituents feel about the issue."[7] This seemingly stable and powerful public support—not merely the attitudes of isolated individuals—provided the cultural and political environment for death penalty legislation. Yet Kansans' support for the death penalty was not absolute.

Citizens who say they support capital punishment laws often express preferences for alternatives to the death penalty. This was true in Kansas at the time of the 1994 legislation, when William Bowers and Patricia Dugan reported that 85 percent of Kansans supported the death penalty.[8] That support decreased to 42 percent when the same Kansans were asked to evaluate several alternatives, with the other 58 percent favoring either life in prison without parole; life in prison without parole, plus substantial payments to victims' families from prison work; or life in prison plus the substantial payments to victims' families, with a chance for parole after forty years if payments were made in full.[9]

There are few data on the attitudes of Kansans toward capital punishment since it has been reinstated. A 2007 poll commissioned by the Kansas Coalition against the Death Penalty interviewed 500 Kansans who had recently voted. The pollsters found that Kansans preferred alternatives to the death penalty. Support for it was only 49 percent when the alternative was fifty years in prison before being considered for parole. And just 35 percent favored the death penalty over "life [in prison] without parole coupled with an element of restitution."[10]

EXECUTIONS, RACE, AND MURDER

From the state's early days, Kansans have vacillated on the death penalty. Fifty-seven people have been executed in Kansas since 1853, all but one by hanging. The sole exception—the first person to be executed,

a Native American condemned for murder—was shot. People of European ancestry and African Americans dominate the list of the fifty-seven
executed. Thirty-nine were white, six were African American, three were
Native American, and the race of the other nine is unknown. The state's
last executions took place on 22 June 1965.[11]

The five Southern states (Texas, Florida, Virginia, Louisiana, and
Georgia) that enacted post-*Furman* death statutes most quickly have accounted for 734 (57.6 percent) of the 12,1271 executions since their resumption in 1977.[12] These states have relatively large African American populations, averaging between 21.1 percent African American in
1994[13] and 21.8 percent African American in 2010.[14] In contrast, when
Kansas reinstated the death penalty, the state's population was 6 percent
African American. The twelve abolition states (excluding the District of
Columbia) at that time averaged 2.8 percent African American.[15]

In Kansas's protracted debate about reestablishing the death penalty,
race was conspicuous by its absence as a contested issue. When it was
considered, both sides were likely to argue for safeguards to prevent discrimination, whether due to the defendant's race, social class, or other
characteristics. Biased application of capital punishment remains a significant concern among Kansans who oppose the death penalty. Consistent with the state's history, however, potential bias based on race
or ethnicity, or class, was rarely a core issue during the 2009 and 2010
committee hearings and legislative debates. Nevertheless, raw data on
post-1994 capital convictions suggest bias.

Since the reenactment of Kansas's death penalty law, 118 capital murder cases have been filed and twenty-six death penalty trials have been
completed, resulting in twelve death sentences. Eight of those sentenced
to death were white, and four were black. All were male. The sentences
of three white death row inmates have been vacated. In 2011, Kansas's
death row population was nine: five white men and four black men.[16]
Ten of the twelve men condemned to death were convicted of killing
one or more whites; one was convicted of killing two African American
women, and one of a Hispanic woman.

As was the case in other states, levels of homicide in Kansas varied
dramatically between 1960 and 2009. Kansas recorded its lowest murder rate in 1961, 1.9 per 100,000 residents. The state's high-water
mark of 6.9 was reached in 1974 and 1980. From 1990 through 2009,
Kansas's mean murder rate ranked twenty-seventh among US states and
the District of Columbia. Stated another way, over this period twenty-
six states and the District of Columbia recorded higher average murder

rates than Kansas. In 2009, Kansas's homicide rate was 4.2, and again twenty-three states recorded higher levels of homicide.[17] In comparison, the mean murder rate of abolition states in 2009 was 3.9.[18]

Although Kansas has historically experienced relatively low homicide rates, these numbers did not typically attract the attention of the media, politicians, and the public, unlike specific acts of especially shocking violence: "Indeed, sensational and brutal homicides can facilitate death penalty legislation."[19] During the 1980s, the crime victims' movement emerged, and the crime victim became a "symbolic figure in the conservative agenda for building crime policy. These policies include[d] a return to the use of the death penalty."[20]

This is clearly illustrated in the 1959 murders of four members of the Clutter family in rural Holcomb, Kansas. The Clutter murders became symbolic of violent crime in Kansas, in large part due to Truman Capote's 1966 bestseller, *In Cold Blood*, and the movie by the same name.[21] A *Los Angeles Times* article stated: "Almost 35 years after the Clutter family homestead became a slaughterhouse, Kansas legislators debating the death penalty still speak movingly, almost intimately, of Herb, Bonnie, Nancy and Kenyon, the four victims no one here can forget." A Republican representative quoted in the article observed: "It [the Clutter case] is like a Bible. . . . We can look at it through our own lenses and substantiate our own viewpoints."[22]

But Kansans pushing for reinstatement of the death penalty would not have to rely only on the 1959 Clutter murders. During the 1994 legislative session, the *Wichita Eagle* noted: "The people most on legislators' minds were Kansans such as Stephanie Schmidt, raped and murdered last year . . . ; 9-year-old Nancy Shoemaker, abducted off a Wichita street in 1990 and later found strangled; and the Clutter family."[23] One Republican representative declared: "There is enough support for . . . [capital punishment] across the state, primarily in connection with the Stephanie Schmidt situation. The time is right for it."[24]

Speaking before a House committee, Gene Schmidt, Stephanie's father, asked rhetorically: "'How many more Stephanies must we kill? . . . When are we going to accept that the death penalty is in the hands of the criminals?'"[25] He added: "By voting no on the death penalty, you are voting to definitely execute innocent lives in the largest of numbers."[26] In March 1994, a Wichita newspaper reported that the Schmidts "have gone nationwide with their fight for tougher laws against sex offenders, appearing with such talk-show hosts as Larry King and Maury Povich. And they formed a not-for-profit corporation called Speak Out for Stephanie that will continue to lobby for tougher laws."[27] In addition, a Kingman couple, Bob and Joelene Fairchild—whose daughter, son-in-law, and two grandchildren were murdered in rural Reno County on 5 November 1993—led a petition drive in 1994 to reinstate capital punishment.[28] They collected more than 21,000 signatures on a petition demanding reinstatement of the death penalty and testified before a House committee.[29]

The murder of young people, coupled with support for capital punishment by surviving family members, appears to have a powerful influence on death penalty politics. While earlier instances of horrific homicides remained in the public conscience, after the two 1993 cases, surviving family members became crusaders in the drive to reinstate the death penalty. These murders and political crusades clearly had an additive character, although others had failed to secure legislative results. In response to Stephanie Schmidt's murder, Governor Joan Finney wrote: "I, too, am appalled with [sic] the recent tragedy. . . . I am personally opposed to capital punishment; however, I believe that most Kansas citizens favor reinstatement of the death penalty. For this reason, should the Legislature pass a law to reinstate the death penalty, I would allow it to become law without my signature."[30] Responding to this letter, a Republican senator stated: "The death penalty will have a good chance to become law in 1994. . . . The governor has changed her position, and if the legislation passes, it can become law."[31] The Republican chair of the Senate Judiciary Committee concurred: "I had not heard of any talk of trying to reimpose capital punishment from my colleagues in the Legislature until I heard the governor's announcement."[32]

The central role that shocking violence played in the reestablishment debate has, likewise, become a core issue in the emerging repeal effort. Although surviving family members remain significant figures in the death penalty repeal narrative, events that occurred in Wichita on 14–15 December 2000 provide opponents of repeal with their most effective ideological and emotional weapons. On 15 December 2000, Wichita police were led to a soccer field, where they discovered "four naked bodies, all lying in the snow with gunshots to the back of the head." The person who brought the police to the field was the fifth victim. She had been gravely wounded, but her life had been saved by a "plastic butterfly hair clip" that had deflected a bullet. The four dead were three men and a woman, all middle class and ranging in age from twenty-five to twenty-nine.[33] Jonathan and Reginald Carr, brothers in their early twenties, were convicted and sentenced to death for these murders plus the murder of a Wichita Symphony cellist slain four days earlier. The horrific nature of the crimes and sustained media attention, combined with the willingness of several surviving family members and friends to actively support the death penalty, provide powerful obstacles to repealing the death penalty.[34]

In January 2007, yet another horrendous crime occurred in the state that affected death penalty repeal efforts.[35] A nineteen-year old woman was raped, sodomized, and murdered in Arkansas City. On 20 March 2009, Justin Thurber was convicted of the murder and sentenced to death by lethal injection.[36] He is currently being held at the El Dorado Correctional Facility. The murdered girl's family strongly and vocally supports the death penalty.

The political use of shocking violence to justify executions brings challenges as well benefits for death penalty advocates. For example, media and community reaction to a multiple murder that occurred in Wichita just eight days before the Carr case exposes a potential source of bias: the interaction between shocking violence, media attention, legislative action, and judicial processes. On 7 December 2000, nineteen-year-old Cornelius Oliver took a gun to a Wichita residence and shot his girlfriend along with one other female and two males also at the home, killing all four. The victims ranged in age from sixteen to twenty.[37] Prosecutors sought the death penalty. Oliver was convicted but sentenced to life in prison.[38] The lack of media attention to the Oliver case, in contrast to the Carr case, led some neighbors and friends to "nickname [the victims as] the Forgotten Four."[39] The uncomfortable thought that race had an indirect effect on these disparate outcomes motivates opponents of the death penalty.[40] The Carr bothers were African Americans, and their five victims were white. In the Thurber case, both the offender and the victim were white. Oliver and his four victims were African American.

THE PROTRACTED REINSTATEMENT DEBATE

Although advocates of capital punishment in the Kansas legislature after *Furman* were not successful in enacting a death penalty law until 1994, this was not due to any lack of effort on their part. Indeed, only New York had as many floor debates and committee hearings on capital punishment during these years as Kansas.[41] There were twenty-two sessions of the Kansas Legislature between 1973 (the year following *Furman*) and 1994, and forty-eight death penalty bills were considered in eighteen of those sessions. Only the sessions of 1974, 1984, 1988, and 1993 had no death penalty activity. The discussion below summarizes this dynamic, volatile legislative history, beginning with the administration of Republican Governor Robert Bennett. This legislative history is also presented in table 1. In some legislative sessions, a death penalty bill introduced in both chambers seemed certain to pass and be signed by the governor, yet this did not happen. In other sessions, death penalty bills were defeated while the Legislature passed alternatives of long, mandatory prison sentences that met varied receptions by the governor. Finally, legislators who opposed the death penalty compromised and agreed to a narrow death penalty bill that became law without the signature of a governor who staunchly opposed capital punishment.

The Bennett Years: 1975–78

During the Bennett administration, there were four Senate votes on death penalty bills, with two of the bills passing, and four House votes, with three passing. However, there was no common death penalty bill passed by both chambers. Although there were Democrats and Republicans on both sides of the debate, the death penalty was a partisan issue from the beginning, as indicated in table 1. In both the Senate and House, the majority of Republicans supported the death penalty in seven of eight votes, while the majority of Democrats opposed the death penalty in all eight votes. The highlight of this period was SB 0156, a "death-in-prison bill"—imposing a twenty-five-year prison sentence without parole—passed in 1977 by both the House and Senate and sent to Governor Bennett, who vetoed it. According to Bennett, a strong proponent of capital punishment, the bill's penalty was not a suitable alternative to the death penalty, and its passage might make reinstatement of capital punishment more difficult. SB 0156 also reflected partisan politics: most Democrats from both chambers supported it (80 percent in the House, 76 percent in the Senate) while most Republicans did not (only 45 percent and 37 percent in the Senate voted in favor of the bill).

The Carlin Years: 1979–87

In 1979, Democratic Governor John Carlin took office in what would be the first of two four-year terms. During his campaign against Governor Bennett, Carlin, an avid opponent of capital punishment, stated that if he became governor he would nevertheless sign a constitutionally valid death penalty bill.[42] In 1979, the House and Senate took him at his word, passed a death penalty bill (HB 2160), and sent it to him for approval. Much to the dismay of death penalty supporters, he did not sign it even though he did not question its constitutionality. Rather, he

TABLE 1   VOTING AND OUTCOMES BY LEGISLATIVE CHAMBER AND POLITICAL PARTY
ON DEATH PENALTY AND IMPRISONMENT BILLS IN KANSAS, 1975–94

Year	Bill[1]	Chamber	Percent voting yes by party Republicans	Percent voting yes by party Democrats	Outcome, Vote Count	Governor's Action
The Bennett Years						
1975	HB 2472	House	46	33	Failed, 48–71	
1975	SB 0503	Senate	58	36	Failed, 19–19	
1975	HB 2141	Senate	54	36	Failed, 19–21	
1976	SB 0740[2]	Senate	69	21	Passed, 21–10	
1976	SB 0740[2]	House	64	35	Passed, 64–60	
1976	SB 1027	Senate	72	36	Passed, 23–16	
1976	SB 1027	House	66	35	Passed, 65–58	
1977	SB 0156[2]	Senate	40	90	Passed, 25–14	
977	SB 0156[2]	House	45	80	Passed, 77–45	
1977	SB 0156[2]	Senate	37	76	Passed, 23–17	Vetoed
1978	HB 2683	House	75	39	Passed, 66–48	
The Carlin Years						
1979	HB 2160	House	80	49	Passed, 82–42	
1979	HB 2160[2]	Senate	48	74	Passed, 24–16	
1979	HB 2160	House	80	41	Passed, 78–47	
1979	HB 2160	Senate	67	37	Passed, 21–19	Vetoed
1980	HB 2988	House	81	46	Passed, 81–43	
1980	HB 2988	Senate	67	37	Passed, 21–19	
1980	HB 2988	Senate	68	33	Passed, 21–19	
1980	HB 2988	House	82	46	Passed, 81–42	Vetoed
1981	SB 0456	Senate	79	40	Passed, 25–14	
1981	SB 0081	House	81	41	Passed, 79–44	
1981	SB 0081	Senate	47	33	Passed, 23–15	Vetoed
1985	SB 2135	House	78	40	Passed, 78–46	
1985	SB 2135	Senate	67	50	Passed, 24–16	Vetoed
1986	HB 2980	House	78	43	Passed, 80–45	
The Hayden Years						
1987	HB 2062	House	77	28	Passed, 71–53	
1987	HB 2062	Senate	58	25	Failed, 18–22	
1989	SB 0038	Senate	73	11	Failed, 18–22	
1989	SB 0077[3]	Senate	96	100	Passed, 39–1	

TABLE 1   (CONTINUED)

Year	Bill[1]	Chamber	Percent voting yes by party		Outcome, Vote Count	Governor's Action
			Republicans	Democrats		
1990	SB 0077[3]	House	75	12	Failed, 57–67	
1990	SB 0077[3]	House	88	98	Passed, 111–9	Signed
The Finney Years						
1994	HB 2578	House	88	19	Passed, 70–55	
1994	HB 2578	Senate	74	15	Passed, 22–18	
1994	HB 2578	House	74	10	Failed, 54–69	
1994	HB 2578[4]	House	88	15	Passed, 67–58	

Source: J. M. Galliher and J. F. Galliher, "'Déjà Vu All Over Again': The Recurring Life and Death of Capital Punishment Legislation in Kansas," *Social Problems* 44 (1997): 369–85.

Notes:

[1]Some bills (such as HB 2988 in 1980) were amended in the House and/or the Senate and thus were voted on more than once.

[2]Different versions of SB 0740 were passed by the House and the Senate.

[3]Non–death penalty bills specifying long mandatory prison terms ("death-in-prison bills").

[4]Became law without Gov. Finney's signature.

rejected it on moral grounds and announced that he would never sign such legislation. When queried years later about his campaign promise and 1979 veto, he stated: "When I ran for governor in 1978, a reporter asked me if I would sign a capital punishment bill even though I had always voted against it as a legislator."[43] Carlin said that he would: "I was simply telling the truth." But after the death penalty bill was passed, "the magnitude of the decision hit me. For the first time I held the power of life and death in my hands, and I knew I couldn't sign it."[44]

Both chambers passed death penalty bills again in 1980 (HB 2988) and 1981 (SB 0081), only to have them vetoed by Carlin. Despite his staunch opposition to capital punishment, in 1982 he won a second term as governor, the maximum allowed by state law. In the 1985 legislative session, capital punishment proponents again passed a death penalty bill (HB 2135), which Carlin vetoed. The partisan nature of the debate remained evident during his tenure: in thirteen death penalty votes, Republicans voted to reestablish the sanction twelve times, while Democrats always voted in opposition.

The Hayden Years: 1987–90

In 1987, Republican Governor Mike Hayden took office. Hayden had campaigned for office on a platform that emphasized the need for the death penalty. After being elected, Hayden remarked: "I am a strong supporter of capital punishment. I'm going to call on the Legislature and hope they would put a bill on my desk in March or April that would make it effective at least by July 1 next year."[45] In January 1987, much to the delight of the new governor, the House passed a death penalty bill (HB 2062) by a vote of seventy-one to fifty-three. Then, in a surprising outcome, the Senate defeated the bill, twenty-two to eighteen. Six senators—two Republicans and four Democrats—changed their 1985 votes in favor of the death penalty to votes against it in 1987. In 1989, Hayden again pushed the legislature for a death penalty bill; this bill (SB 0038) was also defeated in the Senate. In lieu of a death penalty bill, the Senate passed another "death-in-prison bill" (SB 0077), which mandated forty years in prison before the possibility of parole. In 1990, the House handed Hayden another political setback by defeating a death penalty bill. The vote was sixty-seven to fifty-seven, with eight representatives—two Republicans and six Democrats—changing sides to oppose the death penalty. The House then joined the Senate in passing the "death-in-prison bill" (SB 0077) by an overwhelming margin—111 to 9— and the governor signed that bill into law.

During the Hayden years, the death penalty remained a partisan issue: in all four death penalty votes, most Republicans voted favorably, and most Democrats voted negatively. The only nonpartisan support was for SB 0077. With its passage, one Democratic representative predicted: "Death penalty politics will probably die the day the governor signs that bill."[46] Although Hayden signed the bill into law, he did so with some reluctance: "I would say the [death penalty] issue will be around until it's enacted. Among the people, it has not been resolved, and they'll continue to support it."[47] When Hayden ran for reelection in 1990, he lost to a strong death penalty opponent, Democrat Joan Finney. Given that there was now a mandatory forty-year prison sentence as an alternative to the death penalty, and a newly elected governor who opposed capital punishment, death penalty politics in Kansas appeared to be over.

The Finney Years: 1991–94

Except for isolated activities in House committees, there was no organized effort to introduce death penalty legislation during the first three sessions of Finney's term as governor (1991–93). At the beginning of the

1993 session, a Republican representative and strong advocate of capital punishment stated: "I haven't discussed it [the death penalty] with anybody, and nobody has talked to me about it," and "I don't know anybody who plans to bring it up."[48] Although no death penalty bill was proposed during this legislative session, the issue soon became an explosive one among lawmakers and citizens that would carry over into the 1994 legislative session.

On 1 July 1993, Stephanie Schmidt, a nineteen-year-old female college student, was raped and murdered by a co-worker who was on parole for a previous rape conviction. The victim's parents lived in an affluent Kansas City suburb. There were immediate calls for reinstating capital punishment in Kansas. The *Topeka Capital-Journal* declared that the perpetrator "charged into battle armed with a murderous intent, a serpentlike cunning and a blaring criminal record," and that his prey was "sweet [and] unsuspecting Stephanie Schmidt," concluding that "the death penalty . . . would be a valuable tool in [this] case."[49] Legislators could not wait for the 1994 legislative session to begin. The *Wichita Eagle-Beacon* observed: "Lawmakers are falling all over one another to get tough on crime. As expected, the return of the death penalty is the hot-button centerpiece for the tough talk."[50] After amendments and compromises in committees and on the floor of the House, a death penalty bill (HB 2578) passed the House by a vote of seventy to fifty-five and was sent to the Senate for consideration. The Senate Judiciary Committee amended the bill by restricting it to "a handful of premeditated, intentional murders termed 'the worst of the worst.'"[51] The full Senate passed this narrower bill, twenty-two to eighteen.

A joint Senate and House Conference Committee attempted to reconcile the legislators' differences. Senate members of the committee were in no mood to compromise and insisted on a very narrow bill. Continuing dissatisfaction with the Senate version among representatives resulted in its second defeat—sixty-nine to fifty-four—in the House. However, on the last day of the legislative session, two weeks later, the House accepted the Senate's bill by sixty-seven votes to fifty-eight, and sent it to the governor.[52] Finney allowed the bill to become law without her signature. (In Kansas, a bill passed by both legislative chambers can become law without the governor's signature if she or he does not veto it within ten calendar days after the date of receipt.) Thus, after twenty-two legislative sessions and forty-eight death bills, Kansas became the thirty-seventh state to reinstate capital punishment.

Given the previous course of death penalty politics, there was no reason to believe that a death penalty bill would become law during or after Governor Finney's term in office, even if a staunch death penalty supporter followed her as governor. After all, neither Bennett nor Hayden, both strong advocates of capital punishment, had been able to entice majorities in both houses to submit a death bill for the governor's signature. In fact, the two Republicans had lost elections for second terms as governor to liberal Democrats who were vocal critics of capital punishment.

Why then did Finney not veto the final death penalty bill, especially since she testified against the proposed legislation before the Senate Judiciary Committee?[53] According to Finney, she did not wish to break a campaign pledge to allow a death penalty bill to become law without her signature if the Legislature sent her one.[54] She also felt that the death penalty represented the collective will of Kansans.[55]

The bill that became law was approved by the Senate, twenty-two to eighteen, only after amendments were introduced by a Democrat who had voted against previous death bills. He argued that "if a death penalty law were to be enacted, I wanted it to be as narrow as possible, so that the flaws of capital punishment would be minimized."[56] This bill also had the support of the Republican Senate president, who previously had voted against death bills—"I am basically a death penalty opponent"— who voted for the narrow death penalty bill that the Senate passed.[57] If these two death penalty opponents had voted against the bill, it would have been defeated by a vote of twenty to twenty.

FRAMING THE DEATH DEBATE:
PASSAGE OF A NARROW COMPROMISE BILL

Although the enactment of this law can be viewed as an obvious victory for death penalty supporters, it can also be viewed as a symbolic victory for at least some death penalty opponents. The new law applied to few potential offenders. The Legislature had passed a very narrow bill that created the crime of "capital murder,"[58] allowing prosecutors to seek the death penalty for seven specific types of intentional or premeditated killing. Kansas legislative researchers concluded that the Senate's bill might result in the death penalty's being sought about three times a year;[59] the Kansas Department of Corrections estimated that the number could be from two to five per year.[60] With an average of 141 homicides reported annually in Kansas between 1990 and 1993,[61] five capital cases a year would be approximately 3.5 percent of the total. And a spokesperson for the Department of Corrections said that only two of twenty-nine inmates (6.9 percent) sent to prison for first-degree murder convictions in 1993 could have been charged with capital murder as defined by the newly enacted legislation.[62] Coincidentally, the restrictions in the bill would also make its implementation more affordable, with estimated costs of $828,520 in the first fiscal year after passage and $770,976 the next year.[63]

A PERFECT STORM IN KANSAS

Even a cursory review of this legislative history powerfully reinforces the view, attributed to Clarence Darrow, that capital punishment and other such issues are not settled by reason but by prejudices, sentiments, and emotions—and when they are settled, they do not remain settled.[64] The same observation was made time and again by Kansas newspapers and legislators; for example, one reporter wrote: "Another year, another governor, another legislature, and the death penalty will be before Kansas again."[65] In fact, as noted above, the Legislature considered forty-eight death penalty bills in eighteen of twenty-two legislative sessions between 1973 and 1994.

The passage of the 1994 bill required the confluence of a number of events. Clearly the most significant were the two highly publicized murder cases in 1993—that the murders of Stephanie Schmidt and the young family in Reno County. The cases became even more politically influential because the victims' relatives lobbied for capital punishment legislation. Had it not been for these murders and family reactions, there probably would have been no death penalty legislation vote in 1994. After all, there had been no House or Senate vote since 1990, when the bill mandating forty years in prison became law during the Hayden administration.

In addition, passage came only after the House reluctantly compromised and agreed to a very narrow death penalty bill that appealed to both fiscal conservatives and some death penalty opponents. And finally, there was the governor, who—while opposed to capital punishment on moral grounds—disregarded the overwhelming opposition to the death penalty of her fellow Democrats in the House and Senate and allowed the bill to become law without her signature.

During the lengthy reinstatement process, the actions of legislators were affected by political circumstance as much as by their commitment to reinstatement or abolition of capital punishment. Lawmakers knew full well after Governor Carlin's first veto in 1979 that he would not approve a death penalty bill. Yet they went through annual rituals of public hearings, contentious debates, and pointless votes, sending three additional bills for his veto. As evidence that at least some lawmakers' votes served symbolic or political self-interest, several Democrats and Republicans from both chambers changed their votes in favor of the death penalty in 1985 (under Governor Carlin) to votes against it in 1987 and 1989 (under Governor Hayden). These lawmakers knew that Hayden, a staunch death penalty supporter, would sign a death bill if the Legislature passed one. In other words, some legislators voted for death penalty bills when the governor opposed capital punishment, knowing that their votes were meaningless, but they switched sides under a pro–capital punishment governor to avoid actually passing a death penalty bill.

Table 2 shows that Republicans' support for capital punishment legislation generally rose from the Bennett administration (0.630) through the Finney administration (0.810); while Democrats' support generally fell, from 0.339 to 0.148. Although there were important fluctuations, support in both parties rose during the Carlin administration and fell during the Hayden administration, and positions on capital punishment became increasingly polarized along party lines. Contentious legislative debates on the death penalty, given the public sentiments of the time, increasingly benefited Republican political interests.

The 1994 compromise negated a Republican mantra that Democrats were soft on crime by passing a symbolic death penalty statute that applied to only a handful of potential murder cases. Even the most vocal proponents of the death penalty were hard-pressed to argue that the new law would have any measurable effect on criminal violence in the state. For example, Republican Senator Mark Parkinson, chief Senate sponsor of the 1994 capital punishment legislation, asserted: "I'm willing to admit it [the death penalty] might not usually deter these terrible crimes. . . . But if it ever deters, it will be worth the effort."[66] At least some death penalty opponents were willing, albeit reluctantly, to accept the bill because it would apply to only a few cases. Although preferring no capital punishment law at all, they considered the Kansas statute much better than death penalty legislation in states such as Florida, Texas, Georgia, Louisiana, and Virginia, which accounted for most post-*Furman* executions. For other legislators who were moderates on the death penalty, the Kansas statute represented "a compromise between the extreme groups who wanted either no executions or as many as possible,"[67] as well as a welcome end to a long, contentious, partisan debate.

84 Kansas "has purged itself of a certain angry and destructive and distract-

TABLE 2   MEAN PROPORTIONAL SUPPORT FOR DEATH PENALTY LEGISLATION
BY KANSAS REPUBLICAN AND DEMOCRATIC LAWMAKERS, 1975–94

	Mean Proportional Support for Death Penalty Bills	
Governor	Republicans	Democrats
Republican Robert Bennett (1975–79, 8 votes)	0.630	0.339
Democrat John Carlin (1979–87, 13 votes)	0.735	0.412
Republican Mike Hayden (1987–91, 4 votes)	0.708	0.190
Democrat Joan Finney (1991–94, 4 votes)	0.810	0.148

Source: J. M. Galliher and J. F. Galliher, "'Déjà Vu All Over Again': The Recurring Life and Death of Capital Punishment Legislation in Kansas," *Social Problems* 44 (1997): 369–85. *Note*: See table 1 for specific bills and years.

ing populism by getting the law on the books. And it has made the death penalty a non-issue."[68]

REPEAL EFFORTS RESURFACE

As discussed above, the 1994 reinstatement bill was held in judicial limbo until 2008 when the statute passed its last—or latest—constitutional test. While Kansas's highest court and the US Supreme Court were considering challenges to the bill, local prosecutors, defense attorneys, and trial judges were already applying it and anti–capital punishment forces were attempting to repeal it. During the 1997 legislative session, the first repeal effort (HB 2169) was introduced in the House. It cleared committee and was defeated by a vote of sixty-six to sixty on the House floor. Between 1997 and 2011, eight additional abolition bills and two moratorium bills were introduced in the Legislature. Although the bill was largely symbolic, it would still generate real executions, and—according to the coordinator for the Kansas Coalition against the Death Penalty—fairness remains an issue: "Prosecutors can apply the statutes to meet their needs."[69]

A bill (SB 534) calling for a moratorium on executions until a death penalty study commission could review the punishment was introduced in the Senate during the 2002 legislative session. The bill died in committee, but it was resurrected as SB 158 during the 2003 session, only to be withdrawn. The median cost of a death penalty case all the way "through execution" was estimated at $1.2 million.[70] Moreover, fiscal effects multiplied as the state's budget crisis deepened.[71] Democratic Senator Marci Franciso, of Lawrence, credited the combination of the severe budget crisis and the realization that simply prosecuting a death penalty case could cost a million dollars for the renewed legislative interest in repealing the death penalty.[72] On 27 January 2011, the executive director of the Kansas State Board of Indigents' Defense Services reasoned that the economic downturn had helped the repeal effort pick up "additional steam" because the death penalty is so costly.[73]

Death penalty repeal bills were introduced in the Kansas Senate in 2005 (SB 6), 2009 (SB 208), and 2010 (SB 375). A repeal bill (HB 2351) was also introduced in the House during the 2009 legislative session, but it received little attention. In the Senate, however, the Judiciary Committee held public hearings on the three bills that it received and sent them to the Senate floor for consideration by the Committee of the Whole. In the 2005 hearing, Judiciary Committee members heard from the usual suspects. Those speaking in favor of the bill included representatives of the Kansas Catholic Conference, Amnesty International, and Murder Victims' Families for Reconciliation. Those speaking in opposition included a county district attorney. The committee also received written testimony supporting the death penalty from six family members of murder victims. The committee reported the bill out with no recommendation.[74] Anticipating a US Supreme Court decision on the death penalty law in Kansas v. Marsh, the Senate returned the bill to the Judiciary Committee.

Republican Senator Carolyn McGinn cited respect for human life and the belief that money could be better spent during the budget crisis as her motivation for introducing the 2009 death penalty repeal bill.[75] The Senate Judiciary Committee held two hearings on SB 208. Those testifying in support of repeal included representatives from religious, social service, and human rights organizations, including the Kansas Catholic Conference, the Kansas Board of Indigents' Defense Services, and the Kansas Coalition against the Death Penalty. Those speaking against the bill included representatives of the Kansas attorney general's office, the Kansas County and District Attorneys Association, and the Johnson County Police Chiefs and Sheriff's Association, and two relatives of one of the people murdered by the Carr brothers on 15 December 2000.[76]

At the 2010 hearings of the Senate Judiciary Committee, Michael Radelet, a professor at the University of Colorado, noted that "after a while, increases in the severity don't contribute to the deterrent effect of the penalty."[77] Crime, on the other hand, could be reduced by using the money saved from abolishing the death penalty to catch more offenders. Bishop Michael Jackels, representing the Kansas Catholic Conference, told committee members: "In today's world, especially in our country, there is no need to impose the death penalty. . . . There are other means to protect the common good against an unjust aggressor."[78] The Episcopal, Catholic, Lutheran, and Methodist bishops of Kansas wrote the committee a rare joint letter that argued "when governments execute persons, our society is weakened because the value of life is cheapened."[79] Senator McGinn reasoned that the money saved by abolishing capital punishment could help fund programs that would prevent future violence. Moreover, executions violated her pro-life values: "We pass abortion laws because we say 'Child of God.' . . . Please, somebody let me know, although these people become terrible people, tell me at what point in time did they lose that status and who made that decision?"[80]

In the end, the repeal effort was rejected by a twenty-twenty tie. Twelve Republicans and eight Democrats supported repeal.[81] Senator Tom Holland, a candidate for governor, was the only Democrat to vote against the bill. These numbers suggest that support for the death penalty among Republican senators declined between 1994 and 2010. When capital punishment was reestablished in 1994, only seven of twenty-seven Republican senators voted against the measure. In 2010, twelve of thirty-one voted to repeal the statute.[82]

The data reviewed here suggest that death penalty abolition in Kansas remains a reachable goal. Although abolition gains in the legislature or governor's mansion can be eliminated in a single election cycle, or with significant increases in state financial resources, Kansas's tradition regarding the death penalty resembles those of other abolitionist states. Even when the death penalty was available, Kansas rarely used it. Given this tradition and current death penalty law, it is unlikely that Kansas will become another of the states in which hundreds of inmates are condemned to death rows and scores receive a final sanitized needle.

On the other hand, it appears unlikely that Kansas will avoid post-*Furman* executions. A number of death row inmates in the state have been, and continue to be, a focus of media, community, victim advocacy, and legislative attention. In its review of the 2010 death penalty bill, the Judiciary Council Death Penalty Advisory Committee noted: "Under this approach, defendants who are already under a death sentence will remain under a death sentence."[83] It appears unlikely that a repeal bill could become law in Kansas without making this concession. Unless the governor or courts intervene, the execution of one or more of the people now on death row seems probable. Thus a "symbolic" law—a narrowly defined statute offering no crime control benefit—will probably have deadly consequences in Kansas. But newly elected Catholic Republican Governor Sam Brownback, whose views are extremely troubling to people concerned with "a woman's right to choose," poverty, or civil rights, has nonetheless made statements suggesting that he might commute death sentences:

> We need a culture of life in the United States. . . . I have difficulty with the death penalty. This is an individual, though, in that case, that has committed a heinous crime. I think we should limit the death penalty to cases only where we cannot protect the society from the individual, such as when Osama bin Laden is caught. We need to be able to use it then. But we should use this [in] very limited [ways] and only in that circumstance, in order to talk and to teach a culture of life in America.[84]

<table>
<tr><td>**7**</td><td>Death Penalty Near
Misses in New England
New Hampshire and
Connecticut</td></tr>
</table>

Since 1976, no region in the United States has been less likely to execute people convicted of first-degree murder than the Northeast. Only four post-*Furman* executions have occurred there, one in Connecticut and three in Pennsylvania between 1995 and 1999.[1] In all four cases, the inmates rescinded their appellate rights and essentially volunteered for execution. New Hampshire and Connecticut appear close to abolishing the death penalty.

NEW HAMPSHIRE

Since 1739, New Hampshire has executed twenty-four people, all by hanging.[2] Just three of the executions occurred during the twentieth century, the last in 1939. Two people were on death row in the state when the US Supreme Court handed down its 1972 Furman v. Georgia decision. The death sentences of both inmates were vacated by the New Hampshire Supreme Court.[3] The state enacted its post-*Furman* death penalty statute in 1974,[4] and in 1977 the legislature made sure that the statute met the requirements specified in the *Gregg* decision by adding the appropriate sentencing and review components.[5] The current (2011) death statute retains the option of hanging should lethal injections become impossible to administer.[6]

The murder rates in New Hampshire have consistently been among the lowest in the United States. When the state broadened the scope of its death statute in 1991 to include individuals who kill while committing or attempting to commit a sexual assault and individuals who kill while committing or attempting to commit specific drug crimes—the "manufacture, sale, [or] possession with intent to distribute [of] large quantities of controlled drugs"[7]—its murder and non-negligent manslaughter rate was 3.6 per 100,000 population.[8] Between 1960 and 2009, the rate varied between a high of 3.5 in 1974 to a low of 0.8 in 2009.[9] From 2005 through 2009, no more than three states reported lower homicide rates than New Hampshire.[10] In 2000, when the New Hampshire legislature came closest to abolishing capital punishment, a Northeastern University poll found that 55 percent of the state's residents favored repeal, 35 percent opposed it, and 10 percent had no opinion.[11]

Legislative Efforts to Repeal the Death Penalty

In 1998, the New Hampshire Senate voted fourteen to ten in favor of a bill, proposed by Governor Jeanne Shaheen, that expanded the death penalty to include a long list of heinous crimes—including the killing of children and the killing of people because of their race or religion. The House rejected the bill and simultaneously produced a death penalty repeal bill (HB 1548). Exactly what propelled the repeal bill to the governor's desk just two years later is unclear. Without a doubt, the backdrop of numerous wrongful convictions in Illinois played a role in the 2000 New Hampshire death penalty narrative.

The main sponsor of HB 1548 was Democratic Representative James Splaine, a political liberal with some key conservative backing. Early in 2000, the House Committee on Criminal Justice and Public Safety held public hearings on the bill. Records show that 127 people attended the hearing, fifty-one of whom were witnesses and seventy-six of whom simply signed in and registered their support for or opposition to the bill. Forty-seven of the fifty-one witnesses, spoke in favor of repealing the death penalty. Seventy-two of the seventy-six spectators favored repeal. Abolitionists cited issues of excessive cost, lack of deterrence, and sanctity of life as reasons to repeal. However, wrongful convictions played the core role in HB 1548's journey to the House floor. The most powerful testimony heard by the committee, later discussed in numerous newspaper articles, came from Paris Carriger. He gave a moving account of his wrongful murder conviction and the twenty-one years he spent on Arizona's death row, once coming within three hours of execution.[12] One of the four witnesses favoring retention of the death penalty, a New Hampshire representative, argued: "If someone rapes your family member, kills them, and it's definite, I have no problem with the death penalty. I'll pull the switch if no one is available." Another, a prosecutor, claimed that having "the death penalty on the books is a support for our law enforcement officers." The third, a high-school student, stated that executions were "worth the risk," reasoning that if she were wrongly executed she would accept her fate as necessary for saving others' lives. And the fourth, a Bible-quoting minister, said: "To you all on this committee and all the other legislators I have to say that the use of capital punishment against the criminal is not murder. It is justice."[13] With six members absent or not voting, the committee was tied, eight to eight—which meant that HB 1548 went to the House floor for consideration.[14] The influence that anti–death penalty activists had on HB 1548 did not end with the committee vote, as the House and Senate debates that followed included frequent references to their testimony.

The House floor debate on HB 1548 consumed less than two hours.[15] One representative argued that since no one had been executed in New Hampshire in sixty-one years, the law did not require alteration—New Hampshire was not a state like Texas. Another representative argued that this long period with no executions demonstrated that capital punishment in New Hampshire was merely a tool used to pressure those accused of capital murder to plead guilty and save the state the time and money required to pursue a capital case. Another representative countered that the costs of the death penalty had spiked in recent years. Republican Representative Anthony DiFruscia emphasized the death penalty's unfairness and lack of consistency, reminding House members that there were "no millionaires on death row." He noted that the "pro-life" message is inconsistent with support for the death penalty, adding that the United States is the "only democracy in the world" that practices capital punishment. Challenging the belief that abolishing the death penalty necessarily denies justice to the family and friends of murder victims, one representative noted that two of his sister's children had been murdered, yet he and his sister remained opposed to the death penalty. His sister considered capital punishment "premeditated murder by the state."[16] Donna Sytek, Speaker of the overwhelmingly Republican House and someone known for her ability to control party votes, encouraged Republicans to vote their conscience on capital punishment.[17] The House passed HB 1548, 191 to 163, and forwarded it to the Senate for consideration.[18]

The *New Hampshire Union Leader*, the state's well-known conservative newspaper, launched an effort to determine the sentiments of New Hampshire's twenty-four senators toward the recently passed death penalty repeal bill. The paper polled twenty-one senators and found that eleven of them favored abolition and ten opposed it. Votes cut across party and ideological lines. Senator Patricia Krueger, a conservative Republican, stated she had consulted a priest on the issue: "I can't in good conscience be arguing in favor of the sanctity of life to push for my bill to ban partial birth abortion if I'm not accepting the sanctity of life through the death penalty."[19] Concern with executing an innocent person was the most frequently cited reason to abandon the death penalty. Deterrence and just dessert were most often cited as reasons to retain capital punishment.[20]

On 24 April 2000, the Senate Committee on Judiciary held a second public hearing on HB 1548. Testimony differed little from what the House committee had heard three months earlier. In the Senate, thirty-nine of forty-five favored repealing the death penalty, while five favored retention;[21] the testimony lasted five hours. Concern with judicial mistakes and executing an innocent person remained core to the abolitionists' testimony. The committee voted five to one to move HB 1548 to the Senate floor with an "ought to pass" recommendation.[22] As had been the case in the House, the Senate debate on HB 1548 frequently cited anti-death penalty committee testimony.

The full Senate debate on HB 1548 began almost immediately. Of the thirteen Senators participating, nine spoke in favor of abolishing the death penalty, while four opposed the legislation. Echoing arguments made in an editorial chastising prosecutors for attempting to rebrand the death penalty as a tool to coerce people to plead guilty, thereby saving the state time and money, Senator Burt Cohen, the Senate sponsor of HB 1548, said: "As the law stands, a school teacher who kills a police officer could be executed, but a police officer who killed a school teacher could not. . . . A law that places different values on different lives cannot be a just law."[23] Consistent with her statements to the *New Hampshire Union Leader*, Senator Krueger explained that her pro-life stance on abortion moved her to oppose capital punishment. Senator James Squires expressed concern over lack of deterrence: "The State of Massachusetts, which does not have the death penalty, has [a] homicide rate [that is] a fraction of the state of Texas, which does."[24] Senator Debora B. Pignatelli was one of numerous senators concerned with wrongful convictions: "I don't believe the system is infallible. Innocent people do get convicted. We know that the governor of Illinois has come to see that. We know that the state of Maryland knows it. . . . [A former prisoner] came before our Judiciary Committee to tell his story. He was sentenced to death."[25]

Senator Clifton Below told about an epiphany he had had after a drunk driver killed one of his close friends:[26] "I have felt the anger and outrage of one who has seen the precious life of another extinguished by senseless homicide. I have felt such rage, such a passion to see evil brought to justice, that if given the chance, I thought that I could volunteer to be the executioner."[27] The senator noted that he had since come to view life without parole as sufficient punishment for murderers.

Senators favoring the retention of capital punishment argued that justice or retribution necessitated the death penalty. The possibility of executing an innocent person, however, weighed on those favoring capital punishment. Senator Richard Russman noted: "If we had the problems that Texas had, if we had the problems that Illinois had, perhaps it would be another matter."[28] Alteration in the sentiments of three senators pushed HB 1548 over the finish line. Democratic Senator Rick Trombley stated that he had been moved to support abolition after hearing reports of wrongful convictions during the hearing on the bill held by the House Committee on Criminal Justice and Public Safety. Republican Senator Pignatelli credited the January testimony of exonerated death row inmate Paris Carriger for her change of heart. Republican Senator Leo Fraser credited the death penalty's lack of deterrence and a letter from a constituent for his: "And as my agent . . . I'd be devastated if I thought you'd put someone to death."[29]

The Governor Vetoes the Abolition Bill

Governor Jeanne Shaheen wasted little time and few words when, on 20 May 2000, ignoring the pleas of President Jimmy Carter, she formally vetoed HB 1548. In forty words, she explained that New Hampshire's capital punishment statute "is designed to make the carrying out of the death penalty extraordinarily difficult." She reminded her critics that no one had been executed since 1939, no one was on death row, and capital charges were brought only in the most heinous cases.[30] Shaheen stated her belief that "there are some murders that are so brutal and heinous that the death penalty is the only appropriate penalty."[31] And she argued that the fact that the death penalty was not used showed that it was working, although many opposed to capital punishment felt that if the law was not enforced it should be repealed.

The prime sponsor of HB 1548, Democratic Representative James Splaine, said that he was surprised how quickly the veto came: "I suggested that she at least take the weekend to talk with those Senate and House members who underwent the journey of changing their minds." A joint statement by the state safety commissioner and the state police director expressed extreme satisfaction with the governor: "For the men and women who put their lives on the line each and every day to protect all citizens of this state, this law has extreme importance. The death penalty sends an important message to criminals that the most severe consequence will occur if they commit such acts of intolerable violence."[32]

The Debate Continues

Death penalty abolition bills failed to reach the governor's desk during the first decade of the twenty-first century. A 2001 abolition bill passed committee on a vote of nine to six, but failed to pass a roll call vote of the full House. In 2004, SB 513 sought to reduce the scope of capital punishment by prohibiting the execution of anyone who committed a capital offense before reaching eighteen years of age. The bill passed the Senate and the House before being vetoed by the governor.

Three events shaped New Hampshire's post-2005 death penalty narrative. In 2008, the state conducted its first and second post-*Furman* capital murder (death penalty) trials. A brutal home invasion murder in 2009 provided the third catalyst. John Brooks, a fifty-five year old white millionaire, was convicted of hiring others to kill a handyman. Murder for hire and kidnapping during the course of a murder qualified him for the death penalty. Brooks was represented by high-powered private counsel and sentenced to life in prison. Meanwhile, Michael Addison—a young, poor, African American—was convicted of murdering a police officer. Addison was represented by public counsel and was sentenced to death. He remains the state's lone post-*Furman* death row inmate. Former New Hampshire Attorney General Philip McLaughlin "described Addison as 'a young, poor, black man' and Brooks as 'a middle-aged, wealthy white man who acted with planning and deliberation.'"[33]

HB 556 sought, once again, to abolish the state's death penalty. The 2009 repeal effort was led by Democratic Representative Robert "Renny" Cushing, a long-term abolitionist, son of a murder victim, and founder of Murder Victims' Families for Reconciliation who had recently been elected to the New Hampshire House. Members of Murder Victims' Families for Reconciliation challenge the assumption that executions benefit and provide psychological closure for families and friends of murder victims. Cushing asked members of the New Hampshire House to repeal the death penalty "in the name of my [murdered] father." In spite of a veto threat by Governor John Lynch, the chamber responded by voting 193 to 174 in favor of abolition. Gubernatorial intervention was not necessary, however, as the Senate voted to table the issue, 13 to 11.[34]

Even though another abolition bill, HB 520, failed, a 2009 bill calling for the establishment of a committee to study the New Hampshire death penalty became law. The resulting twenty-two-member commission studied the history of executions nationally and in New Hampshire, heard from public officials, and conducted four public hearings.

On 1 December 2010, it released its final report, containing a majority and minority opinion. Twelve members voted in favor of retaining the death penalty, while ten favored repealing it. Of the twelve supporters of capital punishment, ten were associated with law enforcement or prosecution, and one was the father of a slain police officer.[35]

A strong showing by more conservative elements in the New Hampshire electorate, combined with the October 2006 murder of Kimberly Cates, moved the 2011 death penalty narrative from abolition to expansion. The Republican Speaker of the House, William O'Brien, filed a bill (HB 147) seeking to expand the death penalty statute to allow the execution of people who kill during home invasions. In a lightly attended hearing on 1 February 2011, members of the House Criminal Justice and Public Safety Committee heard David Cates, joined by Governor Lynch and Speaker O'Brien, argue for expanding the death penalty: "If you need a reason to support this bill, close your eyes and remember the last moments of my wife's life. Imagine her not knowing if her daughter, her best friend, was dead." Cushing, whose father had been murdered by an off-duty police officer, told the committee that "the death penalty doesn't work, it is failed public policy."[36] The debate continues.

CONNECTICUT

Laws calling for the execution of people found guilty of any one of a multitude of offenses typified the criminal codes of seventeenth-century colonial Connecticut. Although alternative sanctions tended to be imposed for religious transgressions, mid-seventeenth-century capital crimes included idolatry, cursing a parent, killing with malice, and rape. Since colonial times, however, the jurisdiction's legal structure has been committed to "a fair trial" (for example, there has never been a lynching in Connecticut), representation by counsel, and fair jury proceedings. Homicides linked to mental incapacity seldom resulted in executions.[37] By the mid-nineteenth century, instrumental and symbolic attraction to the death penalty had definitely waned. In 1846, while Michigan was abolishing its death penalty altogether, the Connecticut General Assembly was—in practice—limiting the application of capital punishment to those convicted of first-degree murder.[38] A century later, in 1955, Connecticut further amended its death statute to allow discretionary capital punishment; juries, for the first time, could recommend death, instead of imprisonment without parole or pardon, for someone convicted of first-degree murder.[39] The state's death statute remained largely unchanged until the 1972 case of Furman v. Georgia. Connecticut was among the first jurisdictions to respond by reenacting its death penalty statute, which it did in 1973. To increase the scope of crimes eligible for the death penalty, the statute was amended in 1985 and 1995.[40]

Since 1639 Connecticut has carried out 127 executions.[41] With little demographic change over the decades, early-twenty-first century data suggest a xenophobic bias in the state. As of 2010, Connecticut's death row contained ten inmates: six African Americans, three whites, and one Latino.[42] Thus, 70 percent of those on the state's Connecticut's death row are members of minority groups–the highest percentage among states with a death row population of ten or more.[43]

On 14 May 2005, nearly forty-five years after executing Joseph Taborsky, a convicted serial killer, Connecticut became the first and only New England state to conduct a post-*Furman* execution. Another convicted serial killer, Michael Ross—a white man with an Ivy League education—abandoned all remaining judicial appeals and was killed by lethal injection. In a letter to the state prosecutor, Ross wrote: "I am willing to hand you the death penalty 'on a silver platter' on the condition that you will work with me to get this over with as quickly and as painlessly as possible. There is no need to drag the families of my victims through more lengthy and disturbing court proceedings."[44] Since Ross actively sought execution, he can be considered a "volunteer." Indeed, lawyers with the Public Defenders Service attempted to halt the lethal injection, reasoning that Connecticut was involved in a "state-assisted suicide."[45] Connecticut has not carried out an execution since.

The state's traditionally low murder rate probably facilitates its limited use of the death penalty in recent decades. Between 1990 and 2003, Connecticut's murder and non-negligent manslaughter rate ranged from a low of 2.4 in 2002 to a high of 6.6 in 1994.[46] During this time, the state's murder rate remained between 36 percent and 46 percent lower than national murder rates.[47] The first decade of the twenty-first century continued that trend: The murder rate in 2009 was 3.0 per 100,000.[48]

The Abolition Narrative Begins

Paralleling Connecticut's history of executions is a history of continuing efforts to abolish the practice. The first significant threat to the state's death penalty occurred in the 1840s and 1850s. Opposition to capital punishment took on the intensity of the crusade to abolish slavery: "A tally of petitions from 1843 to 1854 indicates that more than 1,700 residents protested the death penalty."[49] Governor Cleveland Chauncey and a significant number of the General Assembly's members supported repeal efforts in 1842–43. The *New Haven Journal* credited three successive speeches given by a religious leader for convincing the House of Representatives to vote two to one in favor of retaining the death penalty.[50] Efforts to repeal it were narrowly defeated in the Senate in 1842 and 1843. A decade later, Governor Thomas H. Seymour informed the General Assembly that the construction of the state's new penitentiary rendered the death penalty unnecessary and therefore "immoral." In 1852 and 1853, the Senate voted to support the governor's reasoning and repeal the death penalty. The House remained intransigent and once more soundly defeated abolition.[51]Legislators then turned their attention to other issues, and death penalty abolition was not seriously considered again until the mid 1950s.

The 1955 abolition debate in the General Assembly mirrored the debates that would occur throughout much of the United States for the next five decades. Newspapers were far less supportive than the legislature of capital punishment. Dominant religious organizations totally abandoned their support for it. Prosecutors, police, and occasionally relatives and friends of murder victims provided the death penalty with its few remaining sources of public support. Connecticut's prosecutors and police gave legislators justification that remains a core to twenty-first-century abolition politics: The punishment is seldom applied, used in only the most extreme cases, and there is an automatic review by the state's Supreme Court and the Board of Pardons. Thus, there was no reason to repeal the death penalty. In spite of this reasoning, the 1955 abolition bill was moved along by the relationship between increasing numbers of execution reprieves and the declining physical and mental health of death row inmates, as periods of incarceration lengthened. Circumstances surrounding George Dortch's execution reprieve doubtless helped the abolition effort: Dortch received a reprieve less than five minutes before his scheduled execution.[52] In the end, however, Democrats failed to support their abolitionist governor, and on 7 June the Senate voted against repeal.

Systemic Bias and Cost

On 6 July 2001, the General Assembly created (but did not fund) a commission to study the state's post-*Furman* capital punishment practices, from 1973 to 2003. The Commission on the Death Penalty was asked to address fourteen specific topics, but it was not asked to make recommendations about retaining or abolishing capital punishment. The most significant conclusions reached by the commission concerned bias in applying the death penalty, and its economic cost. Although committee members were not given sufficient data to identify specific incidents or patterns of racial and ethnic bias, the committee's report suggested that legislators carefully examine a study—funded by the Office of Chief Public Defender—that was due out soon after the report, to see if "any systemic or individual racial or other bias exists in the decision to charge, prosecute, and sentence [an] individual for [a] capital felony" and that legislators adopt procedures that would allow convicted people to challenge their death sentence "based upon proof that their sentence is part of an established discriminatory pattern."[53] The committee also reported that the cost of defending people facing execution from trial through sentencing was nearly 90 percent higher than defending persons facing life without parole: "Of the seven men currently on death row, the defense costs ranged from a low of $101,870 to a high of $1,073,922, with an average defense cost of $380,000 per case." In contrast, the average defense cost was just over $200,000 for defendants who received a life sentence.[54]

Little changed during the latter half of the decade, although a Connecticut Office of Legislative Research (OLR) pamphlet revisited the 2003 report's findings on racial or ethnic bias and geographic disparities. The pamphlet also provided statistics on racial and ethnic disparities throughout the state's correctional system: "Connecticut ranks highest in the United States in its level of disparity in the rates of incarceration of whites, blacks, and Hispanics [and] almost 50% of the male prison population in 2000 came from Hartford, New Haven, and Bridgeport."[55] In December 2007, a long-awaited study of bias in Connecticut's death penalty practice, led by Yale Law Professor John J. Donahue III, was released, and the findings—consistent with those in other states—were troubling. Black people convicted of killing a white person were three times more likely to be sentenced to death than white people convicted of killing a white person. The findings of racial and ethic bias were immediately challenged by Senior Assistant State's Attorney John Massameno, but seven Connecticut death row inmates used the data to challenge their death sentences.[56]

In 2005, Ed Gavin, president of the Connecticut Criminal Defense Lawyers Association, reported that in 2007–8 the state's Capital Defense and Trial Services Unit cost $1,412,860 plus the expense of hiring expert witnesses and "Special Public Defenders." Gavin also noted that American Bar Association standards require capital defendants to be represented by two attorneys.[57] Moreover, in 2006, the yearly cost to house a typical Connecticut prison inmate was $44,165, while the cost to house an inmate convicted of a capital offense was $100,385—an additional $56,220.[58] The Office of Legislative Research reported that Connecticut's Department of Correction had paid $316,000 for the state's last execution.[59]

The Connecticut Legislature Revisits Abolition

Against this backdrop, Senators Mary Ann Handley and Edward Meyer and Representatives Juan R. Candelaria and Gary A. Holder-Winfield introduced bills to abolish the death penalty (SB 744, SB 539, HB 5847, and HB 5459). Meanwhile, Senator Dan Debicella introduced a bill to allow executions for crimes other than murder in the first degree (SB 213). The Legislative Judiciary Committee combined the bills into a single one (HB 6578) calling for the abolition of the death penalty. Of strategic importance, the statute retained the option of death for capital offenses that occurred before HB 6578 became law, allowing abolitionists to pursue repeal without confronting the strong public and legislative sentiments favoring the execution of two people indicted for the home invasion murder of Jennifer Hawke-Petit and her two daughters. Attached to HB 6578 were the names of twenty-nine cosponsors and a fiscal note stating that passage (repealing the death penalty) would save the state "up to $4 million annually."[60] From the beginning, it was relatively certain that HB 6578 would be voted out of the committee, whose cochairs, Representative Michael P. Lawlor and Senator Andrew J. McDonald, strongly favored repeal. The executive director of the conservative Family Institute of Connecticut referred to the committee as "the most radical committee of an already very liberal legislature."[61]

The most emotional testimony of the hearing was delivered by Connecticut's widely recognized crime victim and survivor, Dr. William Petit. Petit was brutalized and his wife and two daughters murdered in the same extremely violent episode: "My family got the death penalty, and you want to give murderers life. That is not justice. Any penalty less than death for murderers is unjust and trivializes the victim and the victim's family. It is immoral and unjust to all of us in our society."[62] On 31 March, the abolition bill made it out of committee by a vote of twenty-four to thirteen.[63] The Hartford Courant voiced support: "A legislative committee has taken a brave step toward abolishing Connecticut's death penalty, a law that is all but unworkable, not to mention expensive, unfair and risky."[64]

The House Debate

On 13 May 2009) the Connecticut House of Representatives turned its attention to death penalty repeal. On one level, the House debate resembled similar debates in many state legislatures outside the South. Representative Steven Mikutel argued that many peer-reviewed studies indicate the death penalty does indeed deter murder. Representative Jeffery Berger said that "the individuals . . . on death row . . . have it pretty good. . . . They've got three square meals a day. They've got a nice room to live in. They've got clothes. They've got health care, all on the state dollar of $62,000 a year. That's a pretty good life for life."[65] Representative Gerald Labriola argued that most Connecticut residents believe that the death penalty is an appropriate punishment for certain heinous crimes. Abolition, he noted, "would be a slap in the face to the families of the victims of those people on death row." Representative John Hetherington questioned the validity of the argument that death penalty appeals are expensive and stated that financial discussions "trivialize" the issue. Representative L. F. Cafero's statement is representative of most legislators voicing opposition to repeal: "Ladies and gentlemen, the death penalty is not for revenge. The death penalty is not a deterrent. The death penalty is not a cost-saving measure. The death penalty in the eyes of the people of the State of Connecticut and its elected representative has been and hopefully will be the ultimate form of justice, rarely used, for the most deplorable, heinous and unspeakable crimes."

The possibility of convicting and executing an innocent person, the economic cost of capital punishment, and the "cruel and unusual" effects of the death penalty on the victim's family and friends were often cited as reasons to repeal. The statements of Representative Christopher Caruso offer a summary of the concerns expressed by abolitionists during the course of the House debate, as well as Caruso's personal opinion: "It's not so much about the cost of incarcerating a prisoner. It's not about the deterrence of the death penalty. It's not even so much about the heinous crimes. It's about compassionate people trying to come to a conclusion as to what is right and wrong."

The House narrative also reflected concerns about an ineffective statute and biased application, issues not applicable in every state. Both representatives favoring repeal and those opposed to it expressed distress over the unworkable nature of the state's death penalty machinery, with both sides arguing that the execution process was far too slow and uncertain. Three of the ten people on death row at the time had committed their crimes in the 1980s. In the words of Representative Michael

Lawlor, a repeal advocate, "that's the dilemma we find ourselves in no matter whether you're for or against the death penalty, you're confronted with this reality that, as a practical matter, in Connecticut, we're never really going to execute somebody against their will." Given the chances of executing an innocent person, the economic cost of the death penalty, and the pain conferred on the families and friends of victims, repealing capital punishment—from the abolitionists' perspective—was the reasonable alternative.

The harshest exchanges between the two sides occurred toward the end of the debate when Holder-Winfield, the bill's prime sponsor, addressed the House. He began by asking why legislators remembered the testimony of Dr. Petit and not that of victims renouncing the death penalty. At the core of his argument was the issue of justice: "We have a problem with the way that the death penalty is practiced in this state. This is not my opinion. This is a fact." According to Holder-Winfield, an African American, the problem was that whether or not a person was subjected to a capital trial was determined by jurisdiction and race, rather than by the severity of the offense:

> This is not about justice because justice is supposed to be blind. Well, it's not blind where I live, and it's not blind for the people that I know. This is not about what we've [been] talking about today. This is about some people are special. That's what it's about. And Representative McCrory is right, depending on who you are and what you look like, it may or may not apply. Representative McCrory gets mistaken for Representative Hewitt, [sic] and I can kind of understand that, but I get mistaken for both of them, and I can't understand that at all. But that is what we deal with, when we deal with all of these questions.

Following Holder-Winfield's statement, five representatives spoke in favoring of repealing capital punishment. Three of them discussed the issues of class, race, and ethnic bias. The last, Representative Demetrios Giannaros, concluded: "I was just looking at the photographs of the people who are in death row in Connecticut, and I can tell you that they're not like me in terms of color by and large. And that may be an indicator of what I'm talking about." Mikutel, an outspoken supporter of capital punishment, countered: "It's quite unfair to infer that Connecticut's legal system is racially biased." In the end, ninety representatives voted in favor of repeal and fifty-six against it; only seventy-four votes were necessary for passage.

The Senate Debate

On 21–22 May 2009, the Senate considered the death penalty repeal bill that the House had approved. The Senate debate took more than twice as long as the House's. The twenty-six amendments offered (only five of them were debated and voted on) and the length of debates became a point of contention between Democrats and Republicans. The majority party accused Republican lawmakers of filibustering.

Senator McDonald, cochair of the judiciary committee, noted that Connecticut's death statute was unworkable: the state had executed only one convicted capital murderer in fifty years, and that person had volunteered to die.[66] McDonald further reasoned that support for capital punishment was based on a desire for "revenge or vengeance or retribution,"[67] and that most of those on Connecticut's death row had been sentenced in one city, thus creating geographical bias and the potential for racial and ethnic bias. He also reviewed the failure of capital punishment to deter murder, noting that the nation's two execution mills, Texas and Louisiana, have murder rates two and four times higher than Connecticut's.[68] Numerous senators were troubled by the potential of wrongful convictions. Senator Martin Looney reasoned that "witnesses can be wrong. . . . there may be perjury . . . prosecutorial misconduct . . . juried bias."[69] Senator Jonathan Harris reminded his colleagues that "there is human error." Senator Donald Williams agreed that human error must be considered, stating that since 1973 there had been 4,700 murders in the state and only thirteen murderers had been sentenced to death. Senator Meyer testified that executions cost approximately $4 million each and that long delays torture victims' families, not to mention the problem of convicts who are later exonerated by DNA evidence. Senator Eric Coleman argued that the imposition of the death penalty depended on the defendant's location in the state, race or ethnicity, and poverty.

Senators opposed to repeal restated familiar themes. Senator Toni Boucher was straightforward in asserting human values: "Any penalty less than death for murder is unjust and trivializes the victim and the victim's family." Senator John Kissel spoke about deterrence and the country club stereotype of prison, arguing that we are safer with the death penalty since "people do enormous things to stay alive." It was also mentioned that dead people no longer threaten society and that death row inmates lead comfortable lives when compared with some who are "poor" and "homeless." In the same vein, Senator Debicella argued that preserving the life of a single murder victim justified the death penalty, calling the trade-off "a huge societal benefit." Executions in Texas, he argued, were responsible for a 60 percent decline in that state's murder rate between the 1970s and the 1990s, and he noted that Isaac Ehrlich. a death penalty researcher, had come to a similar conclusion in 1973. Senator Rob Kane said that he was from an Irish Catholic family, had attended Roman Catholic schools, and was in favor of the death penalty because it deterred murder, noting that Connecticut's death row population had decreased over the previous five years. Senator Sam Caligiuri agreed, stating that the "death penalty . . . does . . . have a deterrent effect."

A 2009 *New Haven Register* editorial noted that the expensive capital appeals process was often used to justify abolition of the death penalty. The author compared this argument to "ending laws against drunken driving because of their cost to the courts" and blamed lawmakers who call the death penalty "unworkable" for changing the law in such a way as to allow capital defendants "multiple and endless appeals."[70] A letter to the editor of the *Norwich Bulletin* asked: "In these times of such financial crunch, is it time for Connecticut to consider a huge financial savings by eliminating—finally—the costly death penalty?"[71] The author noted that the state was spending $4 million annually on capital punishment, even though life without parole was far less expensive and still protected society. She added that recent studies helped to dismiss the notion that the death penalty deterred crime. Accordingly, the Senate on May 22, 2009 at 4:11 a.m., followed the lead of the House and voted 19 to 17 in favor of death penalty repeal. The vote was far from bipartisan. Only one Republican joined eighteen of the Senate's twenty-four Democrats voting in favor of repeal.

The Governor's Veto

Republican Governor M. Jodi Rell's reaction to HB 6578 was never in doubt. Before the House passed the death penalty repeal bill, Rell told reporters that "she believed in the death penalty . . . 'I don't consider it revenge,' . . . 'It's justice.'"[72] In a letter to the governor, Connecticut's Roman Catholic bishops attempted to alter her opinion by emphasizing the expensive and lengthy death penalty appeals process, as well as the "'inconsistent and uneven'" manner in which the state enforced the law.[73] In her veto of the abolition bill, Governor Rell stated: "The death penalty is, and ought to be, reserved for those who have committed crimes that are revolting to our humanity and civilized society. The death penalty sends a clear message to those who may contemplate such cold, calculated crimes."[74] She quoted an English judge who stated: "*Punishment is the way in which society expresses its denunciation of wrong doing."* Rell continued: "There is no doubt that the death penalty is a deterrent to those who contemplate such monstrous acts."

The governor noted that issues of application of the death penalty were addressed in a study whose results had been reported to the legislature on 8 January 2003. She praised the recommendations of the report, which included "training for public defenders and prosecutors" and noted that the ideas had been overlooked by the legislature. She explained that the report had been designed to guarantee that prosecutors' decisions to seek the death penalty were informed by the facts and the law relevant to the case, and that the law was applied in a "consistent" and "even-handed" manner, without reference to "arbitrary or impermissible factors such as the defendant's race, ethnicity or religion."

The Evolving Debate

Although Governor Rell ended the 2009 Connecticut death penalty repeal effort, the efforts of the state's abolitionists continued unabated. Death penalty repeal was a core issue during the 2010 gubernatorial race. A televised debate, held on the same day that Steven Hayes became the first person convicted in the Petit case, began with a question concerning the candidates' stand on the death penalty. It was generally understood that Connecticut residents favored execution in this particular case.[75] Dannel P. Malloy, the Democratic candidate, reasoned that Connecticut's death statute was unworkable. Therefore, he supported repeal of capital punishment for "future" crimes, a statute that would not affect the Petit killers: "If these two gentlemen [the defendants in the Petit murders] are sentenced to death, that sentence will be carried out. Period."[76] The Republican candidate expressed support for the death penalty and asserted that "it is almost certain that [the Petit killer] and his accomplice in this crime will not be put to death [if Malloy is elected governor]."[77]

By the end of 2010, Dan Malloy, a death penalty abolitionist, had been elected governor of Connecticut, and Representative Holder-Winfield, cosponsor of the 2009 repeal bill, was poised to assume the position of vice cochair of the 2011 Legislative Judiciary Committee. The pieces were in place for a successful repeal movement. On 7 March 2011, the committee held public hearings on HB 5036, Holder-Winfield's 2011 repeal bill. After hearing fourteen hours of testimony, the committee cleared the bill, which appeared to have the necessary support in the General Assembly for passage. While this manuscript was being prepared for publication, however, Dr. Petit, the lone survivor of the mass murder that took the life of his wife and two daughters, successfully lobbied two senators to withhold their support for death penalty repeal until the completion of the trial of Joshua Komisarjevsky, the second defendant accused of killing Petit's family. Although the bill would not apply to that case, Petit expressed fear that abolishing the death penalty would reduce the likelihood that the jury would sentence the killer to death. In spite of his lobbying efforts, the chances of a successful repeal effort in 2012 are good.[78]

| 8 | Recent Abolition Near Misses |
| | Nebraska and Maryland |

Maryland and Nebraska became unlikely participants in the abolition movement of the post-*Furman* era more by the legislative skill and
charisma of core actors than by the structural foundations of the states.
Execution levels in Nebraska—with its western-leaning geography,
economy, and culture—reflected those in agrarian, sparsely populated,
highly homogeneous western states. With the rise of a gifted and tena-
cious state senator, however, Nebraska became a hotbed of abolitionist
debate for three decades. And if the abolition effort in Nebraska was unlikely, a strong abolitionist movement in Maryland should have been
impossible. In reality, Maryland is currently involved in an abolition narrative that will probably halt executions, if the state does not abolish the
death penalty.

NEBRASKA

The history of legal executions in Nebraska is relatively short in comparison with the history of states further to the east. Since 1879 the
state has carried out thirty-seven legally sanctioned executions, three
of which were post-*Furman*.[1] The electrocution of Charles Starkweather
on 25 June 1959 remains, without a doubt, Nebraska's most infamous
execution. The nineteen-year-old man's eight-day drive across the Nebraska countryside during January 1958 that resulted in the murder of
ten people has provided plots for books, movies, and songs.[2]

Since the enactment of Nebraska's post-*Furman* death penalty statute
in 1973, the state's juries have handed down thirty-three death sentences. Three Nebraska inmates have been executed; four died on death
row; thirteen had their sentences commuted; and one had his sentenced
vacated. Eleven men remain on death row, awaiting either execution or
appellate relief.[3]

Enter Senator Ernie Chambers

Even a cursory review of Nebraska's post-*Furman* death penalty narrative attests to the central role that human agency played in keeping executions on the minds of legislators. Senator Ernie Chambers entered the Nebraska Unicameral Legislature in 1970. A barber, Chambers holds a law degree from Creighton University. Unlike the majority of his colleagues, he did not supplement his $12,000 salary with other income.[4] Thus, he led a near-poverty existence. In a state that is less than 5 percent African American, he remained the sole black legislator until 2008, when a newly enacted term-limit law directed at him forced him out. Referring to the forty-nine member Senate, he stated: "By getting rid of me, they got rid of the other forty-eight."[5]

A progressive, he consistently and overtly supported pro-choice legislation.[6] His efforts in the 1980s moved Nebraska to lead all states in divesting from companies that did business with apartheid-era South Africa.[7] Abolishing the state's death penalty, however, drove his legislative efforts. During every legislative session between 1976 and 2008, Chambers introduced a bill calling for the abolition of executions. Although Nebraska's unicameral legislature allowed the state to assume a leadership role in reducing the penalty for marijuana possession in the late 1960s,[8] that legislature structure did little to facilitate Chambers's efforts to abolish the death penalty. Rather than coalition building, his legislative strengths were skillful oratory, humanistic values, the power of persuasion, and an unwavering belief in the righteousness of the cause. As a consequence, he often found himself at odds with his abolitionist allies, the Catholic and Jewish communities.

1979: Replace Executions with Thirty-Year Prison Sentences

LB 262, Chambers's first legislative achievement in the area, brought Nebraska closer to abolishing the death penalty than any of his subsequent efforts. The legislative history of LB 262 began on 28 February 1979 when the Judiciary Committee held public hearings on death penalty repeal. There, Chambers noted that all eight Nebraska death row inmates had been sent there for murdering white people. This fact, he argued, illustrated the "freakishness" and "arbitrariness" of the way that Nebraska's death penalty was applied. Martin Gardner, an associate professor of law at the University of Nebraska, argued that the death penalty promotes murder because of the "glamour" of executions. He stated: "I am a Mormon, and my church opposes abortion, therefore I favor the life of the fetus as well as the convicted murderer." Sam Walker, an associate professor of criminal justice at the University of Nebraska in Omaha, argued that there is no evidence of deterrence in a growing body of literature. No police, prison, or judicial officials appeared to testify in opposition to repeal.[9] The Judiciary Committee passed the bill to the floor of the Legislature for consideration.

The Legislature began consideration of LB 262 on 26 April. Senator Martin Kahle, knowing that Governor Charles Thone would veto a death penalty repeal bill, reasoned that twenty-five votes would move the bill out of the Legislature, but it took thirty votes to override a veto—and since the bill lacked that level of support, it was foolish to debate the issue. Senator Orval Keyes countered: "I think that the people of this state are entitled to know what the senators that they have elected will do."[10] The Legislature proceeded to hold a relatively intense debate on deterrence and morality. Senator Christopher Beutler argued that the death penalty was clearly a deterrent, citing the work of Isaac Ehrlich, "common sense," and the human "apprehension of death" as proof. Senator Carol Pirsch argued that biased application did not justifying repealing capital punishment, reasoning that all criminal sanctions are unfairly applied, but the point is never used as an argument to throw out noncapital punishments. The death penalty, she said, is not a deterrent because it is seldom applied. Senators favoring repeal gleaned fundamentally different conclusions from Nebraska's execution history. Senator Loran Schmit viewed sporadic application as a reason for repeal, noting that it had been nearly twenty years since the state's last execution. Senator Vard Johnson compared Nebraska's death penalty to a lottery, in which enforcement—or winning—depended on "geography" and "prosecutorial discretion." Senator John DeCamp referred to the mythical conclusions associated with executions and added: "Execution seems to have a mystique about it [that] can completely reverse conditions. It makes heroes out of hobos." Senator Donald Dworak cited the famed criminologist Thorsten Sellin, who found that capital punishment had no deterrent impact. Senator William Nichol concluded that there was no way to accurately judge whether or not the death penalty was a deterrent.

Senators who supported repeal often pointed to the inherent contradiction between opposing abortion and favoring capital punishment. Senator Bernice Labedz, an opponent of legalized abortion, reacted by noting that pro-choice advocates accused her of attempting to "impose" her Roman Catholic abortion policy on the Nebraska populace. But on the issue of capital punishment, she was criticized for disagreeing with Catholic policy. If an execution saved just one innocent life, she concluded, it would be worth it.[11] Senator Thomas Fitzgerald referred to Senator Chambers as a "sob sister."[12] At the conclusion of the debate, the legislators voted twenty-six to twenty-two in favor of repeal.[13] Shortly thereafter Governor Thone vetoed the bill. Thone said: "In the final analysis, the death penalty can only be justified if it serves as a deterrent to murder and thereby saves the lives of some innocent persons who would otherwise become murder victims. It appears to me that the death penalty serves as a deterrent in some cases."[14] Unable to marshal the thirty votes necessary to override the governor's veto, the 1979 effort to replace execution with a thirty-year prison sentence came to an end.

1992: Life without Parole

Although LB 327, the 1992 repeal effort, was not seriously considered by the Legislature, as initially presented, the bill appeared poised to equal or surpass the 1979 effort. Substituting for execution the sentence of life in prison without the possibility of parole, the bill began with twenty-five cosponsors, enough votes to gain legislative approval. Indicative of their support for the death penalty repeal, the senators voted twenty-five to twenty to move the bill out of the deadlocked Judiciary Committee for consideration on the floor of the Legislature. As was the case in 1979, however, the governor promised to veto the bill if it reached his desk. As the bill moved to final legislative action, cosponsors began to withdraw their support. Eventually there were only seventeen.

Senator John Lindsay, a repeal advocate, cited the recent media attention given to the cases of two convicted killers, Harold Otey and John Joubert, and noted that the friends and relatives of some of their victims had urged Nebraska legislators to keep the death penalty. Thus, according to Lindsay, it was not surprising that some legislators would remove their support from LB 327. Senator Carol Pirsch reasoned that Chambers had lost support for his repeal effort when senators began to question the meaning of "life without parole." Those concerns were, without a doubt, facilitated by a 27 September 1990 letter written by Chambers to Otey outlining how "life without parole" would affect his case. Senator Chambers concluded: "The 'without parole' won't mean much in reality because the Pardons Board always will have the power to reduce any sentence. If that provision allows me to obtain passage of the bill, plenty of time will be available to seek later mitigation." Chambers claimed that "nothing in the letters is different than what I've said from the beginning."[15] He had harsh words for those legislators who bowed to public pressure: "It would be different if a person said, 'I changed my philosophical outlook.' But when they say they changed because of pressure, I have no respect for them."[16] LB 327 died in the Legislature. Otey became Nebraska's first, and Joubert its third, post-*Furman* executions.

1999: Moratorium and Study

With concerns about racial bias and wrongful convictions reaching alarming levels, the American Bar Association in 1997 recommended that states place a moratorium on executions until structures could be implemented to ensure fairness and accuracy.[17] At the turn of the century, Florida led the nation with eighteen exonerations from its death row, while Illinois—as discussed above—was second, with twelve.[18] Nebraska's legislators were either unaware of or unconcerned about this unfolding narrative. During the 1999 legislative session, Senator Kermit A. Brashear, a conservative Republican who supported the death penalty, joined Senator Chambers in an effort to pass legislation authorizing a study of the state's death penalty procedures and a moratorium on executions until that study was completed. Senator Brashear emphasized that he remained supportive of the death penalty but was concerned about its fairness: "If you love the law and you love justice, you must be committed to fairness."[19] The Senate proceeded to endorse the measure twenty-seven to twenty-one, thereby becoming the first legislature in the nation to pass a post-*Furman* bill authorizing a death penalty moratorium.[20] As threatened however, Mike Johanns—the state's first-term Roman Catholic, Republican governor—ignored a plea from the pope and vetoed the measure.[21] The governor contended the moratorium was poor public policy, and that it would lengthen unnecessary appeals and further harm the family and friends of victims: "I focus on the families of the victims and the victim themselves. . . . The death penalty is the law of our state. I feel strongly that part of my role as governor is to do all that I can to carry out the law for the benefit of the victims and their families. The moratorium would be just one more roadblock to bringing closure for them."[22]

Senator Chambers's reaction to the governor's decision, along with the reactions of Catholic leaders, were soon published in the *National Catholic Register*. Chambers, according to the *Register*, called the governor "a political opportunist and hypocrite" for being "pro-life" while supporting the death penalty: "To be anti-abortion in Nebraska is politically popular, but to be anti-death penalty is not politically popular. . . . The governor wants to please as many politically active people as possible."[23] Jim Cunningham, executive director of the Nebraska Catholic Conference, was not as hard on the governor, challenging Chambers's contention that "opponent[s] of abortion must also oppose the death penalty." Although abortion, given the innocent victim, is always wrong, "the Catechism says there are limited, extremely rare, practically nonexistent cases where capital punishment is permissible."[24] Thus, according to Cunningham, it was unjustified to criticize the governor for opposing abortion and supporting the death penalty.

In the end, the Legislature was unable to override the governor's veto of the moratorium. It did, however, successfully override his veto of the proposed "death penalty study," thereby allowing senators to commission a research team headed by David C. Baldus, a prominent death penalty researcher, to investigate the disposition of Nebraska's post-*Furman* homicide cases. In practice, until these data were analyzed, an informal moratorium was placed on executions in the state.

The team's findings on cases between 1973 and 1999 were released on 25 July 2001, and an amended version was released a year later. Although the researchers uncovered some troubling trends in the data, they concluded "There is No Significant Evidence of the Disparate Treatment of Defendants Based on The Race of the Defendant or the Race of the Victim."[25] In addition, the study found significant geographical variations in the administration of the death penalty that disfavored African Americans, but the reduced tendency of judges in urban areas to impose death sentences negated any racial effect on execution outcomes. The researchers also found that the killing of wealthy and prominent individuals significantly increased the likelihood that a prosecutor would seek the death penalty against the accused perpetrator.

The release of the nation's first study of death penalty procedures and outcomes proved to be a double-edged sword. The negative findings on racial bias were welcome news to humanists. At the same time, these findings strengthened the resolve of death penalty advocates. Michael Rushford, president of the pro-death-penalty group Criminal Justice Foundation, dismissed findings of economic disparity, reasoning that such biases were inevitable. Governor Johanns welcomed the findings, saying that they would strengthen his efforts to accelerate the pace of executions in the state.[26]

2007: A Proper Ending

On 31 January 2007, with the threat of a governor's veto yet again hanging over Nebraska's Unicameral Legislature, the Judiciary Committee held a public hearing on LB 476, a bill replacing execution with the sentence of life without the possibility of parole and with restitution. Issues of cost, morality, racial bias, proportionality of punishment, and wrongful convictions dominated the hearing. Senator Chambers argued: "I don't believe there will ever be a fair, equitable, or just means of inflicting a punishment which, in my mind, is inherently barbaric, unjustified, and beneath the dignity of any civilized society."[27]

Omaha Attorney Larry Myers discussed the 1994 execution of Harold Otey, who had been defended by a totally inexperienced public defender right out of law school, concluding that, given the high potential for error in capital cases, some innocent people are executed while some of the worst murderers receive life in prison.[28] Professor Michael Radelet, a death penalty researcher at the University of Colorado, asked: "What have we learned in the 30 years since Gary Gilmore was executed in Utah? The first thing we've learned is that the death penalty is tremendously expensive, up to six times more than the cost of life without parole."[29] Coleen Nielsen, representing the Nebraska Association of Criminal Defense Attorneys, agreed, citing studies in Kansas and Indiana. While noting that a Nebraska study comparing the cost of life in prison without parole to execution did not exist, Nielsen stated that the cost of defending a capital case had risen from $80,000 in 1996 to $200,000 in 2006. She reasoned that the cost of prosecution had increased similarly.[30] The legal director of the Nebraska chapter of the American Civil Liberties Union (ACLU) noted that although minorities made up only 9 percent of the state's population, five of the ten men on death row "are not white . . . that means it's five times overrepresented on death row for people of color"[31] A representative of the Lincoln chapter of the NAACP agreed, arguing that the NAACP "stands firmly against any and all methods of capital punishment."[32] Two lay representatives of Nebraska's Roman Catholic Church, the executive director of the Nebraska Catholic Conference and the director of ministry for the Archdiocese of Omaha and Catholic Charities, testified in support of abolition, but no Catholic clergy appeared.[33] Perhaps they were unwilling to publicly align themselves with Senator Chambers, given his aggressive support for abortion rights. No one offered testimony in opposition to the legislation.[34] The Judiciary Committee forwarded LB 476 to the floor of the Legislature, with six members in favor, one member not voting, and one absent. This was the first time an abolition bill had reached that step in twenty years.[35]

Senator Chambers led off the floor debate on LB 476: "The death penalty is cruel and it is unusual because it is not uniformly imposed."[36]

He noted that most people who committed capital crimes were not sentenced to death. He asked his colleagues: "[Do] you know what electrocution is like? It's like a high-tech burning at the stake."[37] To show that he understood what it is like to have a loved one killed, he spoke of his nephew's murder: "He was shot in the head several times."[38] Senator Donald Preister spoke of his conversation with a Catholic nun, who had reminded him that 123 death row prisoners had been exonerated by DNA evidence.[39] Senator Tom Carlson offered Chambers a deal: if Chambers would support an anti-abortion bill next year, Carlson would vote for LB 476. He said: "If it's correct to be concerned about the rights of and the lives of the lowest . . . it has got to be even more right to be concerned about the defenseless and innocent of our society—the unborn."[40] Senator Chambers—reacting to those challenging his concern for homicide victims—asked: "Would people say that John Paul II and Benedict XVI have no concern for murder victims because they think the death penalty is morally indefensible?"[41]

Senator Mike Friend noted that he was a Catholic who had studied the death penalty, and he would not support its abolition in Nebraska.[42] Shortly before noon, the Legislature rejected death penalty repeal by a single vote, twenty-five to twenty-four.[43] Senator Mike Flood, the most outspoken opponent of repeal, stated that he had not known the Legislature was so divided on the issue. Reflecting on the defeat, Senator Chambers lamented: "I've been fighting this issue for three decades so expectations are never high that success will come."[44] His defiant message to the Legislature was: "'I have another year.'"[45] On 11 November 2007, churches across Lincoln, the state capital, organized a special worship service called "A Witness against the Death Penalty" in support of the next year's abolition effort.[46]

As promised, the 2008 Nebraska Legislature was greeted with Senator Chambers's last death penalty repeal bill. Public testimony supporting repeal differed little from what the Judiciary Committee had heard the previous year. Unlike in 2007, however, representatives of the state's Police Chiefs Association and County Attorneys' Association spoke in opposition to repeal. Lancaster County Chief Deputy Attorney Joe Kelly reasoned that having two different penalties for murder, life and life without the possibility of parole, was unconstitutional. Senator Chambers concluded the testimony before the committee by criticizing the attempts of the police and courts to make sense of the opposing position: "Police officers lie. Courts know that they lie, and courts say it's all right for them to lie. That's a part of the business. Police officers feed information to snitches." His final death penalty bill cleared the Judiciary Committee by the same margin as his 2007 effort. As was the case in 2007, Governor David Heineman informed the Legislature that he would veto the bill if it passed.[47]

On 25 March 2008, the Legislature debated death penalty repeal for the third time in three years. The third time was not the charm, with repeal failing by a larger margin than in 2007, twenty-eight to twenty.[48] Senator Chambers expressed his hope "that someday people in the Legislature would reach the point where they realize, as those in other industrialized countries have, that the death penalty does not advance the cause of civilization."[49] He stated: 'I end my [legislative] career holding to that one unwavering, unshakeable belief and conviction—that the state should not kill anybody."[50]

Senator Chambers had nonetheless seen some success. Motivated by the belief that someday the Nebraska Supreme Court or the us Supreme Court would rule death by electrocution unconstitutional, throughout his legislative career Chambers filibustered, prolonged debates, filed amendments, and used every legislative method possible to block lethal injection bills.[51] In February 2008, that dream had been realized when the Nebraska Supreme Court ruled execution by electrocution unconstitutional.[52] For the last year of Chambers's tenure in the Legislature, Nebraska lacked a legal method of enacting its death penalty statute.

Although Senator Brenda Council, who succeeded Senator Chambers, continues to introduce death penalty repeal bills, the future does not look promising for opponents of the death penalty in Nebraska. In 2009 the Legislature overwhelmingly passed a bill establishing lethal injection as the state's method of execution.[53] An amendment to that bill introduced by Senator Council, calling for the repeal of the death penalty, failed by a vote of thirty-three to thirteen.[54] The Nebraska Department of Correctional Services has created a lethal injection protocol.[55] Moreover, senators in favor of the death penalty have temporarily squelched an effort to focus attention on one troubling aspect of executions: cost. On 21 January 2010, by a vote of thirty to fifteen, the Legislature "shot down a proposal by Omaha Sen. Brenda Council to have the State Auditor's Office study how much money is spent prosecuting and appealing death penalty cases, as well as the potential savings of repealing capital punishment."[56] In April 2011, the Nebraska Supreme Court set June 14 as the execution date for Carey Dean Moore. Questions over the quality of death drugs procured from India resulted in Moore's execution being stayed on 25 May 2011.[57]

Maryland's death penalty statute extends far back into colonial times. Originally, someone could be executed for a number of violent and property crimes. In 1810, the state limited the use of the death penalty to the offenses of "first-degree murder, rape, arson, and treason."[58] In more recent times, the state did not reinstate its death statute until 1978, nearly six years after *Furman*. The legislature excluded juveniles and the "mentally retarded" from execution during the 1980s, long before US Supreme Court decisions in Roper v. Simmons (2005) and Atkins v. Virginia (2002) required those exclusions.[59] Maryland's death statute was amended in 1987 to allow life without the possibility of parole as a sentencing option in capital cases.[60]

Maryland has executed 314 people since 1638,[61] including five post-*Furman* executions.[62] Hanging was the primary method of execution until 1957. Maryland's last state killing occurred in December 2005.[63] At least eleven women are among those executed, five of whom were white and six African American. The sex of seven African Americans executed in the state is unknown, but the last execution of a woman occurred in 1871. Of the 314 people killed, 209, approximately two-thirds, were African American.[64] From the last decades of the nineteenth century through the middle of the twentieth century, at least twenty-nine Maryland residents (the majority of whom were African American) also fell victim to lynching.[65] These statistics are not just the product of pre-twentieth-century racial dynamics. For the years 1900 through 1961, at least 90 of the 112 persons executed in Maryland jurisdiction were African Americans (36 of whom were executed for rape), while only 20 were white.[66] Maryland's post-*Furman* executions followed a familiar course. Three of the five people executed were African Americans, and the victims of all five were white.[67]

The racial makeup of Maryland's post-*Furman* death row population provides equally troubling evidence of administrative bias. Of the seven men awaiting execution on 13 October 2004, five were black, all of whom had been condemned for killing white persons.[68] Of the eleven people removed from Maryland's death row after *Furman*, seven were African American and four where white.[69] As of 1 April 2010, five people remained on Maryland's death row, four of whom were African American.[70]

As the twentieth century came to a close, it was no longer possible to ignore the overrepresentation of African Americans in Maryland's criminal justice system, on the state's death row, and in its capital punishment history. Ironically, elected officials seemed oblivious to the correctional practices and race history of their own state. To fix the death penalty, the execution process needed study, and study it they did. Over the following half-decade, the list of problems worthy of study expanded to include cost and, with the DNA exoneration of Kirk Bloodsworth in 1993, the possibility of executing innocent persons.

Maryland legislators first heard troubling research data concerning the administration of the state's death penalty in 1962, when the Committee on Capital Punishment reported that African Americans sentenced to death were more likely to be executed than whites under the same sentence. These data moved the Capital Punishment Committee of the Legislative Council to vote five to two to recommend that the death penalty be abolished. The committee "recommended a phased in approach: 'that the Legislature accept the principle of abolition as a goal and adopt a plan for the gradual removal of capital punishment in our state.'"[71] The recommendation was never acted on. A quarter-century later, in 1987, Maryland legislators were again presented with problematic data. The Maryland Office of the Public Defender, at the request of the Maryland Court of Appeals, gathered information on 415 cases it considered "death eligible": "They found substantial county-to-county variation in the rate at which state's attorneys file death notices. They also reported that state's attorneys were approximately twice as likely to file a notification to seek a death sentence and not withdraw that notification when the homicide victim was white rather than black."[72]

In 1996, Governor Parris Glendening's Task Force on the Fair Imposition of Capital Punishment delivered the last disturbing information of the twentieth century on the death penalty in Maryland. The nonfunded task force's examination of the racial composition of death row inmates concluded: "The high percentage of African-American prisoners under sentence of death and the low percentage of prisoners under sentence of death whose victims were African-American remains a cause for concern." The Task Force recommended a more thorough examination of Maryland's capital sentencing procedures.[73]

In 2000, Governor Glendening—a Roman Catholic supporter of the death penalty with three post-*Furman* executions on his executive résumé—committed $225,000 of the Maryland Department of Public Safety and Correctional Services' budget to a study directed by Raymond Paternoster, a well-respected University of Maryland criminologist. The purpose of the research was to examine the role that race played in the sentencing of capital offenders in Maryland. Approximately one year before the release of the Paternoster findings, David Baldus and George Woodworth released an analysis of a narrower sample of Maryland cases. They concluded that those in Maryland "who killed white victims were more likely to advance to a penalty trial and are more likely to be sentenced to death than those who killed a black. This was particularly true for black offenders who killed white victims."[74] Ignoring these data was not an option. On 9 May 2002, Governor Glendening—succumbing to the demands of Maryland's Legislative Black Caucus, among other groups—suspended the execution of Wesley Eugene Baker and imposed a moratorium on executions pending completion of the Paternoster study, the most pervasive empirical examination of Maryland's capital sentencing system yet. Paternoster's findings proved to be every bit as troubling as the Baldus analysis foresaw. After controlling for variables that could influence outcomes, the researchers found that "offenders who kill white victims, especially if the offender is black, are significantly and substantially more likely to be charged with a capital crime. . . . Those who kill white victims are also significantly more likely to have their death notification 'stick' than those who kill non-whites."[75]

Robert Ehrlich, the new Republican governor, appeared unimpressed by these data. In January 2003, he lifted the moratorium on executions. Eighteen months later, in June 2004, the state carried out its first execution in nearly six years.[76] Governor Ehrlich presided over an additional execution–on 6 December 2005—during his single term in office.[77] His relations with opponents of the death penalty were far from harmonious. During his time in office, they accused him of using the state police to spy on them, even though there were no reported plans of violent protests.[78]

Governor Ehrlich was succeeded by Martin O'Malley, a Catholic and a passionate opponent of capital punishment who argued that the practice was "inherently unjust," was not a deterrent, and used resources needed for other phases of law enforcement.[79] Almost immediately after assuming office, Governor O'Malley called on the General Assembly to abolish the death penalty. The 2007 repeal effort was rejected by the Senate Judicial Proceedings Committee on a tie vote, five to five.[80] After failing for a second consecutive year to get a repeal bill to the floor of either house, abolitionists in 2008 turned to a time-tested tool in their quest to eliminate Maryland's death statute: they commissioned a study. The two Senate bills to establish the Maryland Commission on Capital Punishment (SB 614 and SB 1111) easily passed the Maryland House and Senate, ninety-one to forty-seven and thirty-two to fifteen, respectively.[81]

Although this legislation represented the fourth time in fifteen years that the General Assembly had mandated a study of capital punishment, the charge given the 2008 commission extended beyond traditional concerns about racially biased administration to include the risk of executing an innocent person, the deterrent effect of the death penalty, and cost. The commission relied on existing data and the testimony of expert witnesses and members of the public in its final report, which was delivered to the General Assembly on 12 December 2008. Based largely on the testimonies of Professor Ray Paternoster and David Baldus, twenty of the twenty-one commissioners concluded: "Racial disparities exist in Maryland's capital sentencing system. While there is no evidence of purposeful discrimination, the statistics examined from death penalty cases from 1978 to 1999 demonstrate racial disparities when the factors of the race of the defendant and the race of the victim are combined."[82]

Commissioners cited national statistics on exonerations from death row, problems with eyewitness identifications, false confessions, and faulty laboratory (forensic) evidence to justify their concluding, eighteen to three, that "despite the advance of forensic sciences, particularly DNA testing, the risk of execution of an innocent person is a real possibility."[83] On a seventeen to four vote, commissioners rejected the notion that capital punishment was a deterrent to murder.[84] Relying heavily on the findings of an Urban Institute study released in March 2008 and the testimony from that study's principal investigators, John Roman and Aaron Chalfin, the commission concluded by a margin of seventeen to four that "the costs associated with cases in which a death sentence is sought are substantially higher than the costs associated with cases in which a sentence of life without the possibility of parole is sought."[85]

The Urban Institute report gave commissioners, Maryland legislators, and the public the following facts about the average case eligible for the death penalty: when the death penalty was not pursued, the cost to Maryland taxpayers in excess of $1.1 million, of which $870,000 was prison costs and $250,000 was adjudication expenses; when the death penalty was sought unsuccessfully, the cost was $1.8 million in prison and adjudication costs; and when the sentence of death was sought successfully, the cost was $3 million. The predicted cost of bringing closure to the 162 capital cases initiated between 1978 and 1999 was $186 million.[86] In the end, the Maryland Commission on Capital Punishment recommended by a thirteen to nine vote that the state's death penalty be abolished.[87] Since Governor O'Malley had appointed thirteen of the commissioners, Republican delegates tended to criticize the Commission—and thus its conclusions and recommendations—for including too many opponents of capital punishment. The *Baltimore Sun* editorialized that the state's death penalty law should be repealed if it couldn't be applied fairly[88] and noted: "The only way we can say we are not executing the innocent is simply not to execute."[89]

In 2009 the General Assembly considered death penalty abolition for the third consecutive year. The recommendation of the 2008 commission, along with the Urban Institute's findings on cost, provided additional momentum to that year's effort. The governor was optimistic as he addressed the eleven members of the Senate Judiciary Proceedings Committee.[90] He told the committee that had rejected abolition efforts in the two previous years that capital cases cost three times more than murder cases in which the prosecution does not seek the death penalty, "and we can't afford that . . . when there are better and cheaper ways to reduce crime."[91] House Speaker Michael E. Bush believed that the repeal bill would easily pass his chamber. If the bill was not released from the Senate Judiciary Committee, senators favoring repeal said that they might resort to a rarely used procedural move to bring the issue to the floor, which would involve asking sixteen senators to sign a petition.[92] The governor contemplated asking the electorate to decide the issue by referendum if the General Assembly failed to act.[93] Yet, even with the strong support of the Legislative Black Caucus, O'Malley did not have the votes necessary to abolish Maryland's death penalty.[94] A *Baltimore Sun* survey found that nineteen senators supported the repeal of Maryland's death penalty while twenty-four opposed it.[95]

The 2009 effort did not reach the same end as earlier repeal efforts. Rather than discard the 2009 bill, legislators amended it—at Governor O'Malley's urging—to curtail the circumstances in which the death penalty can be sought. The resulting law allowed prosecutors to seek capital punishment only in cases where there is DNA or other biological evidence (including fingerprints), a videotape connecting the accused with the crime, or a voluntary, videotaped confession.[96] Maryland's attorney general called the bill "ill-conceived, ill-thought out and awkward."[97] The governor's abolitionist activities did not appear to trouble the electorate: O'Malley easily won reelection on 2 November 2010.[98]

Although it is true that a repeal bill has never reached the floor of either chamber of the General Assembly, three factors suggest that executions are not on the immediate horizon in Maryland. First, there is good chance that Governor O'Malley would commute the sentence of the inmate to life without the possibility of parole. Second, the 2009 restriction bill will reduce execution candidates. And third, as of 28 September 2011, the state has yet to specify a court-approved lethal injection protocol, as mandated by the Maryland Court of Appeals in December 2006.[99] Before executions can begin, a protocol must be in place. According to Amnesty International, European proscriptions against selling execution drugs to the United States, along with Governor O'Malley's active and passive resistance, have made the task of defining a death protocol for Maryland extremely difficult.[100] Moreover, 40 percent of the state's legislators—sixty-one delegates and twenty-one senators—cosponsored the 2011 death penalty repeal bill. Maryland Citizens against State Executions argues that the votes are there to repeal the death penalty in 2012 if—unlike in 2011—both houses are given the opportunity to vote on the issue.[101]

9 De Facto Abolition States

Our information on executions and death row populations in this chapter was taken from the Death Penalty Information Center website. We began by comparing the total number of executions between 17 January 1977 (when Gary Gilmore was executed in Utah) and 4 July 2010 with the total number of death row inmates. We then listed the remaining states that had fewer executions than California's thirteen, resulting in a total of fourteen states. All of the West Coast states are represented: California (690 on death row and 13 executions), Oregon (33 and 2), and Washington (9 and 4). Other western states represented are Nevada (78 and 12), Idaho (18 and one), Montana (2 and 3), Wyoming (1 and 1), Colorado (3 and 1), and Utah (9 and 7). In this region, only Arizona (129 and 23) has a relatively active execution program. The Midwest is represented by South Dakota (3 and 1). The mid-Atlantic region is represented by Pennsylvania (225 and 3). The South is also surprisingly represented—by Kentucky (36 and 3), Tennessee (92 and 6), and Mississippi (59 and 12). This is so surprising that we devote another chapter to the South.

CALIFORNIA

Prior to 1976 California carried out 709 executions. Nevertheless, the state has seen relatively few executions in recent years despite having a large death row population. Authors have expressed concern over the amount of money being spent on the legal processing of those inmates.[1] A *Contra Costa Times* reader may have expressed the feelings of many of the state's residents in noting that "the death penalty is effectively eliminated in California. It is stupid to be paying this much for something that gets us nothing."[2] Franklin Zimring, a law professor at the University of California, Berkeley, described the situation by stating: "We try to maintain the apparatus of state killing and another apparatus that almost guarantees that it won't happen. The public pays for both sides."[3] Similarly, Mark Drozdowski, a deputy public defender and head of the Los Angeles Capital Case Unit, compared California's death row to "a college where nobody ever graduates, where they just keep building more dorms."[4] To put the situation in perspective, one article stated that, as of late 2009, California had carried out thirteen executions in thirty-one years, and at that rate, it would take 1,600 years to execute everybody on death row.[5]

In trying to account for this situation, several authors have indicated that California's death penalty appeals process lasts twenty-five years.[6] Additionally, two articles noted that two-thirds of California's death sentences have been vacated by the federal courts due to ineffective assistance of counsel.[7] Since California has the largest death row population in the United States, it is fitting to show multiple views of this environment.

In a telephone conversation with Galliher on 27 January 2011, a former California public defender noted that the death penalty in California "costs a fortune." Under state law, appeals can drag on for decades, jury selection can take four or five months, and the trial can last another six to seven months. The guilt and penalty phase require separate attorneys. The consequent delays have led to a situation where, in recent years, half of the state's death row inmates have died of natural causes, and approximately half of the prisoners on death row have not yet been assigned attorneys.[8] In a telephone conversation with Galliher on 31 January 2011, David Andersen, a California attorney in private practice, noted that he had spent most of the previous year on one death penalty trial. He estimated that a defendant in a death penalty case must now wait six or seven years after the original conviction to be appointed an attorney for appeals because there are few qualified attorneys, and the state won't appoint unqualified ones.[9] The California public defender argued that "most prosecutors and judges don't have much experience with death penalty cases and don't know what they are doing, and thus they make mistakes that are picked up on appeal."[10]

OREGON

Oregon made the death penalty illegal three times in the twentieth century: 1914–20, 1964–78, and 1981–84.[11] This reflects a continuing and profound distrust of the death penalty and also a distrust of abolition. Whatever exists is subject to change. In 2010 Oregon had thirty-three people on its death row and had executed two since 1976.[12] Before 1976, however, Oregon had executed 122 prisoners.

Oregon's current death penalty statute was approved by the state's voters in 1984.[13] As of September 2009, the state had imposed seventy-three death sentences under the new statute.[14] Thus far, two inmates have been executed—one in 1996 and one in 1997.[15] Both were executed after dropping their appeals and thus were "volunteers" for death.[16]

Because Oregon has sentenced a large number of people to death but executed relatively few of them, complaints have surfaced in the media. A former Marion County judge, for example, sent a letter to the state's Senate Judiciary Committee categorizing Oregon's death penalty as a "largely futile attempt'" that has sapped "'years and years of criminal justice resources, and millions and millions of tax dollars."[17] One author states that Oregon's capital punishment system is "a waste of money" and argues that the state "cannot afford any program that does not work, especially when it hasn't for 25 years."[18] The journalist James Pitkin stated: "Oregon remains stuck with a backward system in which the state has the power to kill criminals yet refuses to do so."[19] Richard Dieter, of the Death Penalty Information Center, notes that Oregon is spending millions of dollars for "one execution every 10 years" and contends that "that's not a lot to show for all that money."[20] The director of the Oregon Capital Resource Center expressed a similar sentiment.[21]

The low number of executions may be due to a variety of factors. According to the *Catholic Sentinel*, half of Oregon's death sentences have been overturned by the state's Supreme Court.[22] Moreover, the appeals process for death row inmates in Oregon "can take nearly 15 years to complete."[23] Pitkin states that Oregon's appeals process lasts twenty to forty-five years and that, in comparison to other states, "additional wrenches have been thrown into Oregon's system." He blames the slow pace of Oregon's Supreme Court, along with recent changes in the law that have hindered the progress of existing death penalty cases: "Several local decisions have forced cases back to square one, including a 1989 state law allowing juries to sentence for life without parole, a 1996 ballot measure changing mandatory minimum sentences, and a 1999 court decision challenging the inclusion of victim-impact evidence."[24]

Judge Michael McShane of the Multnomah County Circuit Court commented on capital punishment in Oregon: "Clearly, in terms of quick justice, it's a system that's not working."[25] Pitkin remarks that the state houses death row inmates for decades, "essentially paying for a life sentence anyway."

Some blame death penalty abolitionists for creating the lengthy appeals process and purposely inflating costs in an effort to gain support for their cause.[26] Others believe that judges and lawyers have lengthened the appeals process in order to prevent executions, rather than trying to abolish the death penalty outright. One Oregon politician argued that members of the Oregon State Bar favor abolishing the death penalty and have "cook[ed] the books" accordingly.[27]

WASHINGTON

Washington abolished its death penalty in 1913. This action was at least in part a consequence of having four executions in Oregon on one day in the previous year. These killings convinced the Washington governor and the press that the process was out of control and capital punishment should be abandoned.[28] In 1919 Washington reinstated capital punishment due to fears of growing unemployment, poverty, and labor unrest led by the Industrial Workers of the world (IWW). Currently Washington houses nine prisoners on its death row; the state has executed four people since 1976, and 105 prisoners before them.[29]

A 2009 guest editorial by Robert Utter in the *Seattle Times* passionately rejected capital punishment.[30] In 1995 Utter had resigned from the state's Supreme Court after twenty-three years to protest the death penalty. Since that time, he noted, there has been a "dramatic" decline in public support for capital punishment. And the number of executions has declined more than 60 percent. The death penalty is not typically imposed on the worst offenders. In addition, the cost of capital cases is three times as much as homicide cases where the death penalty is not sought.

NEVADA

The 2009 Nevada Assembly Bill 190 called for a two-year moratorium on executions in Nevada.[31] Assemblywoman Shelia Leslie (D-Reno) was one of the sponsors of the moratorium, as was Assemblyman Bernie Anderson (D-Sparks). Capital cases are more expensive than life sentence cases because jury selection is more complex, juries are more likely to be sequestered, and more attorneys and expert witnesses are involved. Supporters of executions noted that death cases involve "endless appeals."[32] Prior to 1976, Nevada executed sixty-one prisoners. Since 1977, however, Nevada juries have imposed 130 death sentences, but the state has executed only twelve people, eleven of which were volunteers. The high ratio of volunteers raises questions about the quality of life on the state's death row.[33] In addition, nearly as many death row inmates die from natural causes as from executions.[34]

Some Nevadans note that it is offensive to tell the families of murder victims that the death penalty should be abolished because of cost.[35] So it is not surprising that a plan to study the costs of the death penalty in Nevada passed the state Assembly by a vote of thirty to twelve, after a proposed moratorium for the period of the study was dropped.[36]

IDAHO

Idaho's current death penalty statute was enacted in 1977, and as of 19 August 2011, the state had sentenced forty people to death under it.[37] Perhaps this is why Idaho Senior Deputy Attorney General LaMont Anderson has called Idaho "one of the most pro-death-penalty sentencing states in the country."[38] Despite the high number of death sentences, the state has carried out only one execution in recent years: in 1994 a prisoner was executed after dropping his appeals.[39] Prior to 1976, Idaho executed twenty-six prisoners.

Idaho's large number of death sentences with relatively few executions has led one journalist to question why the state is spending so much money on the death penalty and to ask: "Is it really a punishment if almost nobody is being executed?"[40] An *Idaho Statesman* editorial quotes the father of a murder victim, who asks why the state has a death penalty if it is never enforced.[41] Another journalist points out that Idaho prosecutors must remember that the state's death penalty is a largely "symbolic" and expensive process, which (because of lengthy appeals) can prolong the suffering of victims' families.[42] Similarly, a Boise defense attorney who has represented clients on death row states: "We no longer as a society have any confidence in the certainty of a prosecution that necessarily results in the death penalty."[43]

The high number of death sentences in Idaho may be partly due to the fact that the state's judges and prosecutors are elected every four years and thus are held accountable by the voters for their decisions about what to charge defendants with.[44] In looking at the reasons why the state has executed so few people, it should be noted that (as of 2003) Idaho death sentences have been overturned at a rate that is higher than all but five of the states that have the death penalty.[45] Another author quotes an Idaho prosecutor who blames the state's lack of executions on the US Court of Appeals for the Ninth Circuit, which hears Idaho's death penalty cases. The prosecutor claims: "There are certain judges in the 9th circuit that have never affirmed a death penalty case."[46] A document published by the Idaho Department of Correction seems to shed some light on this controversy. It lists the status for all forty prisoners sentenced to death in the state as of 19 November 2009.[47] As we already noted, Idaho has had one execution in recent years. Of the remaining thirty-nine people who have been sent to death row:

1. Nine inmates had their sentences reversed by the Idaho Supreme Court.
2. Fifteen inmates have "appeals pending."
3. Four inmates had their sentences reversed in Federal District Court.
4. Three inmates died in prison.
5. Two inmates had their convictions reversed in Federal District Court. (One of these inmates also had his sentence commuted by Idaho's governor.)
6. One inmate had his sentence reversed by the US Supreme Court.
7. One inmate had his sentence reversed by the US Court of Appeals for the Ninth Circuit.
8. One inmate had his conviction reversed by the US Court of Appeals for the Ninth Circuit.
9. One inmate was resentenced after reaching a "negotiated settlement" in the US Court of Appeals for the Ninth Circuit.
10. One inmate had his sentence reversed by state district court.
11. One inmate had his sentence modified and reduced by state district court.

In a telephone conversation with Galliher on 31 January 2011, LaMont Anderson expressed deep frustration with the current situation and noted that judges in the Ninth Circuit Court of Appeals have the highest reversal rate of any court in the nation. One judge has never affirmed a death penalty case. As a result, the federal district judges and state circuit judges have significantly raised their standards to make sure that their findings are not reversed by the Ninth Circuit.[48]

MONTANA

A former court administrator in Montana called the state court "underfunded and understaffed" and noted that death penalty cases are unusually complicated and require twice as many attorneys, additional pretrial motions, expert witnesses, a lengthier jury selection process, and "far more preparation and time spent in court than other cases," along with an appeals process that "can last decades."[49] Recently the longtime chief special prosecutor—who had served for twenty-one years and prosecuted five death penalty cases—came to the conclusion that correctional officers are not protected by the death penalty and that it is "an incalculable drain on our limited criminal justice resources."[50] Dan Testa quoted Ed Sheehy, a Missoula public defender with capital case experience, who stated that legal fees for capital defense are "exorbitant" and predicted that two existing capital cases would deplete the resources of the Office of the State Public Defender.[51] Montana has sentenced thirteen people to death since capital punishment was reinstated, of whom three were executed. Two remain on death row. Five had their cases were overturned. Two inmates committed suicide, and one had his sentence commuted by the governor.[52] Prior to 1976, the state executed seventy-one prisoners. Vigilante groups also carried out numerous extralegal executions during the nineteenth century. Between December 1863 and January 1864, twenty-five people were lynched. In 1884, thirty five suspected cattle rustlers were hanged by a single group of vigilantes known as Stewart's Stranglers.[53]

Montana Senator Dave Wanzenried sponsored abolition bills in 2009 and 2011, both of which passed the state Senate but died in a House committee.[54] These defeats came even though Mike Menahan, a state representative and county prosecutor, supported the repeal measure because of the high cost of capital punishment.[55] An editorial noted that an increasing number of legislators are realizing that the death penalty is not cost effective. The writer stated: "Given the high cost of maintaining capital punishment, and rising deficits faced by state governments across the country, abolishing the death penalty increasingly becomes a matter of dollars and cents."[56]

WYOMING

An entry in the *Capital Defense Weekly* blog—"Wyoming's Death Row Down to Just One"—told readers that the state had reduced its death row population by 50 percent after the conviction of a condemned inmate was thrown out because the court found that his public defender had been told that the only way he could keep his job was to stop representing his client so aggressively.[57] The prisoner had been convicted of killing a corrections officer in the state penitentiary, but the federal district court ruled that the state public defender's office had not provided the funds needed for his defense. Wyoming executed twenty-two prisoners prior to 1976. However, with only one prisoner executed since then and only one other currently on death row, the state's debate about expenses involves precious few human beings, yet remains expensive. The inmate who become the sole victim of Wyoming's post-*Furman* death statute, Mark Hopkinson, estimated that instead of paying for his numerous court hearings and the filing of thousands of documents during his thirteen-year appeal process, Wyoming could have paid to keep the state School for the Deaf and Blind open.[58] Hopkinson's observation was confirmed by others. A former state public defender testifying before the Senate Judiciary Committee in 2001 noted that her office had required an additional $800,000 the previous year to deal with an unusually high number of capital cases.[59]

COLORADO

Although some prosecutors argue that the death penalty actually saves money by pressuring defendants into pleading guilty to a lesser charge and avoiding the expense of a trial, there is evidence to the contrary. According to Colorado Democratic House Majority Leader Paul Weissmann, his state has seen only one execution in the past forty years even though Colorado spends $4 million to $5 million annually on capital punishment. Weissmann said that in the last death penalty case, the cost of the prosecution was $1.4 million.[60] The costs start in the trial court and run through the appeal process. Moreover, when public defenders are involved, the entire process is funded by tax dollars.[61] A proposed abolition bill in Colorado would have diverted about $1 million from death penalty funding to state law enforcement efforts to solve cold cases.[62] The mother of a murder victim argued that it was better to spend money on tracking down the person who slit her daughter's throat than to retain the death penalty.[63] When voters were given a choice in 2007 between spending $3 million a year on capital punishment and using the funds to solve open murder cases, 70 percent chose the latter option.[64] In a letter to the editor, Patrick Gallagher argued against the death penalty due to its lack of deterrence, racism, and costs.[65] An editorial in a Greeley newspaper stated: "We understand perfectly why families of victims would want to see the ones who caused them so much pain put to death. But in these times, we simply can't afford it."[66] The high costs are partly due to the fact that since 1980, 124 Colorado defendants had been prosecuted for capital murder.[67] All the debate about abolition involves three people on the state's death row. Proponents of abolition say the death penalty is so rarely used that it cannot be a deterrent. The current governor, Bill Ritter, expressed doubts about capital punishment while he was a prosecutor but sought the death penalty seven times, not succeeding in any of the cases.[68]

A Colorado district attorney billed the state for more than $200,000 in her effort to convict and condemn to death two inmates charged with killing another prisoner. Under Colorado law, counties can be reimbursed by the state Department of Corrections for prosecution of "crimes committed in the state prisons."[69] State Attorney General Ken Salazar protested cuts to a fund that helps rural communities prosecute death penalty cases since "the viability of Colorado's death penalty law is at issue."[70] Accordingly, one Colorado newspaper argued that execution is not costly in itself but is made expensive by those "bent on thwarting this ultimate form of justice."[71]

Michael Radelet and his colleagues at the University of Colorado have recently addressed the seeming contradiction in the state between relatively frequent murder charges and infrequent executions.[72] They found that from 1972 through 2005, prosecutors who pushed for the death penalty were successful in only 21 of more than 100 cases. Moreover, when the victims were white, there was a much higher likelihood that prosecutors would seek the death penalty. Prior to 1976, Colorado had carried out 101 executions. However, of those that have been sentenced to death since then, only one prisoner had been executed, and two were on death row at a cost of "unknown millions."[73] This situation helped "politicians and prosecutors . . . convince the public that they are tough on crime."[74]

UTAH

Marijuana: The Impact of Mormons on the Passage of a Liberal Law

In the 1970s, Utah was a leader in decriminalizing marijuana.[75] It did so when a study found that most Mormon young people had used marijuana. Suddenly the Mormon church realized that such behavior was best handled by the family, rather than by the state legal system, since the church had always emphasized the importance of family life.

Mormons and the Death Penalty

As of July 2010, Utah had executed seven people since 1976 and had nine inmates on its death row.[76] Prior to 1976, however, the state had executed forty-three prisoners. The *Deseret News* is a right-leaning daily newspaper that caters to the state's Mormon population. Although it has taken no explicit editorial position on executions, it published a 2009 article on the death penalty that is revealing: "While many states are trading the death penalty for life sentences to save millions of dollars, the Utah Attorney General's Office is pushing to strengthen the state's ultimate punishment by limiting the appeals process."[77] The last person executed in Utah had been on death row for eleven years; now the average time on death row is in excess of twenty years. According to Jacob Hancock, the state has yet to conduct a study comparing the costs of the death penalty with those of life in prison.[78] However, states that have conducted such a study typically have found a large difference in costs. In Utah, capital prosecutors are paid the same regardless of their record in securing death sentences. The implication is that Utah is spending a lot more for executions than it would for life in prison. In addition, it seems likely that there is an economy of scale whereby states with the most executions spend the least per execution because the fixed bureaucratic costs are constant. If this formula is correct, then Utah spends much more per execution than, say, Texas.

Until 2004, Utah death row prisoners were allowed to choose between lethal injection or the firing squad. Death by gunshot is a consequence of the traditional Mormon belief in blood atonement. The first post-*Furman* execution was in Utah in 1977, when Gary Gilmore volunteered for his execution and died by firing squad. The execution process involves pinning a white cloth over the prisoner's heart and placing a black hood over his or her head. The condemned person is seated in an execution chair, with restraints on his or her legs, arms, chest, and head. Five volunteers from the prison staff and the community shoot simultaneously, and one rifle is loaded with blanks—so those firing do not know if they actually helped kill the prisoner. John Taylor was the next prisoner shot in Utah. He was executed in 1996, and "only hours before he had to be given medication because [understandably] his stomach was doing flip-flops."[79]

The small Roman Catholic community in Utah publicly opposes the state's death penalty. Bishop John C. Wester of Utah's Catholic diocese called the firing squad "archaic" and "violent," stating that "'it simply expands on the violence that we already experience from guns as a society.'"[80] Elsewhere the bishop was quoted as saying that the death penalty "diminishes us and erodes our respect for the sanctity of all human life."[81] Mormon leaders feel that it is not appropriate to speak out on executions, in contrast to the church's energetic support of the initiative to ban gay marriage in California. On 18 June 2010, the state used its firing squad once more, carrying out the first execution in approximately eleven years. This occurred after twenty-five years of legal maneuvering at an estimated cost of $3 million.[82]

SOUTH DAKOTA

Prior to 1976, South Dakota carried out fifteen executions. However, since then the state has executed only one person and has sent seventeen people to death row, with three currently there.[83] In February 2010, the South Dakota attorney general stated that he intended to seek the death penalty against a man accused of killing a sheriff's deputy. A local news report indicated that the county would be paying for it, and that the county auditor had estimated that trial and defense costs associated with the case would total $300,000. The auditor noted that the county had already spent $175,000 on the case and would have to spend more. One prisoner who has been on death row for approximately twenty years has cost the state $1.5 million—a sum that is considerably more than the $600,000 that the state would have spent to keep him in the general prison population during that time.[84] A state senator who sponsored an abolition bill in 2007 was quoted as saying: "It doesn't make sense to me. Not only is the death penalty morally wrong, but the money spent during the lengthy appeals process could be put to better use by the state."[85]

PENNSYLVANIA

Prior to 1976, Pennsylvania executed 1,040 people. However, the state has carried out only three executions in recent years, despite maintaining the country's fourth largest death row population.[86] This has led at least two authors to question the costs of Pennsylvania's capital punishment system.[87] Indeed, a number of articles and editorials have pointed to the high costs of Pennsylvania's death penalty.[88] In trying to account for the discrepancy between death sentences and executions, one article noted that 117 death sentences in the state have been overturned due to trial attorneys' errors.[89] Another journalist noted that 68 percent of Pennsylvania's death sentences were vacated after appeal,[90] and still others reported that six of the state's death row inmates had been exonerated.[91] In a telephone interview, Marshall Dayan, the chair of Pennsylvanians for Alternatives to the Death Penalty, argued that the best answer to the large death row and the small number of executions is as follows: Defense funds are county-based in Pennsylvania, and death cases did not get much in the way of financial support in the early stages and thus did not have the best legal talent. But as the death row cases progress, these prisoners get great legal talent because at that point federal funds can be used to keep the prisoners alive.[92]

131

KENTUCKY

Kentucky carried out 424 executions before 1976. Since then, the state has sentenced ninety-two people to death but executed only three.[93] Not surprisingly, a number of articles and editorials have expressed concern that the state is spending money on a capital punishment system that produces little in the way of executions. In 2005 this sentiment was expressed by Ed Monahan, a former public defender and the director of the Catholic Conference of Kentucky.[94] Similarly, Ernie Lewis, a journalist, questioned whether or not the death penalty itself is a failed social policy, noting that Kentucky has spent millions of dollars on capital punishment.[95] Jane Chiles and Rev. Patrick Delahanty stated that many of the state's citizens were disappointed with Kentucky's capital punishment system.[96] They pointed out that the state had spent nearly $300 million on a death penalty system that had produced just two executions, and that many Kentuckians were experiencing "buyer's remorse" after learning how the state's capital punishment program "really works." In 2005 Ernie Lewis, director of Kentucky's Department of Public Advocacy, estimated that each of the state's executions cost $50 million, while noting that more than half of the state's death sentences had been reversed. Regarding the prosecution of capital cases in Kentucky, he stated: "'we're not doing it very well.'"[97] R. G. Dunlop, a journalist, noted that both opponents and proponents of the death penalty are concerned that the state is spending millions of dollars on an "irreparably broken" capital punishment system that rarely executes people and is hindered by "endless legal delays."[98] In another article, Dunlop reported that the state is spending "millions of dollars" annually on a death penalty system that is "so ineffective that more death-row inmates are dying of natural causes than are being executed." He also stated that some people have asked if Kentucky can afford a capital punishment system that allows cases to "drag on interminably."[99]

Some Kentuckians have argued that the money spent on the state's death penalty could be used for other things. Dunlop quoted Jason Nemes, former director of the State Administrative Office of the Courts, who argued that it was "unwise" to continue funding Kentucky's "ineffective" capital punishment system when it took money from vital services.[100]

Several factors may have contributed to Kentucky's relatively low number of executions. Dunlop noted that five inmates died during the appeals process.[101] Also (as noted above) by 2005, more than half of the state's death sentences had been reversed.[102] Dunlop noted that over the last three decades, thirty people have had their death sentences reduced during the appeals process, a situation that indicates "widespread flaws at the trial level."[103] Similarly Lewis states that over half of Kentucky's death sentences "have been reversed due to the unconstitutionality of their conviction or sentence or a serious and prejudicial error during their trial."[104] Many believe that Kentucky's high rate of reversals and extensive delays are caused by "a broken system that was vastly underfunded and badly flawed when most of the older capital cases were tried."[105] In a telephone interview, Edward Monahan, the state's chief public defender, indicated that part of the reason for Kentucky's few executions is a "top-notch" statewide public defender system. This system is extremely effective even though public defenders do not have adequate resources. Their postconviction skills, however, have resulted in forty of the ninety-six death sentences imposed in the state since 1976 being reversed.

TENNESSEE

Tennessee abolished capital punishment in 1915 but reinstated it in 1919.[106] Racism and the threat and reality of lynching spawned the return of executions. Tennessee currently has ninety-two inmates on its death row, and the state imposed 166 death sentences between 1977 and 2008.[107] Nevertheless only six executions were carried out during this time, all of which have taken place since 2000.[108] Like the pattern in some other states, this is somewhat surprising given that Tennessee carried out 335 executions prior to 1976. Several authors expressed concern about the resources that the state is devoting to capital punishment. In 2004, one noted that Tennessee's "nearly half-dozen" capital prosecutors "aren't doing so hot," given that only one person had been executed in the state since the 1960s.[109] Josh Tinley noted that "these days in the South the economics of capital punishment cannot be ignored."[110] He quoted a United Church of Christ pastor who served as a counselor to a number of Tennessee death row inmates: 'When you're having a fiscal crisis . . . you look at what your policies are, what you're funding and whether you're getting the bang for your buck."[111] Brad MacLean, assistant director of the Tennessee Justice Project, may have had this in mind when he noted that the state's capital punishment system was "broken."[112]

Tennessee's reluctance to carry out executions has not gone unnoticed. Journalists lined up to oppose executions. One editorial writer stated that Tennessee "has been among the most cautious of the pro-death penalty states."[113] Similarly, David Spates noted that "Tennesseans don't have much of a stomach for capital punishment,"[114] while Steve Reddick claimed that the state's residents have an "historic ambivalence toward the death penalty."[115]

This attitude may be reflected in some of the actions of Tennessee's courts. A recent article noted that over half of the state's death sentences have been overturned on appeal, with the author noting that "things are not working as they should at the trial level."[116] An Associated Press article stated that 32 of 109 death sentences were reversed by the Tennessee Court of Criminal Appeals due to "trial errors."[117]

MISSISSIPPI

Mississippi carried out 351 executions prior to 1976 and 13 executions since it reinstated the death penalty.[118] An accused killer has a better chance of being tried, convicted, and executed if he commits murder in some Mississippi counties compared to others. This is because counties must pay for capital murder defense, a responsibility affirmed by the state's Supreme Court in 2005.[119] Counties without large tax bases cannot afford to do so. Quitman County, for example, borrowed hundreds of thousands of dollars to defend two men who allegedly killed four members of a family.[120] The county spent more to defend the men than most of the area's residents earn in a decade.[121] To help fund this case, the county raised taxes three years in a row and borrowed $150,000 from a bank;[122] in the process, it was nearly bankrupted.[123] Thus, in 2005, prosecutors were reported to be hesitant to pursue the death penalty because of the burden to taxpayers.[124]

In 1998 Mississippi passed a bill that would transfer the burden of indigents' defense to the state, but the money to implement the program was never allocated. Two years later, the bill was repealed due to "budget constraints."[125] Thus it is easy to understand why Mississippi had one of the highest reversal rates in the nation.[126]

CONCLUSION

Some of these states—particularly California and Pennsylvania—have the expense of maintaining a large death row population. In those cases it is understandable why local taxpayers would complain about massive expenditures with almost no payoff. As one pundit said, it is a though the "state is running a hotel where no one ever checks out."[127] At the other extreme are states such as Colorado, Montana, and Wyoming, which execute few people and also have few inmates on their death rows.

Since their death row populations are small, these states avoid massive custodial expenses—but again, few people are ultimately killed. In between these two extremes are many states that continue to convict many but execute few. In an era of tight state budgets, the legal authorities in none of these states seem satisfied with the status quo. Although the triggering events across these states are myriad, all of them have struggling economies. It is also noteworthy that in several of these de facto abolition states, journalists have been outspoken opponents of capital punishment—as was true in many of the other states that we studied.

Postscript: On 22 November 2011 a *New York Times* article "Oregon Governor Says He Will Block Executions" reported that Governor John Kitzhaber would not allow any further executions during his time in office. He allowed two executions during two previous terms (1995–2003). Kitzhaber reasoned: "'I do not believe that those executions made us safer; certainly I don't believe they made us more noble as a society. And I simply cannot participate once again in something I believe to be morally wrong.'" Thus Oregon's tenuous relationship with the death penalty continues.[128]

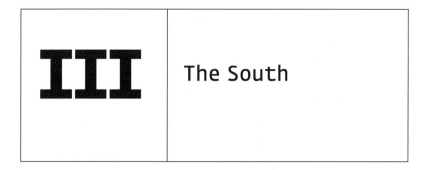

III The South

10. Opposition to Capital Punishment in the South and Texas

The high levels of executions in the southern region of the United States compared to other areas are not surprising. A cursory examination of southern history finds a social structure bound together by substantial amounts of state-condoned violence, fueled by local politics and white populist candidates. The low points of that history include a slave economy; a Jim Crow legal system lasting well into the second half of the twentieth century; Ku Klux Klan terrorism and a lynching craze spanning three-quarters of a century;[1] and regional murder rates that consistently surpass those of other parts of the nation.[2]

Given this historical context, the fact that 8,942 of the 15,269 (58.56 percent) legal executions carried out in the United States between 1608 and 2002 occurred in the sixteen states defined by the US Census Bureau as "the southern region" appears consistent with the culture of the place. In the midst of these troubling data, however, an anti-death-penalty narrative was not foreign to the ears of southerners. One of the ten state legislatures that abolished the death penalty during the first two decades of the twentieth century (the Progressive Era) belonged to that region: there was no death penalty in Tennessee between 1913 and 1915. Oklahoma also witnessed a concerted attack on its execution culture during the same period. The return of capital punishment during the 1970s stirred abolition movements in every southern state. Even the nation's bastion of capital punishment, Texas, seems to have been affected. The base of support for earlier abolitionist efforts tended to be narrow, often led by crusading governors emphasizing the racist and uncivilized nature of capital punishment. Movements in the late twentieth and early twenty-first centuries are considerably more organized and diffused throughout larger segments of society.

EARLY SOUTHERN OPPOSITION TO ABOLITION
Tennessee

Tennessee abolished capital punishment during the Progressive Era, only to reinstate the sanction almost immediately. The swift reversal was partially a consequence of a spate of lynchings, making it apparent to some erstwhile abolitionists that order could be restored only by resuming state-sanctioned killings. In 1915 a Tennessee state legislative committee member succinctly identified the function of capital punishment in his state: "The population of our county is three-fourths colored, and if this abolition bill should become law it would be almost impossible to suppress mobs in the efforts to punish colored criminals."[3] A Tennessee attorney warned the governor against signing a bill that would encourage "lynching and murdering. . . . With the large percent of colored . . . the state legislature has simply let a false feeling of sentiment run away with their judgment."[4] Another citizen warned the governor that abolition was a bad idea because "Negroes fear nothing but death, and this law would increase the crimes of homicide among that race."[5]

It is difficult to identify the factors that moved the Tennessee legislature to experiment with abandoning the gallows. Its execution history differs little from other southern states. Since 1782, 341 executions have taken place there. At least 216 of those executed were African Americans.[6] The Tennessee Department of Correction did not keep records on those who were hanged before 1913. Official records spanning 1916 through 1960 report that 125 persons were killed by electrocution, of whom 85 were African American. The state has carried out six post-*Furman* executions, the last of which occurred in 2009.[7] In 2011 Tennessee's death row housed eighty-five men and one woman: forty-eight were white, and thirty-five were African American.[8] While no post-*Furman* death penalty repeal bill has passed either house in Tennessee's General Assembly, two death sentences were commuted by the governor in the first decade of the twenty-first century. Official records from 2005 to 2006 show that four bills to abolish capital punishment were introduced in the General Assembly.[9] During that same session, the legislature appointed a commission to study the administration of their death penalty.

The commission gathered data and heard testimony from October 2007 through February 2009. One commission member, Republican Representative Bill Dunn, noted: "I think my biggest surprise, though I had an idea, is that the death penalty is a very expensive process."[10] The commission's report found death penalty procedures in the state to be fundamentally flawed and recommended that: (1) the state designate $8 million to establish and support an office of indigent defense to oversee "qualifications, compensation, workload, and training" of attorneys representing persons accused of capital murder; (2) police electronically record all interrogations of homicide suspects; and (3) prosecutors make available to the defense "all documents relevant to the investigation, tangible objects and statements, together with complete files of all investigative agencies."[11]

A commission member representing the Tennessee Bar Association was not optimistic: "The subject of the death penalty is so politicized and prosecutors are so polarized from the other stakeholders in the criminal justice system on the issue that meaningful discussion and consensus on the issue have been difficult, at best. Given the political influence of the prosecutors and their resistance to reform of the administration of the death penalty in Tennessee, it may be unlikely that meaningful reform will be accomplished. Without meaningful reform, however, the death penalty ultimately may not survive."[12] As of March 2011, Tennessee death penalty procedures have not been altered. Abolition bills were introduced in the 2009–10 and 2011–12 sessions of the General Assembly, but there have been no House or Senate votes on the issue.

Oklahoma

The most dramatic Progressive Era effort to abolish capital punishment occurred in Oklahoma. There abolition failed in spite of the fervent actions of Governor Lee Cruce.[13] Prior to Governor Cruce's term in office (1911–14), Oklahoma had executed forty-six African Americans and only two whites. In the words of one historian: "It was the blacks who became the primary beneficiaries of the governor's opposition to capital punishment, a dramatic policy he adopted in July, 1911. . . . [A black man] stood in burial attire prepared for the long walk to the gallows when notified that Cruce had commuted his death sentence to life imprisonment."[14] During his four-year term, the governor commuted twenty death sentences, and "of the first twelve sentences commuted, only one person was white."[15] Response to the governor's actions was swift: "only four of fifty leading state newspapers favored Cruce's policy."[16] Cruce escaped impeachment by only one vote,[17] and he never again held elective office. The remarks of Judge Henry Furman of the Oklahoma Court of Appeals tell the whole story: "No governor has the right to substitute his own views for the law on capital punishment."[18] The data suggest that Governor Lee Cruce's views had little effect on the state's long-term execution traditions. In 2009 Oklahoma had the highest post-*Furman* rate of executions per capita in the United States, and its ratio of executions per death sentence, at 0.291, is the seventh highest in the nation.[19] On 11 January 2011, the state carried out its ninety-sixth post-*Furman* execution.[20] Of the 96 people executed, 28 were African Americans.[21] Prior to 1976 Oklahoma executed 132 people, including at least 40 African Americans.[22]

SOUTHERN COMFORT: NEWFOUND RESPECTABILITY OF DEATH PENALTY OPPOSITION

Georgia's most famous citizen, former President Jimmy Carter, has become an outspoken opponent of executions, as has the state's foremost newspaper, the *Atlanta Journal-Constitution*.[23] President Carter is both a graduate of the US Naval Academy and a 2002 Nobel Peace Prize winner. In 2005, the *Birmingham News*, the newspaper with the largest circulation in Alabama, called for an end to executions.[24] The next year, a retiring circuit judge in the state also called for an end to capital punishment.[25] A Louisianan, Sister Helen Prejean—the author of *Dead Man Walking*[26]—is perhaps the South's most prominent opponent of the death penalty.

South Carolina

In 1974 South Carolina Governor John West—a Presbyterian, an alumnus of The Citadel, and a 1948 graduate of the University of South Carolina School of Law—vetoed a death penalty reinstatement bill that had been passed in response to the 1972 Furman v. Georgia decision. In addition to his religious credentials and undergraduate degree from a conservative military institution, Governor West had served twelve years as a state senator (1954–66) and four years as lieutenant governor (1966–70), before serving a four-year term as governor (1971–75). He had served in the US Army in 1942–46.[27]

Governor West's objections to capital punishment centered on evolving civilization. His veto message reads in part:

> As a matter of personal conviction I cannot accept the premise that man can end a life that God has created. Punishment of offenders including whippings, public torture, the rack and screw, have all been a part of man's attempt to regulate and deter criminal behavior over the course of history. Reinstitution of the death penalty in South Carolina would not—in my opinion . . . serve as a deterrent to crime, but

would rather be a return to a barbaric, savage concept of vengeance which should not be accepted, condoned or permitted in a civilized society. Therefore I veto [the bill].[28]

One day after receiving the governor's message, the South Carolina Senate, without debate, voted to override his veto, thirty-six to two.[29] The House voted to override it the following day, eighty-three to twenty-one.[30] Legislative reaction to West's veto and the history of executions in South Carolina reflected the fact that capital punishment remained a significant institution in that state through the twentieth century. Between 1718 and 1962, 641 executions took place there.[31] West's race, long political career, and perhaps his wartime military service protected him from the negative public reaction experienced by the Progressive Era governor of Oklahoma, who—like West—confronted his state's widely used cultural symbol.

Although troubled by his decision, most Democrats supported Governor West. The lieutenant governor stated: "This is apparently a matter of personal conscience and conviction of the governor. I do respect it."[32] A Democratic candidate for governor went further: "I think it was a very statesmanlike decision. . . . I admire him for his stand."[33] Another Democrat serving in the House said: "South Carolina's Governor stands out like a beacon at a time when a vice president [Spiro Agnew] is a convicted criminal and the President [Richard Nixon] is under grave suspicion."[34] Republicans, on the other hand, were troubled by the veto and the governor's rhetoric. A Republican House member argued: "There's been too much said for the murderers and not enough for the victims. . . . Capital punishment is not savage, barbaric; it is a civilizing factor."[35] Retired General William Westmoreland, a Republican candidate for governor, spoke out against the veto, citing the need for "law, and order" as well as "safety on the streets in every South Carolina community."[36]

A consistent characteristic of the state's execution history is the relative size of the African American population being exposed to the punishment. Of the 684 people that the state has executed since 1718, at least 478 (nearly 70 percent) were African American.[37] The racial makeup of South Carolina's death row population as of 1 March 2011 suggests that not much has changed: thirty-one of the fifty-five inmates (56.36 percent) are African American. The state has carried out forty-three post-*Furman* executions, the latest in 2011.[38] Thus, it appears that Governor West temporarily interrupted rather than altered South Carolina's execution history.

North Carolina

On 30 April 2003, three decades after Governor West's abolitionist efforts in South Carolina, the legislature of North Carolina passed a moratorium bill, motivated by the disclosure that a number of the state's murder convictions and consequent death sentences had been facilitated by prosecutors and police who had withheld evidence of innocence: "After declaring near-unanimous support for capital punishment, the Senate nevertheless voted [twenty-nine to twenty-one] Wednesday to halt executions for two years to study and fix flaws in North Carolina's use of the death penalty."[39] The Senate's action received immediate support from the local press.[40] The North Carolina Bar Association's Board of Governors voted twenty-six to zero in favor of the two-year moratorium.[41] On 5 May 2003, however, a deeply divided Assembly blocked the initiative.[42] In February 2006, the *Fayetteville Observer* ran a headline that said it all: "Execution Objections on Rise."[43] Court interventions, scrutiny by the media, and criticism by numerous death penalty abolitionists inside and outside of government challenged the legitimacy of capital punishment in North Carolina.

In August 2009, North Carolina's abolitionists convinced the General Assembly to join Kentucky and pass the South's second Racial Justice Act; both acts explicitly prohibit racial discrimination in the imposition of the death penalty. The North Carolina law allows the use of statistical studies to demonstrate bias.[44] The legislative action was facilitated by a growing legal processing problem: Between 1726 and 1961, North Carolina executed 784 people, at least 569 of whom (nearly 73 percent) were African American.[45] Between 16 March 1984 and December 2010, forty-three people, including thirteen African Americans, were executed by state officials.[46] As of 8 October 2011, no additional executions have occurred in the state.[47] Over roughly the same time period—November 1977 through February 2011—at least 160 North Carolina death row prisoners had their death sentences or convictions overturned.[48] Moreover, the current death row population retains the same troubling racial profile: as of 6 October 2011, of 157 inmates, 83 are African American, and 62 are white.[49]

The strength of North Carolina's Racial Justice Act is set to be tested. Five death row inmates in the state, charging racial bias, have filed motions to have their death sentence reduced to life without the possibility of parole. The research of Michael Radelet and Glenn Pierce on death sentencing in North Carolina over a twenty-eight-year span ending in 2007 is likely to be at the core of their appeals. The researchers found that, in similar cases, people convicted of killing whites were three times more likely to receive a death sentence than those killing African Americans.[50] It remains to be seen if data once again demonstrating the inability of state courts to remain race-neutral in capital sentencing will move the state in an abolitionist direction.

Virginia

Virginia Republican Delegate Frank D. Hargrove sponsored or cosponsored death penalty abolition bills every year from 2001 through 2009.[51] He also sponsored or cosponsored bills calling for a moratorium on capital punishment and the elimination of the death penalty for minors. The moratorium bills were introduced in 2001, 2002, and 2008, while the bills to eliminate capital punishment for minors were introduced in 2004 and 2005.[52] When he introduced his first abolition bill in 2001,[53] Hargrove was a senior member of the state legislature (he had first been elected in 1982), a Methodist, a Mason, a Virginia Tech alumnus, chairman of the board of the Virginia War Memorial, and an insurance agent. He had served in the US Air Force in 1943–45, and he was a member of the Veterans of Foreign Wars (VFW) and the American Legion. The web page of the Legislature noted that Hargrove represented an extremely pro-business district and faced opposition in only two elections.[54] He did not solicit campaign contributions and in 1999 had won 80 percent of the vote.

Hargrove's 2001 abolition bill was introduced three months after a Virginia death row inmate was cleared of the charge of murder by DNA evidence a mere nine days prior to his scheduled execution.[55] As was the case in North Carolina, the possibility of executing an innocent person was the core of Virginia's 2001 abolition debate. Two former attorneys general supported the repeal bill.[56] The Episcopal Diocese of Southern Virginia's Annual Council adopted a resolution condemning capital punishment,[57] as did an interfaith coalition of thirty-three churches, including the state's Roman Catholic bishop.[58] Nevertheless, Hargrove's colleagues who served on the House Courts of Justice Committee voted twenty- three to zero against releasing his bill from committee.[59]

Given the strength, tenacity, and racial composition of the state's execution history, the rejection of Hargrove's abolition effort was not surprising. Virginia has executed more individuals than any other state. Of the 1,385 people killed by the state, at least 1,128 were African Americans.[60] Maintaining racial disparities remained core to Virginia's executing strategy throughout the pre-*Furman* years: "Between October of

1908 and March of 1962, Virginia used the electric chair to execute 236 people. 201 of those were black males; 34 were white males."[61] These data do not lose their troubling character by isolating post-1976 executions. Virginia has the fourth highest number of post-*Furman* executions per capita among the states.[62] The state has executed 108 people since 1976, second only to Texas's 468.[63] Of those 108, 48 were African American.[64]

In spite of this race-based tradition of executions, Representative Hargrove did not suffer politically or stand alone in his opposition to capital punishment. On 17 January 2001, the *Richmond Times-Dispatch* reported on a Roman Catholic–organized public rally against the death penalty. The demonstration took place at the General Assembly Building, and Frank Hargrove was one of the featured speakers.[65] We could find no published criticism of his position. His reputation as a military veteran, supporter of the US military, and conservative Republican undoubtedly insulated him against public condemnation. However, the notion that you must support the death penalty to be elected to public office may be losing its gatekeeper status among Virginia politicians and voters. Although not directly calling for abolition, thirteen Virginia legislators sponsored or cosponsored four death penalty moratorium bills during the same (2001) legislative session that Hargrove introduced his abolition legislation.[66] In 2005 the newly elected governor, Tim Kaine, publicly opposed capital punishment.[67] Throughout the campaign, he had supported a moratorium on executions in the state and noted that his position dated back to his days at Harvard Law School and his Roman Catholic faith.[68] In 2008 the *Washington Examiner* noted that Virginia's Democratic US Senator, Jim Webb, also opposed the death penalty.[69]

But in Virginia's 2010 and 2011 legislative sessions alone, six bills were introduced to further expand the offenses that could be punished by execution. The two successful bills made the killing of an auxiliary law enforcement officer and the killing of fire marshals and deputy and assistant fire marshals with law enforcement powers executable offenses.[70] If it had not been for the political activities of numerous abolitionists testifying before the Senate Courts of Justice Committee, people convicted of killing "firefighters, special forest wardens, emergency medical technicians, lifesaving and rescue squad members, [and] arson investigators [among others]" would also have been subject to the death penalty.[71] As of 9 October 2011, the state had carried out one execution in 2011, moving the state's post-*Furman* execution total to 109.[72]

Mississippi

To many people in the United States and around the world, the state of Mississippi is synonymous with racial bias and the death penalty. According to the Death Penalty Information Center, Mississippi has carried out 365 executions since 1804.[73] At least 275 (75 percent) of those executed were African American.[74] The data on Mississippi's post-*Furman* death machine are no less troubling. Of the 206 people sentenced to death between November 1976 and October 2010, 114 (55.34 percent) were black.[75] The 2011 death row population reflected these numbers: thirty-three of Mississippi's fifty-nine death row inmates were black, and twenty-five were white.

However, the number and racial makeup of those executed by the state since *Furman* are unexpected. As of 21 July 2010, Mississippi has conducted only thirteen post-*Furman* executions. Those executed were ten white males and three black males.[76] The number of death sentences being imposed by the state's criminal courts is declining. From January 1991 through December 2000, seventy-eight death sentences were imposed. The number declined to thirty-five for the period 2001–10.[77]

During the first decade of the twenty-first century, two state legislators introduced numerous bills in the Mississippi Legislature to repeal the death penalty or impose a moratorium on it. Senator Johnnie E. Walls introduced death penalty abolition bills in every session from 2001 (SB 2245) to 2009 (SB 2525). In 2001, newly elected Representative John Mayo, motivated by his Roman Catholic faith, introduced the first of many abolition and moratorium bills that he would sponsor over eleven consecutive sessions of the Legislature. In one reelection bid, he further disaffected his constituents by endorsing the rights of gay couples to adopt.[78] Evidence suggests that neither individual suffered politically from opposing the time-tested Mississippi icon. Senator Walls, an African American representing a principally African American district, left the Legislature to accept a judicial appointment on the Mississippi Circuit Court. And Democratic Representative Mayo appears poised to win his fourth consecutive four-year term in the Mississippi House, representing a district where Republicans are in the majority. Articles in the state's newspapers indicate that he was not subjected to public criticism for his actions. Yet only one of the bills received legislative attention, a brief hearing in 2003. There he was joined in his abolition effort by the bishop of the state's Roman Catholic Diocese, as well as the bishop of the state's Episcopal diocese.[79]

Mayo contended that an individual's stand on the death penalty is no longer a litmus test for holding elected public office in Mississippi. He credited his electoral success to his Roman Catholic faith, up-front attitude, and strong military background, including service in the Vietnam War.[80] Louwlynn Williams, an observer of a recent Mississippi execution and an attorney with the Mississippi Office of Capital Post-Conviction Counsel, agrees with Mayo.[81] To her, low levels of post-*Furman* executions were primarily a consequence of judicial adjustments rather than changing sentiments. Reflecting on the celebration or partying among prosecutors and members of the victim's family that happened with the last execution, she concluded that the state "was excited about the return of executions." But at the same time she remarked that local prosecutors were becoming less likely to seek the death penalty, for two reasons: cost and the increasing difficulty of getting juries to hand down death verdicts. Perhaps the work of abolitionists, the exoneration of two Mississippi death row inmates, and the 1983 Mississippi asphyxiation execution of Jimmy Lee Gray—which went horribly wrong when a drunken executioner accidentally released gas from the death chamber, prolonging Gray's agony—have tarnished the public image of the death penalty.[82] In their dissenting opinion in a 2008 Mississippi Supreme Court ruling, two members of the court expressed their sympathy, calling the death penalty "unconstitutional." Outgoing Mississippi Supreme Court Presiding Justice Oliver E. Diaz Jr., after recounting Mississippi's biased death penalty history, reasoned:

> Innocent men can be, and have been, sentenced to die for crimes they did not commit. . . . The Mississippi indigent defense system is wholly inadequate to provide meaningful representation to the poorest criminal defendants. . . . In 2008 alone, two men—both black— convicted of murders in Mississippi in the mid-1990s have been exonerated fully. . . . Just as a cockroach scurrying across a kitchen floor at night invariably proves the presence of thousands unseen, these cases leave little room for doubt that innocent men, at unknown and terrible moments in our history, have gone unexonerated and been sent baselessly to their deaths. . . . But I am convinced that the progress of our maturing society is pointed toward a day when our nation and state recognize that, even as murderers commit the most cruel and unusual crime, so too do executioners render cruel and unusual punishment.[83]

The judicial adjustment explanation of Mississippi's uncharacteristically low execution rate offers a less optimistic view of the future of the death penalty in the state. Mississippi, like most southern states, reestablished the death penalty after *Furman* with little concern over evolving US Supreme Court restrictions on capital punishment. As a consequence, poorly trained local prosecutors immediately returned to litigating death sentences against defendants who were generally represented by poorly trained and poorly paid counsel appointed by the court.[84] Exacerbating this problem, Mississippi left the funding of capital cases to county governments. With increasing post-*Furman* requirements, these governments were unable or unwilling to provide adequate counsel.[85] Twelve post-*Furman* death sentences were vacated on the basis of ineffective assistance of trial attorneys.[86] Once direct appeals were exhausted, those sentenced to death were unable to secure post-conviction counsel. The combination of limited access and poor counsel ground the state's death machine to a halt. A 2000 Columbia University study reported that appellate review found a 91 percent error rate in Mississippi's death penalty cases.[87]

In 2003 a US Magistrate found that incarceration on the state's death row constituted cruel and unusual punishment due to incredible filth from fecal matter, and that prisoners were being driven insane.[88] Three US Supreme Court rulings (Roper v. Simmons, 2005; Atkins v. Virginia, 2002; and Ford v. Wainwright, 1986) helped reduce the mounting pressure on the state's death row by vacating the sentences of juveniles and people judged mentally incompetent or mentally ill. Living conditions on Mississippi's death row remained unsanitary and violent. The state housed death row inmates, mentally ill inmates, and "28 gang leaders" in the same unit. A 2007 prison riot that ended in the death of an inmate and the serious injury of two others forced the Department of Corrections to restructure death row.[89] This event achieved what US court intervention, US Supreme Court decisions, and an ACLU suit on behalf of the mentally ill could not.

To fix the legal system, the Legislature (HB 1228) created two agencies in 2000: the Mississippi Offices of Capital Defense Counsel and Capital Post-Conviction Counsel. The first provides competent trial and appeal counsel to indigent people accused of capital offenses, and the second provides counsel to indigent people through the state and federal appeals processes. These agencies are moving cases through the backlogged legal system, and it is likely that the error levels of entering cases will be reduced. More skilled, better compensated, and committed counsel will no doubt reduce the number of capital cases resulting in a sentence of death. The cost of capital cases will also help prevent Mississippi's executions from returning to pre-*Furman* numbers.[90] It is equally unlikely that the state will retains its historically low execution levels. The state added two people to its post-*Furman* execution total in 2011.[91]

BUSINESS AS USUAL IN TEXAS?

Texas is the public face of executions in the late twentieth and early twenty-first centuries. Although Oklahoma has a higher per capita execution rate, no state comes close to matching Texas's post-*Furman* execution total of 468. Of those 468 people, 173 were African American and 78 were Hispanic.[92] Prior to 1976, Texas executed 755 people, at least 457 of whom (nearly 61%) were African American and 71 were Hispanic.[93] Since 1976, the state has executed four times more people than Virginia, its closest competitor. But the Texas execution tradition has not gone unchallenged. One of its earliest post-*Furman* critics was African American State Representative Sam Hudson, an attorney. Hudson introduced abolition bills in 1977, 1979, 1981, and 1983. The Texas Legislative Reference Library indicates that he represented a Dallas district and was first elected in January of 1973, serving twelve two-year terms before leaving office in January 1997. He was elected with 86 percent of the vote in 1986 and 1988. His 1990 reelection was uncontested. He represented a district populated by relatively poor, highly transient apartment dwellers, 80 percent of whom were black or Hispanic.[94] During his time in the Texas House, Representative Hudson introduced many progressive bills that championed human rights. According to articles in the Texas Legislative Reference Library's collection of newspaper articles tracing his career, he began a hunger strike in 1977 to ensure that the bills he introduced would get a hearing.[95] These bills included the establishment of a state day-care program, the creation of two new medical schools and a new law school, and the abolition of the death penalty. The *Austin American-Statesman* noted that he had lost forty pounds in sixty-eight days.[96] Another newspaper used blatantly racist language, terming him "Fast Sambo."[97]

Representative Hudson pre-filed sixty-seven bills in the Texas House the next year, including a bill to allow conjugal visits for Texas prisoners.[98] In 1981 he argued that not one of his bills had been enacted into law because "his bills are designed to benefit the 'poor and the common man.'"[99] In the same year he introduced bills intended to teach racial tolerance in the public schools, and to "prevent and control venereal disease"[100] through education, to require that a Native American be appointed to the State Indian Commission, and to provide state-funded child-care assistance for welfare mothers.[101] Taken as a whole, these bills reflect bold and progressive legislative action. Unfortunately, that is not Hudson's public legacy.

In 1976 the *Dallas Times-Herald* reported that Representative Hudson was being investigated by the Dallas Bar Association due to complaints it had received about the quality of his legal representation.[102] Soon thereafter Hudson filed suit to set aside a reprimand from the Texas Bar Association.[103] As a consequence of being one hour late for a court date, he was fined and sentenced to a day in jail.[104] This was in a state where criminal courts have repeatedly appointed defense counsel in capital cases who were insufficiently trained, lacked a permanent license to practice law, and fell asleep during court proceedings.[105] Later that year, the *Dallas Morning News* reported that Hudson was $11,000 in debt and had numerous judgments against him for unpaid bills.[106] In 1978 an article reported that his home was to be auctioned by the Internal Revenue Service (IRS) for nonpayment of federal taxes.[107] Two years later, the *Dallas Morning News* reported that his opponent in the Democratic primary charged that Hudson had been sued twenty times and was over $51,000 in debt. Hudson claimed that his debts "help him to relate" to his largely poor constituents.[108] In 1984 the IRS again sued him, noting that he had failed to file income tax returns for five years.[109] In 1983 the *Texas Monthly* rated him as one of the ten worst legislators in the state, and in 1985 the magazine awarded him a "dishonorable mention" for failing to show up for votes crucial to the interest of his constituents, such as the vote on a bill aimed at creating a state fund for indigent medical care.[110]

Hispanic Representative Paul Moreno enjoyed a longer and somewhat less troubled political career during the same time that Hudson served in the House. Nevertheless, Democratic Representative Moreno's personal attributes—including military service, which protected other politicians who opposed the death penalty from harsh negative reactions—did not shield him from his Texas audience. Prior to being elected to the Texas House from El Paso in 1966, Paul Moreno had served six years in the Marine Corps. A combat veteran, he was highly decorated, having won two Bronze Stars for exceptional valor. While still a Marine, he became a quadriplegic in a swimming accident. After being discharged from the Marines, he became an opponent of all violence, including war: "'Being against war doesn't make me un-American,' Moreno said."[111] Even if not un-American, he was isolated in the Texas Legislature, and the bills he sponsored seldom got a fair hearing: "One veteran colleague, who didn't want to be named, says Moreno's influence is 'a big zero,' mainly because he's considered too strident [and] radical."[112]

Moreno's lack of legislative prowess was demonstrated by the failure of the constitutional amendment to prohibit capital punishment that he proposed in 1977, and the failures of three bills he introduced (in 1985, 1987, and 1989) to offer jurors a life sentence in prison without parole as a possible alternative punishment for those convicted of first-degree murder. During House debate on a similar bill in 2001, Moreno mentioned that he had probably shot a thirteen-year-old boy while serving as a Marine in Korea. He argued that "killing a person is revenge. We can't do those things. We have to be civilized. Executing people such as Oklahoma City bomber Timothy McVeigh is 'only making those people famous.'"[113]

In Moreno's words, "I'm on the sharp lookout for bad bills, bills that are detrimental to the people, bills that are for the greedy, not the needy."[114] In 1993 he opposed "a $1 billion bond issue to build more prisons, saying the money should instead be spent on education."[115] Nevertheless, editorial comments in Moreno's hometown newspaper, the *El Paso Times*, have been negative. He is routinely criticized for lack of success in passing bills.[116] After he recommended that Mexican Americans boycott the Greyhound Lines for discrimination against Mexican Americans, the *El Paso Times* urged him to pay more attention to legislative activities and less to such political maneuvering.[117] Although public comments were sometimes harsh, the marginalization of Representative Moreno was probably muted by his distinguished military history and his confinement to a wheelchair, and perhaps his Hispanic heritage.

Representatives Moreno and Hudson were imperfect messengers for the issue of capital punishment. Admittedly, Hudson had other problems aside from his opposition to the death penalty. But such was the strength of the Texas death penalty at the turn of the twenty-first century that no politically prominent white male championed abolition. Representatives Moreno's and Hudson's claims of moral superiority were thwarted by their lack of cultural capital. In other states, death penalty abolitionists have overwhelmingly been white, middle-class people with professional backgrounds.[118] Those abolitionists cannot be charged with acting on the basis of self-interest. On the other hand, Representatives Moreno and Hudson were criticized for making political points with their largely poor, Hispanic and black constituents—precisely the type of individuals Texas typically executes. The treatment that Moreno and Hudson received from their legislative colleagues and in the Texas press differed substantially from the public reaction directed toward abolitionists in South Carolina, North Carolina, Virginia, and Mississippi. Moreno and Hudson were never singled out as statesmen, motivated by personal conviction rather than political interests.

Little appeared to change as Texas moved into the twenty-first century. Elliott Naishtat, a Democratic Representative from Austin, the state's most liberal district, limited his abolitionist activity to sponsoring a moratorium bill: "You don't want to talk about instituting a state income tax or doing away with the death penalty. They're both considered—no pun intended—the kiss of death in Texas politics."[119] Democratic Representative Harold Dutton, an African American from Houston, ignored that warning and in 2003 began a tradition of introducing abolition bills in each session of the Texas House. He was joined by Democratic Representative Jessica Farrar, who filed her first abolition bill in 2007. The full House Criminal Jurisprudence Committee conducted hearings on Representative Dutton's 2003 bill.[120] Five additional legislators signed on as cosponsors for one or more of the legislative efforts to abolish capital punishment. During the 2009 session, four legislators joined Dutton and Farrar's effort to sponsor two bills explicitly calling for abolition, and two for a moratorium.[121] Public hearings were held on one of the 2009 abolition bills by the Subcommittee on Capital Punishment of the House Criminal Jurisprudence Committee. The full committee held public hearings on a 2011 death penalty repeal bill.[122] Sensing a lessening of the opposition toward the involvement of politicians in abolition activities, Naishtat noted in 2005: "We are seeing a mood change. Legislative and executive branches are responding to a clear change in public confidence."[123] Although the political activity discussed above did not bring an end to executions, it did help reduce their number and secure a degree of legal support for those accused of capital crimes. Among its most visible accomplishments was the passage of "Life without Parole" (SB 60) in 2005, thereby assuring jurors that people convicted of heinous murders can be permanently removed from society without resorting to execution.

The serious harm inflicted on the machinery of death in Texas over the last decade was perpetrated by the machine itself. On 27 October 2010, Anthony Graves became the state's twelfth post-*Furman* death row inmate exonerated of the crime that had led to the death sentence.[124] In the words of the prosecutor overseeing the case: "After months of investigation and talking to every witness who's ever been involved in this case, and people who've never been talked to before, after looking under every rock we could find, we found not one piece of credible evidence that links Anthony Graves to the commission of this capital murder. This is not a case where the evidence went south with time or witnesses passed away or we just couldn't make the case anymore. He is an innocent man."[125] More problematic for death penalty advocates were the executions of two inmates (Cameron Todd Willingham, in 2004, and Claude Jones, in 2000) on the basis of evidence that numerous Texans later understood to be false.[126] Governor Rick Perry's problematic intervention into the state's formal investigation of the 2004 Willingham execution brought increased media and public scrutiny.[127] The refusal of the presiding judge of the Texas Court of Criminal Appeals to keep her office open after 5:00 p.m.—so that a condemned man, who was executed hours later, could have filed a last-minute request for a stay to await a Supreme Court ruling that could have affected his case—attracted yet more troubling media and public attention. Mark White, a former Texas governor and death penalty supporter, now believes that the risk of executing an innocent person is too great to continue the practice.[128]

Probably the most troubling moment for Texas's death penalty machine occurred in March 2010, when a trial judge presiding over a Houston capital murder case declared the Texas death penalty procedures to be unconstitutional, on the ground that they created a risk that innocent people would be convicted and executed. Later the judge began to hold hearings on the risks of wrongful conviction. The defense attorney planned to present expert evidence on faulty eyewitness testimony, flawed confessions, questionable forensic evidence, and unreliable informants. Prosecutors refused to participate in the hearings.[129] In the end, the Texas Court of Criminal Appeals voted six to two that the judge could not litigate "a purely hypothetical claim," and the hearings came to an end.[130] An editorial in the *Fort Worth Star-Telegram* reasoned that the Texas legislature needed to begin where the judge was forced to end. Using the words of a judge on the Texas Court of Criminal Appeals, the paper's editorial staff reasoned that the very real risk of executing innocent people raises "important moral and public policy questions suitable for intense and open debate by legislative policy makers, not by courts considering only the constitutionality of a legal system, not its absolute perfection."[131] The courts, legislature, and media, it appears, are ready for significant policy changes.

Although support for the death penalty in Texas is not as unquestioning as it was a decade ago, the state remains the major executing jurisdiction in the nation. Since 2003, a combination of US Supreme Court decisions that narrowed the scope of people who could be executed, lower murder rates, fewer capital case filings, increased costs, and the option of "life without parole" have reduced the annual number of those condemned to death by 70 percent. Fewer people were sentenced to death in 2010 than in any year since Texas modified its death statute to meet post-*Furman* standards in 1976. Nevertheless, Texas still has the third largest death row population in the United States. According to the Texas Department of Criminal Justice website, African Americans comprise 39.6 percent of the 308 inmates on death row; whites 29.5 percent; and Hispanics another 29.5 percent.[132] As of 29 September 2011, the Texas Department of Corrections has carried out seven additional 2011 executions, bringing this year's total to eleven and state's post-*Furman* total to 475.[133]

11

Summary and Conclusion
The Death Penalty on a Downhill Slope

We have presented a discussion of the length of commitment to abolition in various states. We began with long-term abolition states such as Michigan and Wisconsin and continued with other states, starting with Maine and ending with Washington, D.C. After this came New York, New Jersey, New Mexico, and Illinois. Next we presented states that had nearly missed abolishing the death penalty, and then de facto abolition states. Finally we talked about the death penalty in the South. In this era of economic crisis, the costs of capital punishment are especially significant in efforts to abolish it. What is really important here is that executions, like other products, enjoy an economy of scale. The more frequent the executions, the less each one costs.

Articles examining the deterrent effects of capital punishment can be found in the archives of numerous social science journals. At the beginning of the twenty-first century, our case studies found that this issue had lost its practical salience. In fact, fearing the onslaught of scientific evidence to the contrary, advocates of retaining or reinstating the death penalty seldom cited deterrence as a justification. Those who were unaware of or ignored these data generally hindered their cause and risked being politically marginalized. Capital punishment's lack of deterrence and the ever-increasing economic cost of executions have become the core instrumental issues in the US debate about the death penalty. As we have shown above, public hearings of legislative committees have consistently been inundated with reminders of the lack of deterrence and of the financial savings of a sentence to life in prison without the possibility of parole. Additionally, legislators have been repeatedly told that murder rates are highest in states that have the death penalty. During a time of economic austerity coupled with an antitax mentality, it seems imprudent to spend enormous sums of money on something that does not reduce levels of murder. There is no doubt that legislative efforts in favor of the death penalty in Alaska, Maine, West Virginia, Wisconsin, North Dakota, New Mexico, and New Jersey were, in part, thwarted by this argument. The economic cost of pursuing a capital case further reduced the number of people being sentenced to death in death penalty states.

The economic crisis of 2008 has placed executions beyond the fiscal reach of many death penalty states. In some instances, states have stopped enforcing their statutes. Even states in the Deep South have significantly slowed their execution processes. The choice in many areas boils down to one between spending money on schools, infrastructure, the poor, and the aged, or spending it on killing prisoners. Without the total abolition of the death penalty, however, many of the costs of capital punishment continue, including the seemingly endless appeals and death row security. This quagmire is, in part, economically engulfing California, the state that has both the largest death row population in the nation and one of the country's most crushing fiscal crises.

The Death Penalty Information Center provides a table that lists per capita executions by state from 1976 through 17 April 2009.[1] Not surprisingly, the bottom half of the table (the eighteen states with the lowest per capita execution rates) are either recent abolition states or states that were discussed in our chapters on near misses and de facto abolition states.

PUBLIC OPINION

Appeals to democratic principles allow legislators who support the death penalty to advance larger political interests and a pro-death-penalty agenda without being required to defend the contradictions inherent in capital punishment. Issues of humaneness and fairness are no longer relevant; instead, the mantra is "let the people decide the issue." Thus, pro-death-penalty legislators are instantly transformed into supporters of government by the people, and legislators who oppose capital punishment become supporters of antidemocratic elites. Consistent with the us Supreme Court decision in McCleskey v. Kemp, a punishment is moral if it reflects "the will and consequently the moral values of the people."[2] The tactic reflects the long-held belief that abolition of the death penalty never reflects popular sentiments or values.

The empirical evidence that we have presented here suggests that there is not a one-to-one relationship between responses to polling questions and individuals' sentiments on capital punishment. On three occasions in Michigan, even with polls finding 70 percent support for the death penalty, advocates could not get a relatively small number of

TABLE 3   STATE EXECUTION RATES

State	2008 Population	Number of Executions, 1 January 1976– 17 April 2009	Executions per 10,000 Population
1. Oklahoma	3,642,361	89	0.244
2. Texas	24,326,974	437	0.179
3. Delaware	873,092	14	0.160
4. Virginia	7,769,089	103	0.133
5. Missouri	5,911,605	66	0.112
6. Arkansas	2,855,390	27	0.095
7. South Carolina	4,479,800	41	0.092
8. Alabama	4,661,900	41	0.088
9. Louisiana	4,410,796	27	0.061
10. North Carolina	9,222,414	43	0.047
11. Nevada	2,600,167	12	0.046
12. Georgia	9,685,744	44	0.045
13. Florida	18,328,340	67	0.037
14. Arizona	6,500,180	23	0.035
15. Mississippi	2,938,618	10	0.034
16. Montana	967,440	3	0.031
17. Indiana	6,376,792	19	0.030
18. Ohio	11,485,910	28	0.024
19. Utah	2,736,424	6	0.022
20. Wyoming	532,668	1	0.019

Michigan voters to sign petitions requiring the Legislature to put the issue on the ballot for a general election. Abolition reflects the interests of Native groups in Alaska, Native and immigrant groups in Hawaii, African Americans in Washington, D.C., and Hispanics in New Mexico. In these jurisdictions, abolition was more likely when categories of people negatively affected by local execution policy gained access to the ballot and a place in the state law-making machinery. A review of the abolition of the death penalty in New Mexico, the most recent state to join the abolition group, is telling. Between 1851 and 2001, New Mexico executed seventy-four people, including forty-two Hispanics. During the twentieth century, the state executed thirty-five people, of whom twenty-two were Hispanic. When the death penalty was abolished in 2009, 45.6 percent of New Mexico residents reported their ethnic background as

TABLE 3 (CONTINUED)

State	2008 Population	Number of Executions, 1 January 1976– 17 April 2009	Executions per 10,000 Population
21. Nebraska	1,783,432	3	0.017
22. South Dakota	804,194	1	0.012
23. Illinois	12,901,563	12	0.009
24. Maryland	5,633,597	5	0.009
25. Tennessee	6,214,888	5	0.008
26. Kentucky	4,269,245	3	0.007
27. Idaho	1,523,816	1	0.007
28. Washington	6,549,224	4	0.006
29. New Mexico	1,984,356	1	0.005
30. California	36,756,666	13	0.004
31. Oregon	6,214,888	2	0.003
32. Connecticut	3,501,252	1	0.003
33. Pennsylvania	12,448,279	3	0.002
34. Colorado	4,939,456	1	0.002
35. New Hampshire	1,315,809	0	0.000
36. Kansas	2,802,134	0	0.000

Source: Death Penalty Information Center, "State Execution Rates," 1976–2 August 2011, www.deathpenaltyinfo.org/state-execution-rates.

Hispanic or Latino.[3] As with Alaska, Hawaii, and Washington, D.C., abolition in New Mexico resulted from a minority group's lived experience and increased access to state power, rather than to submission or conversion to an elite ideology. Given the decline in execution numbers across the country, there is reason to believe that although federal civil rights and voting rights legislation sowed the seeds for a political backlash responsible for the resurgence of executions in the Deep South, it also guaranteed African Americans political participation and access to the vote.[4] As was the case in other jurisdictions, current declines in southern executions are likely a long-term consequence of federal intervention in the Jim Crow South.

The attempts to "democratize" capital punishment during the administration of President George W. Bush by pursuing death sentences in federal district courts located in traditional abolition jurisdictions have largely failed. Local resistance to this policy was strong, and it generated no political movements toward reinstatement. Federal juries in abolitionist jurisdictions demonstrated little interest in capital convictions, even in cases involving extreme violence. In Washington, D.C., for example, juries in federal trials routinely fail to enforce the federal death penalty, even for multiple murders.

DIFFERENT THEORETICAL LEVELS

An analysis of the dramatic differences among American states' death penalty laws invites distinctions across different theoretical levels.[5] At the most microscopic level, one can consider the attitudes of individuals as reflected in public opinion polls. In fact, state legislatures' rush to reinstate death penalty laws in the mid-1970s seemed entirely consistent with the prevailing shift in public opinion. The politicians' push to enact death penalty laws and also focus their election campaigns on the issue appear to have "struck a responsive chord with the public."[6] In the years prior to the US Supreme Court's 1976 *Gregg* decision, public support for the death penalty increased dramatically, from 42 percent in 1966 to 65 percent in 1976.[7] Indeed, public opinion has been suggested as the primary reason for the US Supreme Court's approval of post-*Furman* death penalty laws.[8] As Haines has argued, "*Gregg vs. Georgia* can be seen in large part as a surrender to vox populi."[9]

Yet there is contradictory evidence regarding individual attitudes toward capital punishment. Although polls consistently show strong support for the death penalty in the abstract, they also indicate that large majorities agree that capital punishment is typically imposed in an arbitrary manner.[10] As a consequence, support drops precipitously when survey respondents are presented with a reasonable alternative—such as life in prison without parole, combined with restitution for victims' families.[11]

At this same microscopic theoretical level, triggering events can be identified that propel legislative action at a particular time and place, affecting the motivations and tactics of legislative opponents and supporters.[12] Some of these events provide "the link between demands for action and public policy," such as the efforts of "moral entrepreneurs, media attention, election year politics, [and] sensationalized heinous crimes."[13] Of course, although some instances of strong public opinion and triggering events elicit punitive laws, others do not. And even in states with long traditions of abolition, public opinion leans heavily in favor of capital punishment.[14]

At a macroscopic level, the focus is on the cultural factors that are generally conducive to legislation, often referred to as structural foundations.[15] According to Edmund McGarrell and Thomas Castellano, "these are the overriding social structural and cultural factors that produce crime in society and guide society's response to crime."[16] They include economic conditions as well as the local population's racial and religious composition. For example, social units characterized by heterogeneity, inequality, and economic decline are also associated with higher levels of interpersonal and intergroup conflict, increased rates of criminal law invocation, and increased demands for punitive responses to crime.[17] Yet Michigan, the first American state to abolish capital punishment, is not only racially heterogeneous, but it also has high levels of violent crime.[18] Thus at this macroscopic level, contradictions can be just as obvious as at lower theoretical levels. And in many states, including those using capital punishment, we found that most newspapers oppose capital punishment.

In the 1960s, while most Protestant denominations were divided and mute on the issue, the Roman Catholic Church was an outspoken proponent of executions, arguing that "the state may punish by death persons guilty of serious crimes against a just social order."[19] Hugo Bedau recalls: "When I was in New Jersey on the Princeton faculty in the late 1950s local Catholics were solidly for the death penalty."[20] And Sister Helen Prejean remembers that "beginning in 1974 . . . the U.S. Conference of Catholic Bishops had begun to express 'pastoral concerns' about the death penalty," while prior to that time, legislators, prosecutors, judges, and priests used church teaching to legitimate their pro-death-penalty stance."[21]

But in 1973, the US Supreme Court provided a historical event that, combined with relatively large and influential Roman Catholic populations, created a window of opportunity for death penalty abolition in Rhode Island, Massachusetts, New York, New Jersey, New Mexico, and Illinois. After the Court's decision in Roe v. Wade,[22] the Catholic leadership began a vigorous campaign against abortion rights and, for the sake of consistency, against capital punishment. In numerous statements since, the Church has loftily proclaimed that being pro life is a "seamless garment."[23] In 1984 Joseph Cardinal Bernardin coined this term in an address on the "consistent ethic of life," in which he emphasized that "a concern for promoting a public attitude of respect for life has led the bishops of the United States to oppose the exercise" of capital punishment.[24] On 27 January 1999, Pope John Paul II called for an end to the death penalty as "both cruel and unnecessary."[25]

Recent research has found divisions between Roman Catholic clergy and parishioners on the issue of capital punishment,[26] with the clergy being less supportive of the death penalty than the Catholic laity. Surveys have also found that Americans living in the Northeast and those residing in other regions of the nation differed little in their sentiments toward capital punishment; moreover, Protestants and Roman Catholics across the nation had similar views on the death penalty. The majority in all these groups supported the death penalty.[27]

Yet *Roe* seems to have served as an important judicial event in heavily Roman Catholic states. Witness the following:

(1) The Rhode Island State Supreme Court ruled in 1979 that the state's death penalty law, passed in 1973, was unconstitutional.[28] In 1980, 63.7 percent of Rhode Islanders identified themselves as Catholic, making this state the most Catholic in the nation.[29]

(2) In Massachusetts, the Supreme Judicial Court ruled in 1975, 1980, and 1984 that the state's death penalty law was unconstitutional.[30] In 1980, 53 percent of Massachusetts residents identified themselves as Roman Catholic, making this state the second most Catholic in the nation.[31]

(3) In 2004, the New York State Court of Appeals (the highest court in the state) determined that New York's 1994 death penalty law was unconstitutional. This followed nineteen years of death penalty legislative debate and annual vetoes by Roman Catholic governors Hugh Carey and Mario Cuomo.[32] In 2008, 37 percent of New Yorkers identified themselves as Catholic, making this state (tied with California) the 5th most Catholic in the nation.[33]

(4) In New Hampshire, the state legislature abolished capital punishment in 2000, only to have the governor veto the bill. Even so, the state has sent only one person to death row since 1976.[34] In 2000, 34.9 percent of New Hampshire residents identified themselves as Catholic, making this state the seventh most Catholic in the nation.[35]

So we are left trying to reconcile increasingly liberal judicial decisions with punitive public opinion and mixed legislative action.

It is clear that Roman Catholic beliefs provided essential triggering events for abolition legislation. Federal judicial acceptance of abortion was an initial structural foundation for death penalty abolition, but only in heavily Roman Catholic states when their courts began to resist enforcing death penalty laws. Thus the US Supreme Court provided an initial structural foundation, followed by resistance to the death penalty in state courts where there was a heavily Roman Catholic population. The judicial resistance to the death penalty in New Jersey and New Mexico did not emerge until after *Roe*.

In December 2007, New Jersey became the first state in over forty years to abolish capital punishment, followed closely by New Mexico in 2009 and Illinois in 2011. Roman Catholic clergy, activists, and legislators provided significant support for this legislation in all three states. The high percentage of Catholics in these states made this religious coalition a particularly significant cultural foundation. Roman Catholic thinking on capital punishment was in turn influenced by *Roe*'s legalization of some abortions in 1973. Church leaders reasoned that if they were obligated to publicly oppose abortion to protect human life, they must also publicly oppose executions. They joined other Roman Catholic abolitionists in several western and southern states. The shifting role that religion and clergy assumed in the death penalty debate changed dramatically through the twentieth century. Many religious denominations have joined the Quakers, with strong official anti-death-penalty platforms. When legislators attempt to reinstate capital punishment in abolition states, religious laity and clergy can be counted on to challenge the morality of state-sanctioned killing. Those Roman Catholics who attended parochial school prior to the legalization of abortion learned a different moral lesson of state executions than those who attended later. This generational divide among Roman Catholics is clearly seen in the case of the six Roman Catholic men on the Supreme Court who appear to find no fault with capital punishment.

In New Jersey, New Mexico, and Illinois, Roman Catholic state officials and Church leaders played key roles in the successful abolitionist efforts. Earlier, New York Governors Hugh Carey and Mario Cuomo, both Roman Catholics, vetoed nearly twenty death penalty bills before 1994. In 2004, that state's Roman Catholic Attorney General, Andrew Cuomo, failed to appeal to the Supreme Court a New York Appeals Court decision ruling that New York's death penalty statute violated the state's constitution. The deterrence arguments in New York that lasted for nearly two decades now seem to have vanished.

COMPARATIVE ANALYSIS AMONG AMERICAN STATES

Although most states rushed to pass capital punishment laws, some did not. Those states that led the movement to restore capital punishment typically had long traditions of executions, especially the states in the former Confederacy.[36] Franklin Zimring and Gordon Hawkins have argued that "a history of frequent executions . . . serves as a kind of precedent, reassuring political actors that their own participation is neither inhumane nor immoral . . . on grounds that, historically, executions do not violate local community morality."[37] In other words, the death penalty is a normatively accepted legal reaction to homicide and is consistent with the cultural traditions in these states. State governments in the Deep South have always shown great enthusiasm for capital punishment, with Georgia, Florida, and Texas the first three to propose language for constitutionally acceptable death penalty laws after *Furman*.

New York trailed only Virginia in the number of prisoners executed prior to the death penalty moratorium that began in 1967.[38] After *Furman*, its legislature passed death penalty bills continuously between the 1970s and 1990s, only to have them repeatedly vetoed by two Democratic governors.[39] Although the deterrent impact of capital punishment was hotly debated during these decades, the issue is no longer considered significant—largely because the research of social scientists has discredited it. A year after the election of a new Republican governor in 1994, New York reinstated the death penalty. Even though the law easily passed, there clearly remained some ambivalence on the issue in New York. This ambivalence had developed because the long debate itself created a special sensitivity to possible unfairness in the administration of capital punishment, especially when combined with governors' numerous vetoes that were widely recognized as staking out the moral high ground. Indeed, opposition to the death penalty became respectable in that the sanction was no longer viewed as the only appropriate legal reaction to large numbers of homicides. According to Zimring, this ambivalence is reflected in the nature of the legislation that finally passed: "In drafting and debating a death penalty, the New York legislature eventually passed a law that established a minimum standard for a legally acceptable death sentencing system that is substantially higher than set forth by a state legislature anywhere else."[40] The law applies only to narrowly defined crimes and requires constant vigilance to ensure the provision of effective legal counsel and the absence of racial bias in sentencing. After reviewing this statute, Robert Weisberg estimated that no one would actually be executed under the law.[41] The ambivalence in New York was resolved by passing a death penalty bill that might never be used: "The death penalty law itself was the symbolic victory desired, and the remote prospect of an execution was not a major issue. . . . The major focus of the effort was producing a legislative result. The campaign issue was a death penalty, not executions."[42] Such an unenforceable law has been termed symbolic legislation.[43] Even so, capital punishment was declared unconstitutional by the New York Court of Appeals in 2004.

If such ambivalence existed in New York, with its long history of frequent executions,[44] ambivalence can be hypothesized to be even more pronounced in states with long periods of abolition and infrequent executions. Indeed, some states in that category—including Michigan,[45] Minnesota, and North Dakota[46]—did not join the rush to reinstate the death penalty. Other states that executed relatively few people before 1967 still do not have post-*Furman* death penalty laws, including Rhode Island,[47] Iowa,[48] and Maine.[49] Death bills in Michigan are never reported out of committee and are thus not the subject of legislative debate. In the state's 150-year experience with death penalty abolition, nearly all of Michigan's political leaders, including conservative Republicans, have supported this cultural and political tradition.[50] In doing so, they represent to others, and perhaps more importantly to themselves, the moral superiority of their state's government and people, even while Michigan has one of the most decrepit and punitive prison systems in the nation, and one of the nation's highest murder rates. Other jurisdictions still without a death penalty are Alaska, the District of Columbia, Hawaii, Massachusetts, Vermont, West Virginia, and Wisconsin.[51]

The reinstatement of the death penalty in Kansas can be seen as an attempt to fill an ever-shifting, ambivalent cultural space for that state's residents. Proponents could point to the death penalty bill as a representation of both the affirmation of human life and the dramatization of evil. Moreover, the importance of the death penalty may not be in its actual use, but rather in the symbolism of having it on the books: "This may be seen as . . . the supreme weapon, that can be brought out occasionally and used against persons who murder. It is a way of symbolically displaying to actual murderers and would-be murderers that the state can be just as deadly as those who would take another person's life."[52] Weisberg, commenting on the death penalty in California, expresses a similar view on de facto abolition there: "We could say that California has conceived a fiendishly clever way of satisfying the competing demands on the death penalty: We sentence vast numbers of murderers to death, but execute virtually none of them. Simply having many death sentences can satisfy many proponents of the death penalty who demand capital punishment, because in a vague way they want the law to make a statement of social authority and control."[53]

THE AESTHETICS OF DEATH

Western attitudes toward suffering and cruelty have changed considerably over the past 300 years. The civilizing influence of the Enlightenment, accumulated wealth, and increased state security increasingly moved elites to view violence and cruelty as uncivilized.[54] This alteration in social sensibilities had a profound affect on Western institutions. As societies moved through the nineteenth and twentieth centuries, it became increasingly problematic to balance the contradictions between state and economic interests, on the one hand, and emerging civilized sensibilities, on the other.

The strategy most often pursued to maintain the inherently cruel practices of slavery, war, and capital punishment was to isolate elites from the horrors of their social institutions. Current state efforts to hide the human consequence of wars in Iraq and Afghanistan from the eyes of us residents, especially those who will be asked to fight those wars, testifies to the effectiveness of the technique. Consistent with this approach, the death penalty has been sanitized by legislative mandates and judicial acts that occurred a century apart. Nineteenth-century state decisions to move executions behind prison walls and the decisions of the us Supreme Court since *Furman*, mandating less intrusive and less painful instruments of execution, have played a part.

Abolition efforts in the nineteenth and early twentieth centuries were facilitated by public reactions to the cruelty and bloodletting of executions. Visceral reactions to public hangings often led to riots in the street and newspaper editorials that threatened rather than reinforced state power. In Michigan, Maine, and Wisconsin, the perception of possessing a rational and civilized penal system was then, and remains, a core cultural belief. Through the years, legislative attempts to reinstate capital punishment in these states have inevitably resulted in tales of botched executions being published in local newspapers. The press in every abolitionist state continues that tradition. Editorial writers and other journalists provide readers with ongoing descriptions and analyses of capital punishment debates in other, mostly southern, states. Botched executions in Florida and Texas—along with a willingness to execute juveniles and mentally incompetent people and the carnival-like atmosphere surrounding numerous executions in the Deep South—provided the abolitionist press with ample evidence of contemporary cruelty. The introduction of medicalized executions that resemble the administration of anesthesia has done little to alter the death penalty debate in the United States.

Testimony from a murder victim's relative demanding retribution and the ultimate punishment for persons who commit heinous murders and legislative attempts to narrow the scope of execution bills to the most despised offenders, such as those who kill children or police officers, are tactics that advocates of the death penalty often use to neutralize the "uncivilized" challenge. Opponents of the death penalty are often accused of ignoring or excusing the "uncivilized" acts of the offender, and of caring more for the offender than the victim. Although the views of people emotionally attached to murder victims initially provide support to pro-death-penalty agendas, they tend to be counterproductive over time. The sight of the widow of a slain police officer in a shirt labeled "fry 'em in Michigan" ended a somewhat promising death penalty referendum drive in that state. Additionally, members of victims' families often give legislative testimony favoring forgiveness and healing over execution. The US Supreme Court has rejected death statutes that directed the punishment toward specific categories of offenders.[55] This ruling makes it difficult for pro–death penalty legislators to use the sympathy and outrage of citizens and legislators provoked by the brutal murder of a cherished person, such as a child, to pass death penalty statutes.

In every state, death penalty advocates are inevitably faced with a dilemma: If executions are to protect society from violent offenders or from direct retribution of its citizens against those offenders, the number of people executed must be dramatically increased, due process protections must be substantially curtailed, and the violent execution spectacle must be open to public inspection and in some cases televised. But history suggests that these assaults on humanistic values or aesthetics, even in the executing states, are likely to erode the legitimacy of state institutions rather than pacify the populace.

THE MORALITY OF DEATH

Do states have the right to kill their citizens? If states kill their citizens, must executions be fairly applied? The case studies we have reviewed here find that people who testify before legislative committees, whether opposing or supporting capital punishment, use religion to justify their positions. With the exception of the Mormons and the Southern Baptist Convention, however, every major religious organization in the United States has concluded that states do not have the right to execute their citizens. Here the data are startling. Our review of public hearings found few religious leaders of any denomination, in any region of the country, willing to give public testimony in support of the death penalty or executions. Rather, verbal or written testimony opposing capital punishment dominate most legislative hearings. The religious message of the abolitionists is consistent and clear: Only God has the right to take a life. Religious support for capital punishment, seldom publicly stated by religious leaders in legislative hearings, relies on a single biblical statement—"render unto Caesar the things that are Caesar's"—to justify the state's right to take life.

Advocates and detractors of capital punishment tend to agree on the second question above. If the death penalty exists, it should be fair. But there the agreement ends. Advocates contend that death penalty practices are legal and that procedures specified in numerous court decisions ensure that only the guilty will be executed. Thus, the process is fair. The majority of religious figures, attorneys, and academics participating in legislative hearings on capital punishment disagree with these assumptions. Death penalty advocates are unable to contradict either the barrage of social science evidence on race and class bias or the mounting evidence of wrongful convictions and executions. The tension between instrumental and aesthetic interests is further complicated by issues of fairness. These issues determined the structure of post-*Furman* death statutes in New York, Kansas, and New Jersey. In those states, efforts to negate race and class bias led to the construction of statutes that were impossible to implement. New York and New Jersey—the former by judicial decision, the latter by legislative action—have abolished their death statutes. In 2004, the Kansas State Supreme Court ruled that the Kansas capital punishment statute violated the state's constitution. Two years later, the state's attorney general won a one-vote reversal in the US Supreme Court. More recently, in 2010, the Kansas Senate failed by the slimmest of margins, a vote of twenty to twenty, to pass an abolition bill.

PROMINENT SCHOLARS AND POOR PREDICTIONS

Despite the rapid reintroduction of death penalty statutes in most jurisdictions and the ostensible public support for this sanction,[56] after *Furman* prominent death penalty researchers predicted that America's long tradition of capital punishment would soon come to an end, much as it had in most other industrialized nations. In 1974 Bedau wrote that "we will not see another execution in this nation in this century,"[57] and William Bowers confidently predicted the "abandonment of executions in America."[58] Even after executions had begun again, Zimring and Hawkins remained optimistic: "We surmise that the last execution in the United States is more likely to take place in fifteen than in fifty years; and it is not beyond possibility that executions will cease in the near future."[59] They noted that a theoretical basis for their prediction rested on Durkheim's assertion that repressive punishments are more typical of less developed societies.[60] During the years since Zimring and Hawkins made this observation, there has been only mixed evidence to support their prediction: between 1977 and 1986, there were 68 executions; between 1987 and 1996, there were more than 250.[61]

How could these prominent observers of American political culture be so wrong? And how could the patterns predicted by Durkheim have been of so little use in the analysis of American trends in punishment during the last part of the twentieth century? Nearly a decade after his overly optimistic prediction, Bedau pondered the increasing punitiveness: "One is more than a little curious to know what accounts for the reintroduction of the death penalty in several states . . . no more than a few years after it had been abolished. Surprising though it may be . . . the full story has never been told."[62]

It is easy to underestimate the effectiveness of abolitionist movements across the United States. In addition to the sixteen abolition jurisdictions, efforts to eliminate death statutes narrowly failed in four additional jurisdictions—Connecticut, New Hampshire, Maryland, and Nebraska—and fourteen other states have totally or nearly stopped executions. Thus, capital punishment is on the run in thirty-three of fifty states and the District of Columbia. It is no exaggeration to claim that abolition is on the upswing.

With that said, it is also true that most states have court-approved death statutes on the books, and fourteen continue to execute significant numbers of people. David Garland offers a convincing explanation for the persistence of capital punishment statutes in jurisdictions that seldom, if ever, execute anyone: Capital punishment statutes endure because they serve the interests of specific individuals and groups rather than broader social interests such as crime control. The cumulative effect is to normalize capital punishment and make it difficult to abolish, regardless of its obvious ineffectiveness as a crime control measure. Small and declining levels of execution are insignificant. Functional interests are served by the persistence of the death penalty debate, not actual executions. Garland writes:

> For criminal justice professionals, capital punishment is a practical instrument that allows them to harness the power of death in the pur-

suit of professional objectives. For politicians and elected officials, the death penalty is a commodity, an exchange value, a political token in an electoral game that is played before a viewing audience. For the mass media, each capital case promises a suspenseful, dramatic narrative, a classic human interest story that is constantly renewed. And for the onlooking public, the death penalty is variously an edifying morality play, a vehicle for moral outrage, a prurient entertainment, or an opportunity for the expression of hatreds and aggressions otherwise prohibited.[63]

The president of the Texas Coalition to Abolish the Death Penalty referred to this structure as the "Iron Triangle":

> The Iron Triangle consists of right-wing politicians . . . right-wing district attorneys . . . , and right wing victims groups such as "Justice for All." These three groups conspire to defeat anti-death legislation in the state. . . . An argument often used is that LWOP [life without the possibility of parole] would "confuse juries." Former Harris County [Houston] D.A. [District Attorney] John Holmes once said publicly that he opposed LWOP because then we would not execute the people that deserve it. . . . [It] is difficult for many legislators to oppose the positions of the district attorneys as they will be portrayed as being "soft on crime."[64]

Garland likewise locates explanations for the persistence of executions far removed from crime control ideology. Lynching history, the decline of Jim Crow, ethnocentric family values, and extreme social inequality provided the social and economic foundation for the majority of post-*Furman* executions. Accordingly, southerners viewed the social upheaval of the 1960s, most significantly the civil rights and voting rights movements, as an attack on their evangelical religion and family-centered culture. Beliefs that northern elites, often US Supreme Court justices in particular, were responsible for corrupting southern culture brought renewed demands for states' rights. Recognizing the political capital to be secured from supporting these demands, the Republican Party joined the call for local rule and conservative Christian values. The southern strategy of the Republican Party altered the political landscape of the South for the next forty years. Abortion, women's rights, civil rights, gay rights, crime control, and the death penalty dominated the ensuing cultural wars. As a consequence, post-*Furman* executions were primarily a southern phenomenon that expressed hostility for northern encroachment on southern sensibilities. Garland puts it this way:

> After 1972, the death penalty ceased to be a matter of penal policy and became instead a symbolic battlefield — first in the "law and order" backlash against civil rights and later in the cultural wars, functioning alongside issues like abortion, welfare rights, defendants' rights, and affirmative action as a litmus test of political affiliation and cultural belonging. Support for the death penalty became a marker of respect for states' rights and traditional authority; a respectable (that is to say, not openly racist) means of asserting that the civil rights movement had gone too far; and a vehicle for Southern resentment about interference by Northern liberals. . . . Above all, support for the death penalty came to be a short-hand for a political position that was "tough on crime" and assumed to be in tune with popular attitudes.[65]

It remains to be seen if this hegemony can withstand the pressure of declining violence rates, the combination of reduced revenues and high execution costs, growing evidence that innocent people are being executed in Texas, and increased social and political participation by people in the categories most often subjected to the so-called justice of execution in the South.

In the past, death penalty opponents have been savagely criticized in Texas, but shifting demographics may change this in the future. In 2000, there were just over 4 million Roman Catholics in the state.[66] By 2008, that number had grown to 6.5 million, and the US Census estimated that in 2006, 35.7 percent of Texans were Hispanic or Latino, with the Texas Hispanic population numbering 8.3 million — second only to the 12 million Hispanics in California. Immigrant Hispanics come with solid cultural support for abolition because Mexico has abolished capital punishment. The *Christian Science Monitor* reports that Texas's Hispanic population is growing rapidly and will move the state in some instances toward more liberal policies.[67] In the next few years, Texas will probably see "the permanent retirement [of executioners] that is now a generation overdue,"[68] and Texas Representative Paul Moreno's position may not seem so radical.

Notes

INTRODUCTION

1 "Madame Falls Silent," *Economist*, 20 August 1981, 38.

2 Associated Press, "Germany Urges EU Export Ban of U.S. Execution Drug," 1 April 2011; Clare Dyer, "UK Urges Rest of Europe to Also Ban Export of 'Execution Drugs,'" *British Medical Journal*, 18 April 2011.

3 Edmund F. McGarrell and Timothy J. Flanagan, eds., *Sourcebook of Criminal Justice Statistics,1984*, http://bjs.ojp.usdoj.gov/index.cfm/ty=pbdetail&iid=1416.

4 *Furman v. Georgia*, 408 U.S. 238 (1972).

5 *Gregg v. Georgia*, 428 U.S. 153 (1976).

6 *Jurek v. Texas*, 428 U.S. 262 (1976).

7 *Proffitt v. Florida*, 428 U.S. 242 (1976).

8 Joseph Carroll, "Who Supports the Death Penalty?" Gallup, 16 November 2004 (http://www.gallup.com/poll/14050/who-supports-death-penalty.aspx).

1. TRADITIONAL ABOLITIONIST JURISDICTIONS

1 John F. Galliher, Larry W. Koch, David Patrick Keys, and Teresa J. Guess, *America without the Death Penalty: States Leading the Way* (Boston: Northeastern University Press, 2002), 19. See also 11–30.

2 Michigan State Legislature, 95th Legislative Session, House Joint Resolution H and Senate Joint Resolution F, 1999.

3 "Death Penalty Rumblings Are Alive and Well," *Detroit Free Press*, 21 January 1999.

4 "Death Penalty Proponents Act Quickly," *Detroit Free Press*, 20 April 1999.

5 "Jaye, Sister Prejean Spar Over Death Penalty," *Detroit Free Press*, 24 February 1999.

6 "State Hears Out Public on Death Penalty," *Detroit Free Press*, 24 March 1999; "Hundreds Protest GOP Death Penalty Efforts," *Michigan Citizen*, 3 April 1999.

7 "No Vote on Capital Punishment; Plan Dies in House; Won't Go on Ballot," *Detroit Free Press*, 22 April 1999.

8 Norman Sinclair, "Cop's Kin Push Death Penalty—Family of Slain Detroit Officer Kicks Off Drive to Get Issue on State Ballot in Fall," *Detroit News*, 4 April 2004. See also Gary Heinlein, "House Blocks Death Penalty—

Father of Slain Officer Vows to Get Question on Ballot after Lawmakers Vote against It," *Detroit News*, 19 March 2004.

9 "Death Won't Stop Violence: Conyers Rightly Decries Deadly Crime, but a Return to Capital Punishment Would Be Ineffective and, in Practice, Unjust," *Detroit Free Press*, 6 October 2008.

10 "Lasee Applauds Assembly Passage of Death Penalty Advisory Referendum," Alan Lasee, Wisconsin State Senator, 4 May 2006 (www.legis.state.wi.us/senate/sen01/news/Press/2006/ pr2006-007.html- 16.5k – Wisconsin).

11 Ann Babe, "Death Penalty Hearing Stirs Opposition," *Badger Herald*, 27 April 2006 (http://badgerherald.com/news/2006/04/27/death_penalty_hearin.php).

12 Quoted in ibid.

13 Wisconsin Legislative Documents, 2005–06 (https://docs.legis.wisconsin.gov/2005/proposals/sjr5).

14 "Wisconsin Briefs: From the Legislative Reference Bureau," September 2006 (http://legis.wisconsin.gov/lrb/pubs/wb/06wb12.pdf).

15 Brennan Nardi, "Voters Back Resuscitating Death Penalty in Wisconsin," Channe13000.com, 8 November 2006 (www.channe13000.com/politics/10269942/detail.html).

16 Alan Lasee, Wisconsin State Senator, 8 November 2006.

17 Anita Weier, "Death Penalty Not Foreseen Soon Here; Despite Referendum Passing Tuesday," *Capital Times*, 8 November 2006.

18 Galliher et al., *America without the Death Penalty*, 74–77.

19 115th Maine Legislature, Committee on Judiciary, records of proceedings, "An Act to Reinstate Capital Punishment in the State," SB 1238, 1 May 1991 (http://legislature.maine.gov/lawlib).

20 116th Maine Legislature, Committee on Criminal Justice, records of proceedings, "An Act to Reinstate Capital Punishment in the State," LD 42, 16 March 1993 (http://legislature.maine.gov/lawlib).

21 Charlie Brennan, "Taxpayers Also Pay Penalty in Executions: Death Be Not Cheap: State Residents Paid $1.8 Million Last Year," *Rocky Mountain News*, 12 November 1995.

22 "Officials Fear Cost of Penrod Slaying Trial," *Reno Gazette-Journal*, 12 March 1995.

23 118th Maine Legislature, Committee on Criminal Justice, records of proceedings, "An Act to Reinstate the Death Penalty," LD 1524, 5 May 1997 (http://legislature.maine.gov/lawlib).

24 119th Maine Legislature, Committee on Criminal Justice, records of proceedings, "An Act to Reinstate the Death Penalty," LD 2214, 28 April 1999 (http://legislature.maine.gov/lawlib).

25 119th Maine Legislature, House of Representatives, records of proceedings, "Act to Reinstate the Death Penalty," LD 2214, vote to accept "ought not to pass" committee recommendation, roll call no. 241, 18 May 1999 (http://legislature.maine.gov/lawlib).

26 120th Maine Legislature, House of Representatives, records of proceedings, "An Act to Reinstate the Death Penalty for Murder of Children," LD 1493, vote to accept "ought not to pass" committee recommendation, roll call no. 192, 16 May 2001 (http://legislature.maine.gov/lawlib).

27 122nd Maine Legislature, "An Act to Prevent Domestic Abuse by Reinstating the Death Penalty for Persons Who Murder Family or Household Members," LD 1501, "Fiscal Note for Bill as Amended by Committee Amendment," 12 May 2005 (http://legislature.maine.gov/lawlib).

28 "Pair Accused of Murder Appear in Court," WABI TV5, 23 April 2009 (www.wabi.tv/news/5615/waldoboro-homicide-update).

29 Michael Khoo, "Governor to Push for Return of Death Penalty to Minnesota," Minnesota Public Radio, 27 January 2004 (http://news.minnesota.publicradio.org/features/2004/01/27_khoom_deathpenalty/).

30 Ibid.

31 Conrad DeFiebre, "Death Penalty Gets a Hearing; House Panel Takes No Action on Pawlenty's Proposal," *Star Tribune*, 27 February 2004.

32 Conrad DeFiebre, "Death Penalty Bill Is Voted Down," *Star Tribune*, 25 March 2004.

33 Ibid.

34 Quoted in ibid.

35 Ben Steverman, "Death Penalty Splits GOP; Two Legislators Side with the DFL on the Governor's Proposal," *Star Tribune*, 31 March 2004.

36 Galliher et al., *America without the Death Penalty*, 115.

37 Dave Kolpack, "Rodriguez Case May Revive North Dakota Death Penalty Debate," *Bismarck Tribune*, 22 September 2006 (http://bismarcktribune.com/news/local/article_5419ed4c-0ef1-5827-963f-34ba892c3521.html); "Legislature May Reconsider ND Death Penalty," KXnet.com, 22 September 2006 (www.kxnet.com/getArticle.asp?ArticleId=47489).

38 Associated Press, "Attorney General Says He's Not Aware of State Death Penalty Bill," 27 October 2006 (www.dakotpolitics.com/news/59296.asp).

39 Galliher et al., *America without the Death Penalty*, 148–63.

40 Hawaii State Legislature, Bill Status and Documents: SB 348 (2009), SB 214 (2007), SB 2066 (2006), SB 894 (2005), SB 878 (2005), SB 405 (2003), SB 404 (2003), SB 1575 (2003) (www.capitol.hawaii.gov/site1/archives/archives.asp).

41 Pat Omandam, "Lawmaker Calls for Isle Death Penalty: 2 Proposals, Which

Would Punish Crimes against Children, Are Greeted with Concern," Starbulletin.com, 1 January 2003 (www.archives.starbulletin.com/2003/01/01/news/index3.html).

42 Hawaii State Legislature, HRC49 and HRC50, introduced 9 March 2000 (http://capitol.hawaii.gov/session2000/ReferralSheets/HREF_33_03-14-00_.htm).

43 Melissa S. Green, "Senate Bill 60: Advisory Vote on Capital Punishment, 20th Alaska Legislature, 1997–1998," in *Focus on the Death Penalty*, compiled by Melissa S. Green (Anchorage: University of Alaska Justice Center, 20 July 2001; http://justice.uaa.alaska.edu/death/alaska/1998sb60.html).

44 Ibid.

45 Robert Kowalski, "Taylor Defends Call for Vote on Death Penalty," *Anchorage Daily News*, 30 January 1998.

46 Green, "Senate Bill 60."

47 Anne Sutton, "House Debates Death Penalty: New Bill Would Allow Execution by Lethal Injection in Alaska," JuneauEmpire.com, 24 February 2009 (http://juneauempire.com/stories/022409/sta_398043207.shtml).

48 Alaska State Legislature, *House Judiciary Committee Minutes*, 23 and 25 February and 2–3 and 23 March 2009 (www.legis.state.ak.us/basis/get_minutes.asp?session=26&Chamb=B&Date1=02%2F01%2F2009&Date2=03%2F31%2F2009&Comm=JUD&Root=&Button=Display+Minutes+Text+%28Requires+Committee+Code+or+Bill+%23%29).

49 Quoted in Pat Forgey, "Top Lawmaker Defends Death Penalty: Chenault Meets Skepticism at Native Issues Forum," JuneauEmpire.com, 12 March 2009 (http://juneauempire.com/stories/031209/loc_408289536.shtml).

50 Melissa S. Green, Justice Center, University of Alaska, Anchorage, telephone interview with Larry W. Koch, August 2010.

51 Galliher et al., *America without the Death Penalty*, 142–46.

52 Jonathan Roos, "Majority of Iowans Back Death Penalty," *Des Moines Register*, 25 April 2005.

53 Quoted in Thomas Beaumont, "GOP Proposes Death Penalty Law," *Des Moines Register*, 1 December 2005.

54 "Don't Grandstand on Death Penalty," *Des Moines Register*, 28 February 2006.

55 "Cost Would Prohibit Executions? That's Good," *Des Moines Register*, 15 December 2008.

56 Bob Link, "Death Penalty Will Be Imposed Oct. 11," *Globe Gazette*, 24 August 2005 (http://globegazette.com/news/local/article_0aba231c-8369-5407-9aa7-24f98b096e4d.html?print=1).

57 Galliher et al., *America without the Death Penalty*, 201–5.

58 Tom Searls, "Democrats Buck Leadership: The Capitol Report; 2005 Legislature," *Charleston Gazette*, 3 March 2005.

59 Josh Karp, "Events of 1965 Led to Death Penalty's Demise," *Charleston Gazette*, 23 July 2000.

60 Phil Kabler, "Platform Will Attract Democrats, GOP Says," *Charleston Gazette*, 8 June 2004.

61 "Pro-Death Right-Wing Politicians," *Charleston Gazette*, 19 April 2002.

62 Liz Anderson, "Vote Delayed on Bill for Panel to Study Death Penalty," *Providence Journal*, 13 May 2005.

63 Scott MacKay, "Death Penalty Resisted in R.I.," *Providence Journal-Bulletin*, 12 June 2001.

64 Rhode Island General Assembly, "House Judiciary Committee Hearings on the Death Penalty," 7 March 1989; "House Special Legislative Committee Hearings on the Death Penalty," 10 April 1996; "Senate Judiciary Committee Hearings on the Death Penalty," 30 March 2001.

65 Quoted in "Legislators Take Public's Pulse on Reinstating the Death Penalty," *Providence Journal*, 8 March 1989.

66 Scott MacKay, "Pine, Pires Say Voters Should Make Call on Death Penalty; A House Panel Is Considering a Measure on Capital Punishment, Not Used in Rhode Island for 151 Years; But Most at the Hearing Opposed the Measure," *Providence Journal-Bulletin*, 11 April 1996.

67 Quoted in Scott MacKay, "Death Penalty Resisted in R.I.," *Providence Journal-Bulletin*, 12 June 2001.

68 Liz Anderson, "Vote Delayed on Bill for Panel to Study Death Penalty," *Providence Journal*, 13 May 2005.

69 Quoted in "Rhode Island Lawmaker Proposes Death Penalty Study," *Newport Daily News*, 6 May 2005.

70 Scott Mackay, "Bay State Support for Death Penalty Renews R.I. Debate," *Journal-Bulletin*, 31 October 1997.

71 408 U.S. 238, 92, 2726 (1972).

72 Vermont Public Act 60, Acts and Resolves 1987, Section 2.

73 Vermont Statutes, Title 13: Crimes and Criminal Procedures, Chapter 75, Sections 3401 and 3484.

74 Quoted in Associated Press, "Who Knew? Vermont Still Has Death Penalty—For Treason," *Rutland Herald*, 24 September 2006.

75 "Executions in the U.S. 1608–2002: The ESPY File Executions by State," Death Penalty Information Center, 2011, www.deathpenaltyinfo.org/documents/ESPYstate.pdf.

76 Authors' research for 1989–90, 1991–92, 1997–98, 2001–2, and 2003–4 sessions (www.leg.state.vt.us/researchmain.cfm?Session=2012).

77 "GOP Bill Calls for Death Penalty," *Rutland Herald*, 14 February 2001.

78 Tracy Schmaler, "Victim's Family Issues Call for Death Penalty in Vermont," *Times Argus*, 7 December 2000.

79 David Mace, "Legislative Bills Pile Up Early in Session," *Times Argus*, 8 January 2004.

80 Sue Allen, "Barre Mayor Wants Death Penalty for Drug Peddlers," *Rutland Herald*, 26 February 2007.

81 Greg Guma, "Executing Justice: A Murder Trial Reignites Vermont's Death Penalty Debate," *Vermont Guardian*, 17 May 2007.

82 Allen, "Barre Mayor Wants Death Penalty for Drug Peddlers."

83 Wilson Ring, "Feds Want Death Penalty for Slain Vt Girl's Uncle," *Associated Press*, 25 August 2009.

84 "Judge: Jacques Trial to Proceed as Death-Penalty Case," *Burlington Free Press*, 4 May 2011.

85 "Death Penalty Reaffirmed in Jacques Trial," WPTZ.com., http://wptz.com/r/29104110/detail.html.

86 "Executions in the U.S. 1608–2002."

87 Ibid.; "Overview of the Salem Witch Trials: Brief Account," Salem Witch Trials Documentary Archive and Transcription Project, 2002, http://www2.iath.virginia.edu/salem/overview.html.

88 "The Death Penalty in Massachusetts: Facts and History," Resources for Keeping the Death Penalty out of Massachusetts, www.nodp.org/ma/s1.html.

89 Joseph M. Harvey, "SJC Rules Death Penalty is Illegal," *Boston Globe*, 28 October 1980.

90 Nick King, "Fight over Death Penalty Not Yet Ended," *Boston Globe*, 3 November 1982.

91 Joseph M. Harvey, "Mass. Death Penalty Ruled Illegal," *Boston Globe*, 19 October 1984.

92 Adrian Walker and Doris Sue Wong, "No Death Penalty, by One Vote: Momentum for a State Law Is Halted as House Member Changes His Mind," *Boston Globe*, 7 November 1997.

93 Brian MacQuarrie, "Mass. House Rejects Death Penalty Again," *Boston Globe*, 30 March 1999.

94 Erin C. McVeigh, "Death Penalty Bill Soundly Defeated," *Boston Globe*, 13 March 2001.

95 Julie Mehegan, "Debate Yields Little Support for Reinstating Death Penalty," *Sentinel & Enterprise*, 28 March 2003.

96 Scott Helman, "Death Penalty Bill Fails in House: Romney Initiative Roundly Defeated," *Boston Globe*, 16 November 2005.

97 "DC Government History: Chart of DC Government History," Council of the District of Columbia, 2011, www.dccouncil.washington.dc.us/ dcgovernmenthistory.

98 "DC Courts," District of Columbia, http://dc.gov/DC/Government/DC+ Courts+&+Laws.

99 "Executions in the U.S. 1608–2002"; "State by State Database," Death Penalty Information Center, 2011, www.deathpenaltyinfo.org/state_by_state.

100 Rene Sanchez, "Some in D.C. Clergy Fight Death Penalty Measure—Leaders Angry that Congress Forced Vote," *Washington Post*, 26 September 1992; Rene Sanchez, "District Rejects Death-Penalty Measure—Emotional Effort against Issue Pays Off," *Washington Post*, 4 November 1992.

101 Kent Jenkins Jr., "Hill Moves to Put Death Penalty to Vote in D.C.," *Washington Post*, 19 September 1992; Kent Jenkins Jr., "House Votes Referendum on D.C. Death Penalty—Lawmakers Gut City's Domestic Partners Law," *Washington Post*, 25 September 1992; Rene Sanchez, "D.C. Officials Feel Anti-Crime Pressure; Referendum on Death Penalty among Measures Being Proposed," *Washington Post*, 9 March 1992; Kent Jenkins Jr., "Congress, Bush Are Making a Federal Case out of Local Affairs," *Washington Post*, 27 September 1992; Dorothy Gilliam, "A Carrot and Stick for D. C.," *Washington Post*, 3 May 1990.

102 Jenkins, "Hill Moves to Put Death Penalty to Vote in D.C."; Jenkins "House Votes Referendum Referendum on D.C. Death Penalty."

103 Sanchez, "District Rejects Death-Penalty Measure."

104 "Sense of the Council Opposition to the Attorney General of the United States Seeking the Death Penalty for Crimes Committed in the District of Columbia Emergency Declaration Resolution of 2000" and "Sense of the Council Opposition to the Attorney General of the United States Seeking the Death Penalty for Crimes Committed in the District of Columbia Emergency Resolution of 2000," Council of the District of Columbia, PR 13–766 and PR 13–767, www.dccouncil.us/mendelson/CP%2013%20Legislation .pdf.

105 Congresswoman Eleanor Holmes Norton, letter to Jeffrey A. Taylor, interim United States attorney for the District of Columbia, 8 January 2007.

106 Ibid.

107 Quoted in Carol D. Leonnig, "Jury Rejects Death Penalty in Drug Gang Killings," *Washington Post*, 7 June 2007 (www.washingtonpost.com/wp-dyn/ content/article/2007/06/06/AR2007060602557.html).

108 Norton, letter to Taylor.

2. THE NEW YORK STATE DEBATE

1 Franklin E. Zimring and Gordon Hawkins, *Capital Punishment and the American Agenda* (Cambridge: Cambridge University Press, 1986), 144.

2 "Executions in the U.S. 1608–2002: The ESPY File Executions by State," Death Penalty Information Center, 2011, www.deathpenaltyinfo.org/documents/ESPYstate.pdf.

3 Timothy J. Flanagan, Pauline Gasdow Brennan, and Debra Cohen, "Attitudes of New York Legislators toward Crime and Criminal Justice: A Report of the State Legislator Survey," (1991); Timothy J. Flanagan and Edmund F. McGarrell, "Attitudes of New York Legislators toward Crime and Criminal Justice: A Report of the State Legislator Survey—1985" (Albany: State University of New York Press, 1986).

4 New York State Assembly and Senate, Records of Proceedings, 1977–95, New York State Library, Albany.

5 Franklin E. Zimring, "The Wages of Ambivalence: On the Context and Prospects of New York's Death Penalty," *Buffalo Law Review* 44 (Spring 1996): 316.

6 "United States—States: GCT-T1-R; Population Estimates (Geographies Ranked by Estimate) Data Set, 2009 Population Estimates," Census Bureau, Geographic Comparison Table, 2011, http://factfinder.census.gov/servlet/GCTTable?_bm=y&-geo_id=01000US&-_box_head_nbr=GCT-T1-R&-ds_name=PEP_2009_EST&-_lang=en&-format=US-40S&-_sse=on; "Crime in the United States by State, 2009," Federal Bureau of Investigation, Criminal Justice Information Services Division, 2011, http://www2.fbi.gov/ucr/cius2009/data/table_05.html.

7 William J. Bowers, *Legal Homicide: Death as Punishment in America, 1864–1982* (Boston: Northeastern University Press, 1984); Michael Lumer and Nancy Tenney, "The Death Penalty in New York: An Historical Perspective," *Journal of Law and Policy* 4 (1995): 81, 98; "Executions in the U.S. 1608–2002."

8 James R. Acker, "New York's Proposed Death Penalty Legislation: Constitutional and Policy Perspectives," *Albany Law Review* 54 (1990): 515–616.

9 Ibid., 522–23.

10 Ibid., 524.

11 Ibid., 525.

12 Ibid.

13 People v. Fitzpatrick, 346 N.Y.S.2d 793 (1973).

14 Acker, "New York's Proposed Death Penalty Legislation," 531.

15 Jurek v. Texas, 428 U.S. 262 (1976); Profitt v. Florida, 428 U.S. 242 (1976); Gregg v. Georgia 428 U.S. 153 (1976).

16 "Estimated Crime in 1965: Crime Rate per 100,000 Population; Violent Crime," Federal Bureau of Investigation, Uniform Crime Reporting Statistics, 2011, www.ucrdatatool.gov/Search/Crime/State/RunCrimeOneYearofData .cfm.

17 "Estimated Crime in 1990: Crime Rate per 100,000 Population; Violent Crime," Federal Bureau of Investigation, Uniform Crime Reporting Statistics, 2011, www.ucrdatatool.gov/Search/Crime/State/RunCrimeOneYearofData .cfm.

18 "Estimated Murder Rate," Federal Bureau of Investigation, Uniform Crime Reporting Statistics, 2011, www.ucrdatatool.gov/Search/Crime/State/Run CrimeTrendsInOneVar.cfm.

19 Ibid.

20 Assemblyman Mega, New York State Assembly Debate on AB 8815 (1977, 7632). References and quotations from Assembly debates are from the New York State Library, Albany.

21 Senator Volker, New York State Senate Debate on SB 7250 (1978, 1562).

22 Assemblyman Hevesi, New York State Assembly Debate on AB 1070 (1989, 76).

23 Senator Bernstein, New York State Senate Debate on SB 600 (1989, 424).

24 Assemblyman Ortloff, New York State Assembly Debate on AB 8960 (1990, 105).

25 Assemblyman Singer, New York State Assembly Debate on AB 360 (1993, 139).

26 Assemblyman Gromack, New York State Assembly Debate on AB 305 (1991, 95).

27 Assemblyman Robach, New York State Assembly Debate on AB 9028 (1994, 37).

28 Assemblyman Kauffman, New York State Assembly Debate on AB 4843 (1995, 158).

29 Assemblyman Saland, New York State Assembly Debate on AB 1070 (1989, 137).

30 Jack P. Gibbs, *Crime, Punishment, and Deterrence* (New York: Elsevier, 1975), 22.

31 Assemblyman Vitaliano, New York State Assembly Debate on AB 4843 (1995, 77).

32 Assemblyman Skidman, New York State Assembly Debate on AB 9028 (1994, 94–95).

33 Senator Farley, New York State Senate Debate on SB 6600 (1990, 522).

34 Assemblyman Tedisco, New York State Assembly Debate on AB 9028 (1994, 77).

35 Hugo Adam Bedau, "The Controversy over Deterrence and Incapacitation," in *The Death Penalty in America: Current Controversies*, ed. Hugo Adam Bedau (New York: Oxford University Press, 1997), 127–34.

36 Assemblyman Graber, New York State Assembly Debate on AB 8815 (1977, 7586).

37 Senator Knorr, New York State Senate Debate on SB 7250 (1978, 4258).

38 Senator Volker, New York State Senate Debate on SB 6600 (1990, 462).

39 Ibid., 1183.

40 Assemblyman Pataki, New York State Assembly Debate on AB 8657 (1988, 193).

41 Assemblyman Graber, New York State Assembly Debate on AB 1070 (1989, 62).

42 Senator Volker, New York State Senate Debate on SB 4414 (1979, 3731–32).

43 Senator Knorr, New York State Senate Debate on SB 7250 (1978, 4260).

44 Assemblyman Friedman, New York State Assembly Debate on AB 8657 (1988, 83).

45 Assemblyman Hickey, New York State Assembly Debate on AB 9028 (1994, 111).

46 Assemblyman Seminerio, New York State Assembly Debate on AB 8431 (1980, 133).

47 See Richard Nisbett and Lee Ross, *Human Inference: Strategies and Shortcomings of Social Judgment* (Englewood Cliffs, NJ: Prentice-Hall, 1980).

48 See Isaac Ehrlich, "The Deterrent Effect of Capital Punishment: A Question of Life and Death," *American Economic Review* 65, no. 3 (1975): 397–417 (where each legal execution was alleged to reduce homicides severalfold); Isaac Ehrlich, "Capital Punishment and Deterrence: Some Further Thoughts and Additional Evidence," *Journal of Political Economy* 85, no. 4 (1977): 741–88.

49 Assemblyman Walsh, New York State Assembly Debate on AB 843 (1980, 146).

50 Senator Bernstein, New York State Senate Debate on SB 6600 (1990, 512).

51 Assemblyman Ryan, New York State Assembly Debate on AB 8815 (1977, 8920).

52 Senator Goodman, New York State Senate Debate on SB 7250 (1978, 1600).

53 Senator Leichter, New York State Senate Debate on SB 7250 (1978, 4068).

54 Assemblyman McCabe, New York State Assembly Debate on AB 8815 (1977, 8804).

55 Assemblyman Stringer, New York State Assembly Debate on AB 4843 (1995, 282).

56 Assemblyman Hevesi, New York State Assembly Debate on AB 1070 (1989, 84).

57 William J. Bowers and Glenn L. Pierce, "Deterrence or Brutalization: What Is the Effect of Executions?" *Crime & Delinquency* 26 (October 1980): 453, 473.

58 Senator Nolan, New York State Senate Debate on SB 6600 (1990, 473).

59 Senator Leichter, New York State Senate Debate on SB 6350 (1994, 1021).

60 Senator Gold, New York State Senate Debate on SB 2850 (1995, 1961).

61 Senator Volker, New York State Senate Debate on SB 7250 (1978, 4040).

62 Senator Ruiz, New York State Senate Debate on SB 7600 (1982, 2470).

63 Assemblyman Saland, New York State Assembly Debate on AB 9379 (1982, 7019).

64 Assemblyman Saland, New York Assembly Debate on SB 7040 (1986, 59).

65 Senator Volker, New York State Senate Debate on SB 4414 (1979, 3698).

66 Assemblyman Graber, New York State Assembly Debate on AB 12 (1979, 174–75).

67 Assemblyman Nicolosi, New York State Assembly Debate on AB 8815 (1977, 8762–8763).

68 Assemblyman Frisa, New York State Assembly Debate on AB 8657 (1988, 181).

69 Senator Volker, New York State Senate Debate on SB 6600 (1990, 457–458).

70 Senator Volker, New York State Senate Debate on SB 200 (1991, 1290).

71 Assemblyman VanVarnick, New York State Assembly Debate on AB 9031 (1992, 162).

72 Assemblyman Proskin, New York State Assembly Debate on AB 1039 (1987, 150).

73 Assemblyman Friedman, New York State Assembly Debate on AB 9031 (1992, 142).

74 Assemblyman Friedman, New York State Assembly Debate on AB 12 (1979, 205).

75 Assemblyman Kremer, New York State Assembly Debate on AB 8657 (1988, 111).

76 Assemblyman Healey, New York State Assembly Debate on AB 8657 (1988, 124).

77 Assemblyman Friedman, New York State Assembly Debate on AB 8657 (1988, 72–73).

78 Assemblyman Tedisco, New York State Assembly Debate on AB 8657 (1988, 132).

79 Senator Eckert, New York State Senate Debate on SB 7100 (1980, 87–88).

80 Senator Ohrenstein, New York State Senate Debate on SB 7100 (1980, 157).

81 Assemblyman Greenberg, New York State Assembly Debate on AB 8815 (1977, 8800–8801).

82 Assemblyman Kisor, New York State Assembly Debate on AB 12 (1979, 261).

83 Senator Ruiz, New York State Senate Debate on SB 4414 (1979, 3755).

84 Assemblyman Smoler, New York State Assembly Debate on AB 8431 (1980, 150).

85 Michael Davis, *Justice in the Shadow of Death: Rethinking Capital and Lesser Punishments* (Lanham, MD: Rowman and Littlefield, 1996), 13–14.

86 Senator Eckert, New York State Senate Debate on SB 7100 (1980, 2734).

87 Assemblyman Vitaliano, New York State Assembly Debate on AB 4843 (1995, 76–78).

88 Bedau, "The Controversy over Deterrence and Incapacitation," 129.

89 Assemblyman Mega, New York State Assembly Debate on AB 9421 (1978, 2076).

90 Assemblyman Fremming, New York State Assembly Debate on AB 9421 (1978, 2109).

91 Senator Maltese, New York State Senate Debate on SB 200 (1991, 1199).

92 Assemblyman Solomon, New York State Assembly Debate on AB 9421 (1978, 2242).

93 Senator Bloom, New York State Senate Debate on SB 7250 (1978, 4051).

94 Assemblyman Wemple, New York State Assembly Debate on AB 12 (1979, 225).

95 For the argument that life in prison without parole is increasingly seen as a satisfactory alternative to execution, see Phoebe C. Ellsworth and Samuel R. Gross, "Hardening of the Attitudes: Americans' View on the Death Penalty," in *The Death Penalty in America: Current Controversies*, ed. Hugo Adam Bedau (New York: Oxford University Press, 1997), 90–115.

96 See, for example, National Institute of Law Enforcement and Criminal Justice, "The Nation's Toughest Drug Law: Evaluating the New York Experience; Final Report of the Joint Committee on New York Drug Law Evaluation" (Washington: Government Printing Office, 1978).

97 Assemblyman Behan, New York State Assembly Debate on AB 9028 (1994, 129–30).

98 See Nisbett and Ross, *Human Inference.*

99 Benjamin D. Steiner, William J. Bowers, and Austin Sarat, "Folk Knowledge as Legal Action: Death Penalty Judgments and the Tenet of Early Release in a Culture of Mistrust and Punitiveness," *Law & Society Review* 33 (1999): 465.

100 Paul Greenberg, "Liberals Need to Face Reality about Crime," *Kansas City Star*, 30 April 1998.

101 For example, Ehrlich, "The Deterrent Effect of Capital Punishment."

102 Ellsworth and Gross, "Hardening of the Attitudes."

103 Laws of the State of New York, 1995, Chapter 1 (http://criminaljustice.state .ny.us/legalservices/ch1_1995_death_penalty.htm).

104 Lumer and Tenney, "The Death Penalty in New York," 14.

105 People v. Stephen S. Lavalle, 3 N.Y. 3d 88, 817 N.E. 2d 341, 783 N.Y.S. 2d 485 (2004), 18.

106 Ibid.

107 "The Death Penalty in New York," New York State Assembly, 3 April 2005, http://66.147.244.181/~nyadporg/sites/default/files/deathpenaltyreport .pdf, 39.

108 Ibid., 22.

109 Nicholas Confessore, "Big Victory in New York Caps a Long Comeback," New York Times, 3 November 2010 (http://query.nytimes.com/gst/fullpage .html?res=9502EFD9103EF930A35752C1A9669D8B63).

3. ABOLITION IN NEW JERSEY

1 NJ Rev. § Stat. 2C:11–3 (2007).

2 Jeremy W. Peters, "New Jersey Moves to End Its Death Penalty," New York Times, 14 December 2007 (www.nytimes.com/2007/12/14/nyregion/14death .html).

3 Jeremy W. Peters, "Corzine Signs Bill Ending Executions, Then Commutes Sentences of Eight," New York Times, 18 December 2007 (www.nytimes .com/2007/12/18/nyregion/18death.html).

4 Jon Corzine, "Remarks — Elimination of the Death Penalty," State of New Jersey, Office of the Governor, 17 December 2007 (www.state.nj.us/governor/ news/approved/20071217c.html).

5 Jeremy W. Peters, "In Ending Executions, Soul Searching," New York Times, 23 December 2007 (www.nytimes.com/2007/12/23/nyregion/nyregion specia12/23polnj.html).

6 "Gallup Poll Social Series: Crime," Gallup News Service, 7–10 October 2010, www.gallup.com/poll/File/144278/Death_Penalty_Nov_8_2010.pdf.

7 "An Enduring Majority: Americans Continue to Support the Death Penalty," Pew Forum on Religion and Public Life, 19 December 2007, http:// pewforum.org/Death-Penalty/An-Enduring-Majority-Americans-Continue- to-Support-the-Death-Penalty.aspx.

8 "Facts and Issues about the Death Penalty: A Study of New Jersey's Death Penalty Statute and Its Application," League of Women Voters of New Jersey, January 2004, www.lwvnj.org/action/death-penalty/dpfacts.shtml; New Jersey Death Penalty Study Commission Report (Trenton: State of New Jer-

sey, January 2007; (www.njleg.state.nj.us/committees/dpsc_final.pdf), 35; "Most New Jerseyans Support Moratorium on the Death Penalty New Eagleton Poll Reports," Death Penalty Information Center, 30 May 2002 (www .deathpenaltyinfo.org/node/577).

9 "Executions in the United States, 1608–1976, by State," Death Penalty Information Center, 2011, www.deathpenaltyinfo.org/executions-united-states-1608–1976-state.

10 John F. Galliher, Larry W. Koch, David Patrick Keys, and Teresa J. Guess, *America without the Death Penalty: States Leading the Way* (Boston: Northeastern University Press, 2002).

11 "Executions in the United States, 1608–1976, by State."

12 Ibid.

13 Ibid.

14 Hugo A. Bedau, "Death Sentence in New Jersey, 1907–1960," *Rutgers Law Review* 19 (1964): 1–64.

15 "Executions in the U.S. 1608–2002: The ESPY File Executions by State," Death Penalty Information Center, 2011, www.deathpenaltyinfo.org/documents/ ESPYstate.pdf.

16 Campbell Gibson and Kay Jung, "Historical Census Statistics on Population Totals by Race, 1790 to 1990, and by Hispanic Origin, 1790 to 1990, for the United States, Regions, Divisions and States" (Suitland, MD: Census Bureau, September 2002; http:///www.census.gov/population/www/ documentation/twps0056/twps0056.html).

17 "New Jersey," MapStats, 2009, www.fedstats.gov/qf/states/34000.html.

18 "Executions in the U.S. 1608–2002."

19 Franklin E. Zimring and Gordon Hawkins, *The Citizens' Guide to Gun Control* (New York: Macmillan, 1987).

20 "Estimated Crime in New Jersey: Crime Rate per 100,000 Population: Violent Crime," Federal Bureau of Investigation, Uniform Crime Reporting Statistics, 2011, www.ucrdatatool.gov/Search/Crime/State/RunCrimeState byState.cfm.

21 "Estimated Crime in 1990," Federal Bureau of Investigation, Uniform Crime Reporting Statistics, (2011, www.ucrdatatool.gov/Search/Crime/ State/RunCrimeOneYearofData.cfm.

22 "Estimated Crime in 2007," Federal Bureau of Investigation, Uniform Crime Reporting Statistics, 2011, www.ucrdatatool.gov/Search/Crime/ State/RunCrimeOneYearofData.cfm.

23 Galliher et al., *America without the Death Penalty*, 208–11.

24 428 U.S. 153 (1976).

25 Martin Waldron, "Byrne Pocket Vetoes a Bill to Restore Death Penalty" and "Byrne Pocket Vetoes Death-Penalty Bill," *New York Times*, 4 March 1978; Daniel J. O'Hern and Alexander P. Waugh Jr., "Gubernatorial Courtesy: A Reply," *New York Times*, 4 May 1980.

26 Quoted in "The Death Penalty, New Jersey Voices," New Jerseyans for Alternatives to the Death Penalty (www.njadp.org/gdcommentary&what=njvoices).

27 Quoted in *New Jersey Death Penalty Study Commission Report*, 6.

28 Ibid.

29 State v. Biegenwald, 106 N.J. 13 (1987); State v. Ramseur, 106 N.J. 123 (1987).

30 Joseph F. Sullivan, "New Jersey's High Court Upholds Death Sentence after Blocking 26," *New York Times*, 25 January 1991 (www.nytimes.com/1991/01/25/nyregion/new-jersey-s-high-court-upholds-death-sentence-after-blocking-26.html).

31 Quoted in *New Jersey Death Penalty Study Commission Report*, 7.

32 New Jersey v. Robert O. Marshall, 123 N.J.1, 586 A2d 85 (1991).

33 New Jersey Legislature, Assembly Law and Public Safety Committee, Public Hearing on S171, 10 December 2007 (www.nileg.state.nj.us/media/archive_aud02.asp?KEY=S&SESSION=2006).

34 Joseph F. Sullivan, "Is Court Killing Death Penalty in New Jersey?," *New York Times*, 1 December 1990 (http://select.nytimes.com/gst/abstract.html?res=F30616FB3D540C728CDDAB0994D8494D81).

35 Quoted in ibid.

36 Jay Romano, "Legislators Seek to Put Justices on Ballot," *New York Times*, 22 November 1992 (www.nytimes.com/1992/11/22/nyregion/legislators-seek-to-put-justices-on-ballot.html).

37 367 N.J. Super. 61, 842 A.2d 207 (http://law.justia.com/cases/new-jersey/appellate-division-published/2004/a0899-01-opn.html).

38 Ibid. See also New Jerseyans for a Death Penalty Moratorium, "Appellate Court Suspends All Executions: Remands Lethal Injection Back to NJ DOC," 20 February 2004, www.deathpenaltyinfo.org/node/1064.

39 State v. Marcus Toliver and Ryshaone Thomas, 180 N.J. 164, 849 A.2d 1071.

40 Laura Mansnerus, "New Jersey Raises the Bar In Death Cases," *New York Times*, 3 February 2004 (http://query.nytimes.com/gst/fullpage.html?res=9804E4DD123BF937A35751C0A9629C8B63).

41 Lorry Post, e-mail message to John Galliher, 2009.

42 Bob Braun, "For Pro-Life Nun, State's Death Penalty Deserves Execution," *Star-Ledger*, 23 January 2005.

43 Robert Schwaneberg, "Assembly to Decide Soon on Repealing Death Penalty," *Star-Ledger*, 10 November 2007.

44 Bob Braun, "For a Most Unlikely Lobbyist, a Major Death Penalty Victory," *Star-Ledger*, 23 January 2006; Raymond J. Lesniak, *The Road to Abolition* (Union, NJ: Kean University Press, 2007).

45 "Achievements," *Star-Ledger*, 18 January 2008.

46 Raymond J. Lesniak, "Political Leadership and Spiritual Guidance," speech atYale University, New Haven, CT, 9 September 2008 (http//blog.nj.com/ nyv_raymond_lesnick/2008/09/political_leadership_and_leadership_spiri .html).

47 "Assembly, No. 1913," State of New Jersey, 210th Legislature, 3rd reprint, 24 November 2003 (www.njleg.state.nj.us/2002/Bills/A2000/1913_R3.HTM).

48 Ibid.

49 "New Jersey Senate Passes Death Penalty Moratorium," National Coalition to Abolish the Death Penalty, 15 December 2005 (http//www.commondreams .org/news2005/1215-17.htm).

50 Quoted in Nancy Solomon, "New Jersey's Death Penalty Moratorium," NPR, 15 January 2006 (www.npr.org/templates/story/story.php?storyId=5158551).

51 *New Jersey Death Penalty Study Commission Report*, 4–5.

52 Ibid., 51.

53 Ibid., 36.

54 Ibid., 80.

55 Ibid., 2.

56 Ibid., 79.

57 Ibid., 82.

58 Ronald Smothers, "Panel Seeks End to New Jersey's Death Penalty," *New York Times*, 11 May 2007 (www.nytimes.com/2007/05/11/nyregion/11death .html).

59 Quoted in Jeremy W. Peters, "New Jersey Senator Urges Delay on Repeal of Death Penalty," *New York Times*, 21 November 2007 (www.nytimes .com/2007/11/21/nyregion/21death.html).

60 Jeremy W. Peters, "In Ending Executions, Soul Searching," *New York Times*, 23 December 2007 (www.nytimes.com/2007/12/23/nyregion/nyregion specia12/23polnj.html).

61 New Jersey Legislature, Senate Budget and Appropriations Committee, public hearing on S171, 3 December 2007 (www.njleg.state.nj.us/media/ archive_audio2asp?KEY=SBA&SESSION=2006).

62 Ibid.

63 Ibid.

64 New Jersey Legislature, Senate Sessions, Legislative Debate on S171, 10 December 2007 (www.njleg.state.nj.us/media/archive_audio2.asp?KEY+ S&SESSION=2006).

65 Ibid.

66 New Jersey Legislature, Assembly Law and Public Safety Committee. Public Hearings on S171, 10 December 2007 (www.njleg.state.nj.us/media/archive_audio2.ask?KEY=ALP&SESSION=2006).

67 Ibid.

68 Ibid.

69 New Jersey Legislature, Assembly Sessions, 13 December 2007 (www.njleg.state.nj.us/media/archive_audio2.asp?KEY=A&SESSION=2006).

70 Ibid.

71 Ibid.

72 Peters, "In Ending Executions, Soul Searching."

73 "Lesniak Statement on the Signing of the Death Penalty Ban," New Jersey Senate Democrats, 17 December 2007, www.njsendems.com/release.asp?rid=1694.

74 Roe v. Wade, 410 U.S. 113 (1973).

75 New Jersey Legislature, Assembly Sessions, Legislative Debate on S171, 13 December 2007 (www.njleg.state.nj.us/media/archive_audio2.asp?KEY=A&SESSION=2006).

4. ABOLITION IN NEW MEXICO

1 NMSA 1978, §§ 31-20A-1 to -6 (1979, as amended through 2009). See also Associated Press, "Death Penalty Is Repealed in New Mexico," New York Times, 18 March 2009 (www.nytimes.com/2009/03/19/us/19execute.html?scp=1&sq=new%20mexico%20death%20penalty&st=cse).

2 Caitlin Kelleher, "Governor Bill Richardson Continues to Hear from New Mexicans Today on HB 285," State of New Mexico, 17 March 2009 (www.deathpenaltyusa.blogspot.com/2009/03/in-new-mexico-people-speak.html).

3 Associated Press, "Death Penalty Is Repealed in New Mexico."

4 "Governor Bill Richardson Signs Repeal of the Death Penalty," State of New Mexico, 18 March 2009 (www.deathpenaltyinfo.org/documents/richardsonstatement.pdf).

5 Quoted in ibid.

6 Ibid.

7 Barry A. Kosmin and Ariela Keysar, "American Religious Identification Survey (Aris 2008): Summary Report" (Hartford, CT: Trinity College, March 2009; www.americanreligionsurvey-aris.org/reports/ARIS_Report_2008.pdf).

8 Steve Terrell, "Poll: Voters Favor Death Penalty," Santa Fe New Mexican, 4 October 2002.

9 Quoted in Steve Terrell, "Death-Penalty Debate Comes for the Governor," *Santa Fe New Mexican*, 27 February 2005.

10 "Albuquerque Journal On-Line Poll Says REPEAL!," *Abolish the Death Penalty*, 18 March 2009 (http://deathpenaltyusa.blogspot.com/2009/03/albuquerque-journal-on-line-poll-says.html).

11 Ibid.

12 "Executions in the U.S. 1608–2002: The ESPY File Executions by State," Death Penalty Information Center, 2011, www.deathpenaltyinfo.org/documents/ESPYstate.pdf.

13 Campbell Gibson and Kay Jung, "Historical Census Statistics on Population Totals by Race, 1790 to 1990, and by Hispanic Origin, 1970 to 1990, for the United States, Regions, Divisions, and States," Census Bureau, September 2002, "Table 46. New Mexico—Race and Hispanic Origin: 1850 to 1990," www.census.gov/population/www/documentation/twps0056/tab46.pdf.

14 Ibid.; "State & County QuickFacts: New Mexico," Census Bureau, 2009, http://quickfacts.census.gov/qfd/states/35000.html.

15 Don E. Albrecht, "The State of New Mexico: Minority Population Growth" (Logan, UT: Western Rural Development Center, 2008; http://wrdc.usu.edu/files/uploads/Population/NewMexico_WEB.pdf), 1–2.

16 "State & County QuickFacts: New Mexico."

17 "Demographic Profile of Hispanics in New Mexico, 2009," Pew Hispanic Center, 2011, http://pewhispanic.org/states/?stateid=NM.

18 Robert Ruby and Allison Pond, "An Enduring Majority: Americans Continue to Support the Death Penalty" (Washington: Pew Forum on Religion and Public Life, 19 December 2007; http://pewforum.org/Death-Penalty/An-Enduring-Majority-Americans-Continue-to-Support-the-Death-Penalty.aspx).

19 "Estimated Murder Rate: New Mexico," Federal Bureau of Investigation, Uniform Crime Reporting Statistics, 2011, www.ucrdatatool.gov/Search/Crime/State/RunCrimeTrendsInOneVar.cfm.

20 Marcia J. Wilson, "The Application of the Death Penalty in New Mexico, July 1979 through December 2007: An Empirical Analysis," *New Mexico Law Review* 38 (2008): 255–301.

21 "House Bill 285, House Debate on HB 285," New Mexico Legislative Reports, 2009.

22 Ibid.

23 Ibid.

24 Kenneth W. Mentor, "The Death Penalty Returns to New Mexico," paper prepared for the annual meeting of the Western Social Science Association,

Albuquerque, NM, April 2002 (www.kenmentor.com/papers/nm_deathpen .htm).

25 Quoted in "Death Penalty Opponents Seek to Repeal NM Law," Lubbock-Online, 10 December 2000, www.lubbockonline.com/stories/121000/nat_ 121000072.shtml.

26 Steve Terrell, "Thumbs Down on Anti-Execution Bill," *Santa Fe New Mexican*, 10 February 2001; Barry Massey, "N.M. Senate Rejects Death Penalty Repeal," *Denver Post*, 10 February 2001.

27 Steve Terrell, "Facing Death," *Santa Fe New Mexican*, 28 October 2001.

28 Quoted in ibid.

29 Mentor, "The Death Penalty Returns to New Mexico."

30 Quoted in Steve Terrell, "Death Penalty Repeal Clears Crucial Panel Vote," *Santa Fe New Mexican*, 9 March 2009 (www.santafenewmexican.com/ Local%20News/2009-Legislature2009-03-09T21-50-22).

31 "Representative Gail Chasey—(D)," New Mexico Legislature, 2011 (www .nmlegis.gov/lcs/legdetails.aspx?SPONCODE=HCHAS).

32 Viki Elkey, "Abolishing the Death Penalty in New Mexico: Lessons Learned in Long Campaign," unpublished manuscript (http:/www.peaceworkmagazine .org/abolishing-death-penalty-new-mexico-lessions-learned-long-campaign).

33 "Gov. Richardson, Activists Honored in Rome After New Mexico Repeals Death Penalty," Democracy Now! 20 April 2009, (www.democracynow.org/ 2009/4/20/gov_richardson_activists_honored_in_rome).

34 Elkey, "Abolishing the Death Penalty in New Mexico."

35 "Gov. Richardson, Activists Honored in Rome After New Mexico Repeals Death Penalty."

36 Elkey, "Abolishing the Death Penalty in New Mexico."

37 Ibid.

38 Ibid.

39 Viki Elkey, telephone interview with John F. Galliher, 11 May 2009.

40 Ibid.

41 "1999 Regular Session: HB 305: Abolish Death Penalty," New Mexico Legislature, 2011, www.nmlegis.gov/lcs/_session.aspx?chamber=H&legtype=B& legno=305&year=99.

42 "Legislative Accomplishments," New Mexico Coalition to Repeal the Death Penalty, 2011, www.nmrepeal.org/legislative_accomplishments.

43 Ibid.

44 Steve Terrell, "House Votes to End Death Penalty," *Santa Fe New Mexican*, 1 March 2005.

45 "2005 Regular Session: HB 578: Employee Leave for Certain Crime Vic-

tims," New Mexico Legislature, 2011, www.nmlegis.gov/lcs/_session.aspx ?chamber=H&legtype=B&legno=%20578&year=05; "2007 Regular Session: HB 193: Leave for Crime Victims at Legal Proceedings," New Mexico Legislature, 2011, www.nmlegis.gov/lcs/_session.aspx?chamber=H&legtype =B&legno=%20193&year=07.

46 "2005 Regular Session: HB 577: Murder Victim's Children College Tuition," New Mexico Legislature, 2011, www.nmlegis.gov/lcs/_session.aspx ?chamber=H&legtype=B&legno=%20577&year=05; "2007 Regular Session: HB 966: Families of Homicide Victim College Tuition," New Mexico Legislature, 2011, www.nmlegis.gov/lcs/_session.aspx?chamber=H&legtype =B&legno=%20966&year=07.

47 "2009 Regular Session: HB 211: Crime Victim Employment Leave," New Mexico Legislature, 2011, www.nmlegis.gov/lcs/_session.aspx?chamber=H& legtype=B&legno=%20211&year=09.

48 "Fiscal Impact Report," Finance Committee, HB 239, 5 March 2001 (www .nmlegis.gov/lcs/_session.aspx?chamber=H&legtype=B&legno=239& year=01).

49 "Fiscal Impact Report," HB 576, 3 March 2005 (www.nmlegis.gov/lcs/_ session.aspx?chamber=H&legtype=B&legno=%20576&year=05).

50 "Fiscal Impact Report," HB 190, 5 March 2007 (www.nmlegis.gov/Sessions/ 07%20Regular/firs/HB0190.pdf); "Fiscal Impact Report," HB 285, 31 January 2009 (www.nmlegis.gov/lcs/_session.aspx?chamber=H&legtype=B& legno=%20285&year=09).

51 Elkey, "Abolishing the Death Penalty in New Mexico."

52 "Fiscal Impact Report," HB 285, 31 January 2009; Steve Terrell, "Bill to Abolish Death Penalty Moves Forward," SantaFeNewMexican.com, 30 January 2009 (www.santafenewMexican.com/Local%20News/A renewed plea for life).

53 Quoted in Terrell, "Bill to Abolish Death Penalty Moves Forward."

54 Ibid.

55 "Fiscal Impact Report," HB 285, 31 January 2009.

56 Steve Terrell, "Panel Passes Bill to Repeal Death Penalty: Supporters Plan Monday Rally at Capitol Rotunda," SantaFeNewMexican.com, 6 February 2009 (www.santafenewmexican.com/LocalNews/Panel-passes-bill-to-repeal-death-penalty).

57 Quoted in Deborah Baker, "House Panel Approves Death Penalty Abolition," Associated Press, 7 February 2009.

58 Ibid.

59 Quoted in ibid.

60 Quoted in ibid.

61 "House Debate on HB 285," New Mexico Legislative Reports.

62 Ibid. See also "Senate Debate on HB 285," New Mexico Legislative Reports.

63 "House Debate on HB 285."

64 Ibid. See also Deborah Baker, "Death Penalty Opponents Seize on Economic Costs," Associated Press, 12 February 2009.

65 "House Debate on HB 285." See also Gail Chasey, New Mexico State Representative, telephone interview with Larry W. Koch, 2 October 2011.

66 "House Debate on HB 285."

67 Ibid.

68 Ibid.

69 Elkey, "Abolishing the Death Penalty in New Mexico."

70 Terrell, "Death Penalty Repeal Clears Crucial Panel Vote."

71 Ibid.

72 "Senate Debate on HB 285."

73 Ibid.

74 Steve Terrell, "Senate Backs Death-Penalty Repeal," SantaFeNewMexican .com, 13 March 2009 (www.santafenewmexican.com/LocalNews/Death-penalty-repeal-passes).

75 "Senate Debate on HB 285."

76 Ibid.

77 Ibid.

78 Trip Jennings, "One Man Will Decide Fate of the Death Penalty in New Mexico," *New Mexico Independent*, 13 March 2009 (http://newmexico independent.com/21720/one-man-will-decide-fate-of-capital-punishment-in-nm).

79 "Gov. Richardson Meets With Pope," KOAT.com, 15 April 2009 (www.koat .com/r/19191673/detail.html).

80 Elaine de Leon, "Money, Morality, and Repealing the Death Penalty," *Religion & Ethics Newsweekly*, 24 April 2009 (www.pbs.org/wnet/religionandethics/ episodes/april-24–2009/money-morality-and-repealing-the-death-penalty/ 2757/).

81 Terrell, "Senate Backs Death-Penalty Repeal."

5. ABOLITION IN ILLINOIS

1 "Executions in the U.S. 1608–2002: The ESPY File Executions by State," Death Penalty Information Center, 2011, www.deathpenaltyinfo.org/documents/ ESPYstate.pdf.

2 Robert Sherrill, "Death Trip: The American Way of Execution," *Nation*, 21 December 2000 www.thenation.com).

3 Ken Armstrong and Steve Mills,"Failure of the Death Penalty in Illinois,"

Chicago Tribune, 14–18 November 1999 (www.chicagotribune.com/chi-death illinoisseries,0,3159621.special).

4 Ken Armstrong and Steve Mills, "Death Row Justice Derailed," *Chicago Tribune*, 14 November 1999 (www.chicagotrobine.com/news/watchdog/ chi-991114deathillinois1,0,4002543.story). See also Ken Armstrong and Steve Mills, "Inept Defense Cloud Verdict," *Chicago Tribune*, 15 November 1999 (www.chicagotrobine.com/news/watchdog/chi-991115deathillinois2,0 ,5051121.story).

5 Steve Mills and Ken Armstrong, "A Tortured Path to Death Row," *Chicago Tribune*, 17 November 1999 (www.chicagotrobine.com/news/watchdog/ chi-991117deathillinois4,0,7148277.story) and "Convicted by a Hair," *Chicago Tribune*, 18 November 1999 (www.chicagotrobine.com/news/watchdog/ chi-991118deathillinois5,0,196862.story); Armstrong and Mills, "Death Row Justice Derailed."

6 Bill Bell Jr. and Kevin McDermott, "Death Row Hearings Open with Tears, Lawyers' Appeals," *St. Louis Post-Dispatch*, 16 October 2002. See also Armstrong and Mills, "Death Row Justice Derailed."

7 Thomas P. Sullivan, "Preventing Wrongful Convictions—A Current Report from Illinois," *Drake Law Review* 52 (Summer 2004):606.

8 Bruce Shapiro, "Ashcroft's Song: The Attorney General's Trigger-Happy Record on the Death Penalty Is Running against the Tide of Public and Judicial Opinion," *LA Weekly*, 15 July 2002 (www.alternet.org/rights/13592/ ashcroft%27s_song).

9 *Report of the Governor's Commission on Capital Punishment*, State of Illinois, 15 April 2002 (www.idoc.state.il.us/ccp/ccp/reports/commission_report/ index.html). See also Bruce Shapiro, "Rethinking the Death Penalty," *Nation*, 22 July 2002 (www.thenation.com/article/rethinking-death-penalty).

10 Quoted in Ted Cox, "St. George and the Death-Penalty Dragon Deadline Enables a Corrupt Politician to Score Points against Capital Punishment," *Chicago Daily Herald*, 30 July 2004.

11 Bill Ryan, letter to the editor, *Chicago Daily Herald*, 14 January 2001.

12 Glenn L. Pierce and Michael L. Radelet, "Race, Religion, and Death Sentencing in Illinois, 1988–1997," *Oregon Law Review* 81 (2002): 39–96.

13 "Illinois Governor Elevates Justice by Clearing Death Row," *USA Today*, 13 January 2003 (www.usatoday.com/news/opinion/editorials/2003–01–12-our-view_x.htm).

14 Dirk Johnson, "Poor Defense Can Be One-Way Ticket to Death Row," *Contra Costa Times*, 6 February 2000.

15 "Death Penalty Does Not Deter Crime, Costs More," *The Exponent Online*,

13 January 2003 (www.purdueexponent.org/interface/bebop/showstory
.php?date=2003/01/14&section=opinions).

16 Quoted in *Daily Illini* Editorial Board, "It's Time to Abolish the Death
Penalty," DailyIllini.com, 24 February 2010 (www.dailyillini.com/opinions/
editorials/2010/02/23/it-s-time-to-abolish-the-death-penalty).

17 Dave McKinney, "Victory for Death Penalty Reform," *Chicago Sun-Times*,
24 May 2003.

18 Associated Press, "Costs Soar for Death-Row Cases," *Telegraph-Herald*, 28
December 2003.

19 Nicholas C. Pistor, "Judge Declares Coleman Indigent in Murder Case:
Taxpayer-Funded Defense Lawyers Are Named to Represent Him," *St. Louis
Post-Dispatch*, 5 September 2009.

20 Ryan, letter to the editor.

21 Betsy Wilson, "Illinois Can't Afford the Costs: Death Penalty Taxpayers De-
rive No Benefit from the State Spending Hundreds of Millions Annually,"
St. Louis Post-Dispatch, 29 January 2010.

22 Ibid.

23 Natasha Korecki, "How Death Penalty Has Changed Since Commutations,"
Chicago Daily Hearld, 11 January 2004.

24 Ashley Badgley, "Advocates Urge Lawmakers to Abolish Death Penalty," *Illinois Statehouse News Service*, 11 March 2010 (http://illinois.statehousenews
online.com/2323/advocates-urge-lawmakers-to-abolish-death-penalty/).

25 *Illinois Capital Punishment Reform Study Committee: Sixth and Final Report*,
State of Illinois, 28 October 2010 (www. www.icjia.state.il.us/public/pdf/
dpsrc/CPRSC%20-%20Sixth%20and%20Final%20Report.pdf). See also
James Warren, "Exposé Hits Hard at Death Penalty System," *Chicago News
Cooperative*, 13 November 2010 (www.chicagonewscoop.org/expose-hits-
hard-at-death-penalty-system/).

26 Badgley, "Advocates Urge Lawmakers to Abolish Death Penalty."

27 Tim Jones, "Illinois Has Days to Plug $13 Billion Deficit That Took Years to Pro-
duce," *Bloomberg*, 3 January 2011 (www.bloomberg.com/news/2011–01–03/
illinois-must-plug-13-billion-deficit-in-days-that-took-years-to-produce.html).

28 "Murder Victims' Families Support Repealing the Death Penalty," posted
on International Coalition against the Death Penalty Website, 2011 (http://
graphics8.nytimes.com/packages/pdf/us/icadp-victims-letter.pdf).

29 State of Illinois, 96th General Assembly, Regular Session, Senate Transcript,
144th Legislative Day, 11 January 2011 (www.ilga.gov/senate/transcripts/
strans96/09600144.pdf).

30 State of Illinois, 96th General Assembly, House of Representatives, Tran-

scription Debate, 161st Legislature Day, 6 January 2011 (www.ilga.gov/ house/transcripts/htrans96/09600161.pdf).

31 Jeff Finley, "Should Illinois End Death Penalty? Catholic Bishops Say Yes," PioneerLocal.com, 13 January 2011 (http://blogs.pioneerlocal.com/religion/ 2011/01/should_illinois_end_death_pena.html).

32 Monica Davey, "Illinois Bill Eliminating Death Row Is Approved," *New York Times*, 11 January 2011 (www.nytimes.com/2011/01/12/us/12death.html?_ r=1&src=twt&twt=nytimespolitics).

33 David Crary, "Gay Legislators Having Impact in Marriage Debate," *Washington Post*, 6 March 2011 (www.washingtonpost.com/wp-dyn/content/ article/2011/03/06/AR2011030601604.html); Monique Garcia, "Illinois Civil Unions Signed into Law," *Chicago Tribune*, 31 January 2011 (http:// articles.chicagotribune.com/2011–01–31/news/ct-met-quinn-civil-union- signing-20110131_1_civil-unions-lesbian-couples-gay-marriage).

34 Quoted in Tammy Webber, "Quinn Signs Historic Civil Unions Legislation," *State Journal-Register*, 31 January 2011 (www.sj-r.com/top-stories/x122 669191/Quinn-signs-historic-civil-unions-legislation).

35 Dave McKinney, "Gov. Quinn to 'Follow Conscience'" on Unions," *Chicago Sun-Times*, 2 December 2010 (www.suntimes.com/news/metro/2652654–417/ state-senate-bill-vote-illinois.htmlv).

36 Quoted in Doug Finke, "Illinois Gov. Pat Quinn Defends Income Tax Increase," RRStar.com, 12 January 2011 (www.rrstar.com/carousel/x195845 3303/Illinois-Governor-Pat-Quinn-defends-income-tax-increase).

37 Al Lewis, "Lewis: New Jersey, Illinois Governors Attacking Each Other, Rather Than Problems," Denverpost.com, 9 March 2011 (www.denverpost .com/search/ci_17567489).

38 Christopher Wills, "Illinois Abolishes Death Penalty, Clears Death Row," *Washington Post*, 9 March 2011 (www.washingtonpost.com/wp-dyn/content/ article/2011/03/09/AR2011030900319.html?hpid=moreheadlines).

39 John Schwartz and Emma G. Fitzsimmons, "Illinois Governor Signs Capital Punishment Ban," *New York Times*, 9 March 2011 (www.nytimes.com/ 2011/03/10/us/10illinois.html?_r=1).

40 Quoted in "Catholic Leaders Praise Illinois Governor for Ending Death Penalty," *Catholic News Agency*, 9 March 2011 (www.catholicnewsagency .com/news/catholic-leaders-praise-illinois-governor-for-ending-death- penalty/?utm_source=feedburner&utm_medium=feed&utm_campaign= Feed%3A+catholicnewsagency%2Fdailynews-us+%28CNA+Daily+News+- +US%29).

41 "Statement from Governor Pat Quinn on Senate Bill 3539," Illinois Gov-

ernment News Network, 9 March 2011 (www.illinois.gov/PressReleases/ShowPressRelease.cfm?SubjectID=2&RecNum=9265).

42 Quoted in Tom Barker, "Local Officials React to Abolishment of Death Penalty," *Effingham Daily News*, 10 March 2011 (http://effinghamdailynews.com/local/x449488195/Local-officials-react-to-abolishment-of-death-penalty).

43 Quoted in Associated Press, "Illinois Ends Death Penalty, Clears Death Row," CBS News, 9 March 2011 (www.cbsnews.com/stories/2011/03/09/national/main20041207.shtml?tag=mncol;lst;3).

44 "Background—U.S. Catholic Population by State," US Conference of Catholic Bishops, Office of Media Relations, 3 November 2008 (http://old.usccb.org/comm/archives/2008/08-160.shtml).

45 David Carr and John Schwartz, "A Watchdog Professor, Now Defending Himself," *New York Times*, 17 June 2011 (www.nytimes.com/2011/06/18/business/media/18protess.html).

6. THE RECURRING DEATH PENALTY IN KANSAS

1 John F. Galliher, Gregory Ray, and Brent Cook, "Abolition and Reinstatement of Capital Punishment during the Progressive Era and Early 20th Century," *Journal of Criminal Law and Criminology* 83, no. 3 (1992): 538–76.

2 State of Kansas v. Michael L. Marsh II, 278 Kan. 520, 102 P. 3d 445 (2004).

3 Kansas v. Marsh, 548 U.S. 163 (2006).

4 State of Kansas v. Gavin D. Scott, 286 Kan. 54, 183 P.3d 801 (2008).

5 William J. Bowers and Patricia H. Dugan, "Kansans Want an Alternative to the Death Penalty," 1994, unpublished manuscript.

6 Quoted in "Death Penalty 4 Days Away," *Hutchinson News*, 18 April 1994.

7 Quoted in John A. Dvorak, "Death Penalty Gets First OK in Legislature: Kansas House Expected to Give Its Final Approval to the Bill Today," *Kansas City Star*, 11 February 1994.

8 Bowers and Dugan, "Kansans Want an Alternative to the Death Penalty," 1.

9 Ibid., 9.

10 "New Poll: What Kansans Think about the Death Penalty," Kansas Coalition against the Death Penalty, 31 January 2011, www.ksabolition.org/news/poll-kansans-think-about-death-penalty.

11 "Executions in the U.S. 1608–2002: The ESPY File Executions by State," Death Penalty Information Center, 2011, www.deathpenaltyinfo.org/documents/ESPYstate.pdf.

12 "Facts about the Death Penalty," Death Penalty Information Center, 29 September 2011, www.deathpenaltyinfo.org/documents/factsheet.pdf.

13 "Estimates of the Population of States by Race and Hispanic Origin: July 1,

1994," Census Bureau, www.census.gov/population/estimate-extract/state/ sasr/sasr94.txt.

14 "State and County Quickfacts," Census Bureau, http.www.quickfacts.census .gov/qfd/indix.html.

15 "Estimates of the Population of States by Race and Hispanic Origin: July 1, 1994," Census Bureau, www.census.gov/population/estimate-extract/state/ sasr/sasr94.txt.

16 Patricia Scalia, "Records of Kansas State Board of Indigents' Defense Services," March 2011, unpublished paper.

17 "Estimated Murder Rate," Federal Bureau of Investigation, Uniform Crime Reporting Statistics, 2011, www.ucrdatatool.gov/Search/Crime/State/Run CrimeTrendsInOneVar.cfm.

18 "Deterrence: States without the Death Penalty Have Had Consistently Lower Murder Rates," Death Penalty Information Center, 2011, www .deathpenaltyinfo.org/deterrence-states-without-death-penalty-have-had-consistently-lower-murder-rates.

19 Frank J. Weed, *Certainty of Justice: Reform in the Crime Victim Movement* (New York: Aldine de Gruyter, 1995), 132.

20 Ibid.

21 Truman Capote, *In Cold Blood: A True Account of a Multiple Murder and Its Consequences* (New York: Random House, 1966).

22 Quoted in John Hanna, "'In Cold Blood' Murders Haunt Death Penalty Debate," *Los Angeles Times*, 20 March 1994 (http://articles.latimes.com/1994–03–20/news/mn-36257_1_death-penalty).

23 Julie Wright, "Death Penalty Takes Big Step: Final House OK Is Likely Today," *Wichita Eagle*, 11 February 1994.

24 "Will Death Penalty Become Law in '94?" *Johnson County Sun*, 25 August 1993.

25 John A. Dvorak, "Schmidts Push for Death Penalty," *Kansas City Star*, 18 February 1994.

26 "Death Penalty Supported," *Topeka Capital-Journal*, 18 February 1994.

27 Julie Wright, "Family's Crusade Getting Results: Lawmakers Responding to Pleas," *Wichita Eagle*, 27 March 1994.

28 "Death Penalty: Kansas Couple Mounting Own Campaign for Reinstatement," *Kansas City Kansan*, 1 January 1994.

29 Julie Wright, "A Father Tells Why He Wants Death Penalty," *Wichita Eagle*, 26 January 1994.

30 Quoted in "Finney Opens Door to Death Penalty," *Olathe Daily News*, 24 August 1993.

31 Quoted in ibid.

32 Quoted in "Holcomb Murders Haunt Death Penalty Debate," *Hutchinson News*, 14 March 1994.

33 Ron Sylvester, "Ten Years Later, Carr Brothers' Murders Still Haunt," *Wichita Eagle*, 15 December 2010 (www.kansas.com/2010/12/15/1633883/ ten-years-later-carr-brothers.html).

34 Donna Schneweis, chair of the Board, Kansas Coalition against the Death Penalty, telephone interview with Larry W. Koch, 28 February 2011.

35 Liz Dodds, "Murder Charges Filed in Arkansas City Teen's Death," KTKA .com, 17 January 2007 (www.ktka.com/news/2007/jan/17/murder_charges_ filed_students_death/).

36 Shane Farley, "Judge Keeps Delays Brief, Thurber Gets Death," *NewsCow*, 20 March 2009 (www.newscow.net/story.php?StoryID=2850).

37 Ron Sylvester, "Victims in 2000 Quadruple Homicide Aren't Forgotten," *Wichita Eagle*, 7 December 2010 (www.kansas.com/2010/12/07/1621722/ a-vigil-tonight-will-unveil-a.html); Associated Press, "Vigil Planned for 4 Wichita Homicide Victims," El Dorado Times.com, 8 December 2010 (www.eldoradotimes.com/newsnow/x1921989090/Vigil-planned-for-4- Wichita-homicide-victims).

38 State of Kansas v. Cornelius Devon Oliver, 280 Kan. 681, 124 P.3d 493 (2005).

39 Sylvester, "Victims in 2000 Quadruple Homicide Aren't Forgotten"; Associated Press, "Vigil Planned for 4 Wichita Homicide Victims."

40 Schneweis interview.

41 Franklin E. Zimring. "The Wages of Ambivalence: On the Context and Prospects of New York's Death Penalty," *Buffalo Law Review* 44 (Spring 1996): 303–23.

42 "New Legislators and Violent Crime May Boost Death Bill," *Hutchinson News*, 11 January 1979.

43 "I Held the Power of Life and Death," *Topeka Capital-Journal*, 12 March 1994.

44 "Carlin Defends His Death Penalty Stand," *Hutchinson News*, 12 March 1994.

45 "Hayden Wants Death Penalty by July," *Kansas City Times*, 13 December 1986. Also see "Hayden Wants Death Penalty Law by July 1," *Lawrence Journal World*, 13 December 1986 (http://news.google.com/newspapers?nid=2199 &dat=19861213&id=0UoyAAAAIBAJ&sjid=8eUFAAAAIBAJ&pg=6676 ,3095302).

46 "40-Year Prison Term Becomes Law," *Kansas City Times*, 24 February 1990.

47 Ibid.

48 "Death Penalty: Seen as Dead Issue at Capitol," *Topeka Capital-Journal*, 7 January 1993.

49 "Death Walks among Us," *Topeka Capital-Journal*, 30 July 1993.

50 "Inevitable? Death Penalty Picks Up Speed in Topeka," *Wichita Eagle*, 16 January 1994.

51 Julie Wright, "Panel OKs Narrower Death Penalty Bill," *Wichita Eagle*, 25 February 1994.

52 Julie Wright, "House Gives Final Push to Death Bill: Governor Expected to Let Penalty Become Law," *Wichita Eagle*, 9 April 1994.

53 "Finney Testifies against Death Penalty," *Topeka Capital-Journal*, 19 February 1994.

54 "Finney Sticks to Promise to Permit Death Penalty," *Wichita Eagle*, 23 April 1994.

55 "Finney Testifies against Death Penalty."

56 Quoted in "Proposal Was Drafted by Rock," *Hutchinson News*, 9 April 1994.

57 Quoted in Julie Wright, "House Members Offered Broader Death Penalty," *Wichita Eagle*, 25 March 1994.

58 John A. Dvorak, "Kansas Senate Approves Death Penalty," *Kansas City Star*, 2 March 1994; Julie Wright, "No Consensus Is Reached on Death Penalty: Senate Digs In Its Heels," *Wichita Eagle*, 19 March 1994.

59 "Death Penalty in House Today," *Wichita Eagle*, 18 March 1994.

60 "Death Penalty 4 Days Away," *Hutchinson News*, 18 April 1994.

61 "Estimated Murder and Nonnegligent Manslaughter," Federal Bureau of Investigation, Uniform Crime Reporting Statistics, 2011, www.ucrdatatool.gov/Search/Crime/State/RunCrimeTrendsInOneVar.cfm.

62 "Death Penalty 4 Days Away."

63 Wright, "House Gives Final Push to Death Bill."

64 "Death Penalty Debate Age-Old," *Kansas City Star*, 29 April 1979.

65 Ibid.

66 "Senate OKs Death Bill," *Topeka Capital-Journal*, 2 March 1994.

67 Robert Weisberg, "The New York Statute as Cultural Document: Seeking the Morally Optimal Death Penalty," *Buffalo Law Review* 44 (Spring 1996): 286.

68 Ibid., 287.

69 Schneweis interview.

70 "Performance Audit Report: Costs Incurred for Death Penalty Cases; A K-GOAL Audit of the Department of Corrections," State of Kansas Legislative Division of Post Audit, December 2003, www.kansas.gov/postaudit//audits_perform/04pa03a.pdf, 10.

71 Ron Sylvester, "Legislature to Consider End to Death Penalty," *Wichita Eagle*, 19 December 2009 (www.kansas.com/2009/12/19/1104984/legislature-to-consider-end-to.html); Tom Bell, "Death Versus Dollars," *Salina Journal*,

4 January 2010 (www.saljournal.com/Print/death-penalty-edit-for-Monday—Jan—4—2010); Rhonda Holman, "Reasons to Rethink Death Penalty," *Wichita Eagle*, 21 October 2009 (www.kansas.com/2009/10/21/1020316/reasons-to-rethink-death-penalty.html).

72 Erin Brown, "Kansas Could Abolish Death Penalty to Cut Costs," Kansan .com, 27 January 2010 (www.kansan.com/news/2010/jan/27/kansas-could-abolish-death-penalty-cut-costs/).

73 Patricia Scalia, Executive Director of the Kansas State Board of Indigents' Defense Services, telephone interview with Larry W. Koch, 27 January 2011.

74 "Supplemental Note on Senate Bill No. 6: As Reported Without Recommendation by Senate Committee on Judiciary," Kansas Revised Session of 2005, www.kansas.gov/government/legislative/supplemental/2006/SN0006.pdf.

75 Holman, "Reasons to Rethink Death Penalty."

76 "Supplemental Note on Senate Bill No. 208: As Amended by Senate Committee on Judiciary," Kansas Session of 2009, www.kansas.gov/government/legislative/supplemental/2010/SN0208.pdf.

77 Quoted in Jeannine Koranda, "Penalty No Deterrent, Panel Told," *Wichita Eagle*, 20 January 2010.

78 Quoted in ibid.

79 Quoted in David Klepper, "Kansas Senate Takes Up Repeal of Death Penalty," *Kansas City Star*, 30 January 2010.

80 Quoted in Barbara Hollingsworth, "Death Penalty Remains Alive," *Topeka Capital-Journal*, 18 February 2010 (http://cjonline.com/news/legislature/2010-02-18/death_penalty_remains_alive); Rhonda Holman, "At Least Senate Had Debate, Vote," *Wichita Eagle*, 23 February 2010.

81 "Major Victory!," Kansas Coalition against the Death Penalty 2010 (www.ksabolition.org/wp-content/uploads/2011/02/Spring2010.pdf).

82 Holman, "At Least Senate Had Debate."

83 "Report of the Judicial Council Death Penalty Advisory Committee," Kansas Judicial Council, 4 December 2009, www.kansasjudicialcouncil.org/Documents/Studies%20and%20Reports/2009%20Reports/Death%20Penalty.pdf, 4.

84 "Republican Candidates 'All-American Presidential Forum' at Morgan State University in Baltimore, September 27, 2007," American Presidency Project, www.presidency.ucsb.edu/ws/index.php?pid=75913#axzz1QjAfosvL.

7. NEAR MISSES IN NEW ENGLAND

1 "State by State Database," Death Penalty Information Center, 2011, www.deathpenaltyinfo.org/state_by_state.

2 "Executions in the U.S. 1608–2002: The ESPY File Executions by State,"

Death Penalty Information Center, 2011, www.deathpenaltyinfo.org/documents/ESPYstate.pdf.

3 House Committee Research Office, "Legislative History of Death Penalty," (Concord: New Hampshire House of Representatives, 6 November 2009), 175.

4 1974 N.H. Laws 34:1.

5 New Hampshire Criminal Laws, Laws of 1977, Chapter 440.

6 New Hampshire Criminal Laws, 530:1, et seq.

7 House Committee Research Office, "Legislative History of Death Penalty," 2.

8 "Estimated Crime in 1991: Crime Rate Per 100,000 Population: Violent Crime," Federal Bureau of Investigation, Uniform Crime Reporting Statistics, 2011, www.ucrdatatool.gov/Search/Crime/State/RunCrimeOneYearof Data.cfm.

9 "Estimated Crime in New Hampshire: Crime Rate Per 100,000 Population: Violent Crime," Federal Bureau of Investigation, Uniform Crime Reporting Statistics, 2011, www.ucrdatatool.gov/Search/Crime/State/RunCrimeState byState.cfm.

10 "Crime—National or State Level: State-by-State and National Crime Estimates by Year(s)" Federal Bureau of Investigation, Uniform Crime Reporting Statistics, 2011, www.ucrdatatool.gov/Search/Crime/State/RunCrime StatebyState.cfm; "Nationwide Murder Rates, 1996–2008," Death Penalty Information Center, 2010, www.deathpenaltyinfo.org/murder-rates-nationally-and-state.

11 "55 Percent in NH Say They're Against Death Penalty," *New Hampshire Union Leader*, 9 May 2000.

12 "Senate to Vote on Death Penalty Repeal," *New Hampshire Union Leader*, 18 May 2000; "Senate Rejects Death Penalty; Repeal Measure Faces Certain Shaheen Veto," *New Hampshire Union Leader*, 19 May 2000.

13 New Hampshire General Court, House Committee on Criminal Justice and Public Safety hearing on HB 1548, 26 January 2000.

14 New Hampshire General Court, House Committee on Criminal Justice and Public Safety executive session on HB 1548 FN, 26 February 2000.

15 New Hampshire General Court, House session, 9 March 2000.

16 New Hampshire General Court, *Journal of the House of Representatives of the State of New Hampshire, 2000* (Concord: State of New Hampshire, 2000), 831–43.

17 John Kifner, "A State Votes to End Its Death Penalty," *New York Times*, 19 May 2000 (http://partners.nytimes.com/library/national/051900nh-death penalty.html).

18 New Hampshire General Court, *Journal of the House of Representatives*, 643.

19 Quoted in John DiStaso and John Toole, "Death Penalty Fate Still up in Air in Senate," *New Hampshire Union Leader*, 13 March 2000.

20 Ibid.

21 New Hampshire General Court, Senate Committee on Judiciary hearing on HB 1548 FN, 24 April 2000.

22 New Hampshire General Court, Senate, "Report of the Committee on House Bill 1548 FN," 18 May 2000.

23 New Hampshire General Court, *Journal of the Senate of New Hampshire, 2000* (Concord: State of New Hampshire, 2000), 832.

24 Ibid., 836.

25 Ibid., 837.

26 "Senate Rejects Death Penalty."

27 New Hampshire General Court, *Journal of the Senate of New Hampshire*, 832.

28 Ibid., 835.

29 Quoted in Kifner, "A State Votes to End Its Death Penalty."

30 John DiStaso, "Shaheen Vetoes Death Penalty in NH: Legislators React to Veto," *New Hampshire Union Leader*, 20 May 2000.

31 Associated Press, "New Hampshire Veto Saves Death Penalty," *New York Times*, 20 May 2000 (www.nytimes.com/2000/05/20/us/new-hampshire-veto-saves-death-penalty.html).

32 Quoted in DiStaso, "Shaheen Vetoes Death Penalty in NH."

33 Quoted in Lynne Tuohy, "Ex-NH AG Opposes Death Penalty; Panel Favors It," Boston.com, 1 December 2010 (www.boston.com/news/local/new_hampshire/articles/2010/12/01/nh_to_release_report_to_retain_the_death_penalty/).

34 House Committee Research Office, "Legislative History of Death Penalty," 180; Associated Press, "N.H. House Votes to End Death Penalty," Boston.com, 26 March 2009 (http://articles.boston.com/2009–03–26/news/2925 4359_1_death-penalty-repeal-bill-punishment-in-murder-cases).

35 New Hampshire General Court, "Final Report of the Commission to Study the Death Penalty in New Hampshire, HB 520, Chapter 284, Laws of 2009," 1 December 2010.

36 Garry Rayno, "Husband: Expand Death Penalty," *New Hampshire Union Leader*, 2 February 1011.

37 Lawrence B. Goodheart, *The Solemn Sentence of Death: Capital Punishment in Connecticut* (Amherst: University of Massachusetts Press, 2011), 7, 38.

38 Ibid., 100.

39 Ibid., 179.

40 "Death Penalty Fact Sheet for Connecticut: Connecticut's Death Penalty," Connecticut Network to Abolish the Death Penalty, 2011, www.cnadp.org/dpConn.php.

41 "State by State Database"; "Executions in the U.S. 1608–2002: The ESPY File Executions by State," Death Penalty Information Center, 2011, www.deathpenaltyinfo.org/documents/ESPYstate.pdf.

42 "Current Death Row Populations by Race: as of April 1, 2010," Death Penalty Information Center, 2011, www.deathpenaltyinfo.org/race-death-row-inmates-executed-1976#deathrowpop.

43 "Death Penalty Fact Sheet for Connecticut."

44 Quoted in Goodheart, *The Solemn Sentence of Death*, 228.

45 Gregory Hladky, "Rell Considers Delaying Serial Killer's Execution," *Bristol Press*, 3 December 2004.

46 "Estimated Crime in Connecticut: Crime Rate Per 100,000 Population: Violent Crime" Federal Bureau of Investigation, Uniform Crime Reporting Statistics, 2011, www.ucrdatatool.gov/Search/Crime/State/RunCrimeState byState.cfm.

47 George Coppolo and Ryan O'Neil, "Murder Rates in Connecticut and Other States and Certain Cities," State of Connecticut Office of Legislative Research, 14 September 2005, www.cga.ct.gov/2005/rpt/2005-R-0639.htm.

48 "Estimated Crime in Connecticut: Estimated Crime in United States—Total," Federal Bureau of Investigation, Uniform Crime Reporting Statistics, 2011, www.ucrdatatool.gov/Search/Crime/State/RunCrimeStatebyState.cfm.

49 Goodheart, *The Solemn Sentence of Death*, 108.

50 Ibid., 107–8.

51 Ibid., 107–9.

52 Ibid., 181.

53 "Study Pursuant to Public Act No. 01–151 the Imposition of the Death Penalty in Connecticut," Connecticut Commission on the Death Penalty, 8 January 2003, www.scribd.com/doc/16155359/Death-Penalty-Commission-Final-Report, 28.

54 Ibid., 14.

55 Christopher Reinhart, "Disparity in Death Penalty Cases and the Criminal Justice System" State of Connecticut Office of Legislative Research, 16 March 2005, www.cga.ct.gov/2005/rpt/2005-R-0215.htm.

56 Dave Collins, "Yale Study: Race Bias Mars Conn. Death Penalty Cases," *Bay State Banner*, 20 December 2007 (www.baystatebanner.com/nat115–2007–12–20); John J. Donohue III, interview by Lucy Nalpathanchil, "The Death of Capital Punishment: Should We Abolish the Death Penalty in Connecti-

cut?" Connecticut Public Radio, 10 March 2008 (www.cpbn.org/program/ where-we-live/episode/death-capital-punishment).

57 Richard Meehan, "Death Penalty Should Be Repealed in Connecticut," NorwichBulletin.com, 23 May 2009 (www.norwichbulletin.com/opinions/ columnists/x313655374/Richard-Meehan-Death-penalty-should-be-repealed-in-Connecticut).

58 "Testimony of Edward J. Gavin, President of the Connecticut Criminal Defense Lawyers Association, in Support of Raised Bill 6578," Judiciary Committee Public Hearing, 2 March 2009 (www.cga.ct.gov/2009/JUDdata/ Tmy/2009HB-06578-R000304-CT%20Criminal%20Defense%20Lawyer's %20Association,%20Edward%20J.%20Gavin-TMY.PDF).

59 "HB-6578: An Act Concerning the Death Penalty for a Capital Felony: OFA Fiscal Note," Office of Fiscal Analysis, www.cga.ct.gov/2009/FN/2009HB-06578-R000726-FN.htm.

60 Ibid.

61 Quoted in Mark Pazniokas, "On Politics: Judiciary Committee Finds Itself under Heat," *New York Times*, 27 March 2009 (www.nytimes.com/2009/03/ 29/nyregion/connecticut/29polct.html).

62 William Petit, "Testimony to Members of the Connecticut Senate Judiciary Committee, in Opposition to HB 6578, An Act Concerning the Penalty for a Capital Felony," 4 March 2009, www.cga.ct.gov/2009/JUDdata/Tmy/ 2009HB-06578-R000304-William%20Petit-TMY.PDF.

63 "Death Penalty Fact Sheet for Connecticut."

64 "Do Away with Death Penalty," *Hartford Courant*, 7 April 2009 (http:// articles.courant.com/2009-04-07/news/no-death-penalty.art.art_1_death-penalty-death-row-inmates-killers).

65 Connecticut General Assembly, House of Representatives, "House Session Transcript for 05/13/2009," 13 May 2009, http://search.cga.state.ct.us/ dtsearch_lpa.asp?cmd=getdoc&DocId=33195&Index=I%3A\zindex\2009 &HitCount=15&hits=1a18+28f8+2ae6+3979+51d4+599b+7478+7ddf+7de b+9f63+a2ef+b0a9+b0b0+c65e+df5b+&hc=30767&req=isn&Item=298. All the quotes in the text from this debate in the House come from the same source.

66 "State Needs Effective Death Penalty," *New Haven Register*, 31 May 2009 (www .nhregister.com/articles/2009/05/31/opinion/doc4a2085654b50d497172111 .txt); "Senate Session Transcript for 05/21/2009," Connecticut General Assembly, Senate, http://search.cga.state.ct.us/dtsearch_lpa.asp?cmd=getdoc& DocId=33319&Index=I%3A\zindex\2009&HitCount=2&hits=3993+12758+ &hc=6219&req=con&Item=451.

67 "Senate Session Transcript for 05/21/2009."

68 Ibid.; Jon Lender, "Death Penalty Abolition Gets Final Legislative Approval in Senate," Courant.com, 22 May 2009 (http://blogs.courant.com/capitol_watch/2009/05/death-penalty-abolition-gets-f.html).

69 "Senate Session Transcript for 05/21/2009." All the quotes in the text from this debate in the Senate come from the same source.

70 "State Needs Effective Death Penalty."

71 Patricia Cook, "Cutting Death Penalty Could Save Money," NorwichBulletin .com, 8 November 2009 (www.norwichbulletin.com/opinions/letters/x80 1095128/Cutting-death-penalty-could-save-money).

72 Christopher Keating, "House Debates Death Penalty on 4th Anniv. of Michael Ross," CapitolWatch: Connecticut Politics, *Courant.com*, 13 May 2009. Available at http://blogs.courant.com/capitol_watch/2009/05/house-debates-death-penalty-on.html.

73 "Connecticut Bishops Ask Governor to Support Death Penalty Repeal," *Catholic News Service*, 2 June 2009 (www.catholicnews.com/data/stories/cns/0902530.htm).

74 "Governor Rell Vetoes HB 6578, an Act Concerning the Death Penalty for a Capital Felony," Office of Governor M. Jodi Rell, 5 June 2009, www.ct.gov/governorrell/cwp/view.asp?A=3675&Q=441204. All the quotes in the text from this veto come from the same source.

75 Jon Lender, "76% Back Death Penalty for Hayes, New Poll Shows," Courant .com, 13 October 2010 (http://articles.courant.com/2010–10–13/news/hc-death-penalty-poll-1013–20101013_1_death-penalty-issue-death-penalty-favor-capital-punishment).

76 Quoted in "Connecticut Governor Candidates Spar over Death Penalty," FoxNews.com, 5 October 2010 (www.foxnews.com/politics/2010/10/05/connecticut-governor-candidates-spar-debate/).

77 Quoted in ibid. See also Susan Haigh, "Malloy, Foley Fight over Connecticut's Death Penalty," NorwichBulletin.com, 5 October 2010 (www.norwichbulletin.com/carousel/x244486709/Malloy-Foley-fight-over-Connecticuts-death-penalty#axzz10kmFvEZJ).

78 Daniela Altimari, "Senators Withdraw Support for Death Penalty Repeal," Courant.com, 11 May 2001 (http://articles.courant.com/2011–05–11/community/hc-death-penalty-bill-doa-0512–20110511_1_death-penalty-repeal-bill-petit-case/2).

8. NEAR MISSES IN NEBRASKA AND MARYLAND

1 "State by State Database," Death Penalty Information Center, 2011, www .deathpenaltyinfo.org/state_by_state.

2 Lincoln (Nebraska) City Libraries, "Starkweather: Murder on the Plains, 1957–58," www.lincolnlibraries.org/reference/starkweather_case.htm.

3 "Inmates Sentenced to Death Row in Nebraska," Nebraska Department of Correctional Services, 2011, www.corrections.nebraska.gov/pdf/DRHistory .pdf.

4 Sara Catania, "The Importance of Being Ernie," *Mother Jones*, January–February 2006 (http://motherjones.com/politics/2006/01/importance-being-ernie).

5 Ernie Chambers, interview by Ed Gordon, "Sen. Ernie Chambers, a Solo Act in Nebraska," NPR, 24 January 2006 (www.npr.org/templates/story/story .php?storyId=5170002).

6 Ibid.

7 Catania, "The Importance of Being Ernie."

8 John F. Galliher, James L. McCartney, and Barbara E. Baum, "Nebraska's Marijuana Law: A Case of Unexpected Legislative Innovation," *Law and Society Review* 8 (Spring 1974): 441–56.

9 Nebraska Unicameral Legislature, Judiciary Committee hearing on LB262, 28 February 1979, 4052.

10 Nebraska Unicameral Legislature, floor debate on LB262, 26 April, 1979, 4053. All the quotes in this paragraph from the debate come from the same source.

11 Ibid., 4992.

12 Ibid., 4982.

13 Nebraska Unicameral Legislature, *Legislative Journal of the State of Nebraska, Eighty-Sixth Legislature, First Session* (Lincoln: State of Nebraska, 1979) 2:2289-90.

14 Ibid., 2:2302.

15 Quoted in Jason Gertzen, "Death Penalty Foes Watch Support Slip: Death Penalty Chronology," *Omaha World Herald*, 20 January 1992.

16 Quoted in ibid.

17 "The ABA Calls for a Temporary Halt on Executions," American Bar Association Death Penalty Moratorium Implementation Project, 2011, www .americanbar.org/groups/individual_rights/projects/death_penalty_ moratorium_implementation_project/about_us.html.

18 Sunny Kaplan, "Illinois, Nebraska Study Death Penalty as Others Quicken Use," *Stateline*, 23 September 1999 (www.stateline.org/live/ViewPage.action ?siteNodeId=136&languageId=1&contentId=13798).

19 Quoted in Dirk Johnson, "Legislature of Nebraska Votes Pause in Executions," *New York Times*, 21 May 1999 (www.nytimes.com/1999/05/21/us/ legislature-of-nebraska-votes-pause-in-executions.html).

20 Associated Press, "Nebraska Execution Moratorium OKd," *Los Angeles Times*, 21 May 1999 (http://articles.latimes.com/1999/may/21/news/mn-39466); "A Brief History of the American Bar Association Section of Individual Rights and Responsibilities," American Bar Association, www.americanbar .org/groups/individual_rights/about_us/history/dp2.html.

21 Henry Weinstein, "Nebraska Governor Vetoes Moratorium on Executions," *Los Angeles Times*, 27 May 1999 (http://articles.latimes.com/1999/may/27/ news/mn-41554); Greg Chesmore, "Neb. Won't Halt Death Penalty," *National Catholic Register*, 13 June 1999 (www.ncregister.com/site/article/neb_ wont_halt_death_penalty/).

22 Chesmore, "Neb. Won't Halt Death Penalty."

23 Quoted in ibid.

24 Quoted in ibid.

25 David C. Baldus, George Woodworth, Gary L. Young, and Aaron M. Christ, "The Disposition of Nebraska Capital and Non-Capital Homicide Cases (1973–1999): A Legal and Empirical Analysis; Amended July 26, 2002" (Lincoln: State of Nebraska, 4 October 2002; www.ncc.ne.gov/pdf/others/ other_homicide/Rev_v1.pdf), 14.

26 Pam Belluck, "Nebraska Is Said to Use Death Penalty Unequally," *New York Times*, 2 August 2001 (www.nytimes.com/2001/08/02/us/nebraska-is-said-to-use-death-penalty-unequally.html?src=pm).

27 Nebraska Unicameral Legislature, Judiciary Committee, Public Hearing on HB 476, 31 January 2007 (www.nebraskalegisature.gov/bills/view_bill .php?DocumentID=630), 2.

28 Ibid., 3.

29 Ibid., 7.

30 Ibid., 15.

31 Ibid., 18.

32 Ibid., 20–21.

33 Ibid., 1–30.

34 JoAnne Young, "Senators Take Up Matter of Life, Death," *Lincoln Journal Star*, 20 March 2007.

35 Nebraska Unicameral Legislature, Judiciary Committee vote on LB476 (www.nebraskalegislature.gov/bills/view_bill.php?DocumentID=630), 31.

36 Nebraska Unicameral Legislature, Floor Debate, 19 March 2007 (www .legislature.ne.gov.FloorDocs/100/PDF/Transcripts/Floordebate/r1day48 .pdf), 4.

37 Ibid., 21.

38 Ibid., 15.

39 Ibid., 18.

40 Nebraska Unicameral Legislature, Floor Debate on LB476, 20 March 2007 (http://www.legislature.ne.gov/FloorDocs/100/PDF/Transcripts/Floor debate/r1day48.pdf), 12.

41 Ibid., 16.

42 Ibid., 26.

43 Nebraska Unicameral Legislature, *Legislative Journal of the State of Nebraska, One Hundredth Legislature, First Session* (Lincoln: State of Nebraska, 1979), 1:909–10.

44 Quoted in Young, "Death Penalty Repeal Fails."

45 Quoted in Anna Jo Bratton, "Senator: Next Year Could Be 'Best Chance' to Repeal Death Penalty," JournalStar.com, 24 December 2007 (http://journalstar .com/news/local/govt-and-politics/article_c38a8761-d82a-5909–974a-e8ec112b0c69.html).

46 Bob Reeves, "Sunday Service to Focus on Abolition of the Death Penalty," JournalStar.com, 9 November 2007 (http://journalstar.com/lifestyles/faith-and-values/article_c6522e71–3722–53c6-a0e8-ba55e40edd56.html).

47 JoAnne Young, "Bill to Repeal Death Penalty Would Go to Full Legislature," JournalStar.com, 6 February 2008 (http://journalstar.com/news/local/govt-and-politics/article_01ebf3a8–0247–5423–8cb3–682f86c1d47e.html).

48 JoAnne Young, "Senators Kill Death Penalty," *Lincoln Journal Star*, 26 March 2008.

49 Quoted in ibid.

50 Quoted in Leslie Reed, "Death Penalty Stays on Books," *Omaha World-Herald*, 26 March 2008.

51 John Gramlich, "Nebraska Legislator Fights Death Penalty to the End," Stateline.org, 17 August 2007 (www.stateline.org/live/details/story?content Id=232994).

52 Associated Press, "Nebraska Court Deems Electric Chair 'Torture,' Ends Its Use in State Executions," *FoxNews.com*, 8 February 2008 (www.foxnews.com/ story/0,2933,330129,00.html).

53 JoAnne Young, "Senators to Debate Death Penalty Repeal," JournalStar .com, 20 January 2010 (http://journalstar.com/news/local/govt-and-politics/ article_05356a0c-0569–11df-a667–001cc4c002e0.html).

54 Anna Jo Bratton, "Nebraska Lawmakers Reject Death-Penalty Repeal," theindependent.com, 19 May 2009 (http://theindependent.com/articles/ 2009/05/19/news/local/doc4a12fb9a87cef305990392.txt).

55 Young, "Senators to Debate Death Penalty Repeal."

56 Paul Hammel, "How Expensive Is the Death Penalty?," Omaha.com, 21 January 2010 (www.omaha.com/article/20100121/NEWS01/701219867).

57 Robynn Tysver, "Moore Execution Postponed," *Omaha World-Herald*, 25 May 2011 (www.omaha.com/article/20110525/NEWS97/110529819/32).

58 Michael Millemann and Gary W. Christopher, "Preferring White Lives: The Racial Administration of the Death Penalty in Maryland," *University of Maryland Law Journal of Race, Religion, Gender & Class*, 1 (2005): 1 (http://digitalcommons:law.umaryland.edu/cgi/viewcontent.cgi?article =1086&context=fac_pubs&sei-redir=1#search=%22Preferring+White+Lives %22).

59 Art. 27, § 413, Annotated Code of Maryland; "Capital Punishment History: Maryland's Death Penalty: A Synopsis," Maryland Department of Public Safety and Correctional Services, 2011, www.dpscs.state.md.us/publicinfo/ capitalpunishment/synopsis.shtml; Most Rev. Edwin F. O'Brien, Most Rev. Donald W. Wuerl, Most Rev. W. Francis Malooly, "Statement on the Recommendations of the Maryland Commission on Capital Punishment" (Annapolis: Maryland Catholic Conference, 12 December 2008; www.mdcathcon .org/main.asp?page=1194&c=1105).

60 "Chronology of the Death Penalty in Maryland," Maryland Citizens against State Executions, 2011, www.mdcase.org/node/40#1978.

61 "State by State Database"; "Executions in the U.S. 1608–2002: The ESPY File Executions by State," Death Penalty Information Center, 2011, www .deathpenaltyinfo.org/documents/ESPYstate.pdf.

62 "State by State Database."

63 "Searchable Execution Database," Death Penalty Information Center, 2011, www.deathpenaltyinfo.org/executions.

64 "Executions in the U.S. 1608–2002."

65 Millemann and Christopher, "Preferring White Lives," 1.

66 "Executions in the U.S. 1608–2002."

67 "Capital Punishment History"; "Searchable Execution Database."

68 Julie Bykowicz and Jennifer McMenamin, "Death Penalty Review Possible," *Baltimore Sun*, 22 October 2004.

69 "MD Inmates Removed from Death Row (since 1978)," Maryland Citizens against State Executions, 2011, www.mdcase.org/node/24#removed.

70 "Current Death Row Population by Race," Death Penalty Information Center, 2011, www.deathpenaltyinfo.org/race-death-row-inmates-executed-1976 #inmaterace.

71 Millemann and Christopher, "Preferring White Lives," 2.

72 Raymond Paternoster et al., "An Empirical Analysis of Maryland's Death Sentencing System with Respect to the Influence of Race and Legal Jurisdiction: Final Report," www.newsdesk.umd.edu/pdf/finalrep.pdf, 1–2.

73 Ibid., 3.

74 Quoted in ibid.

75 Ibid., 36–37.

76 "Searchable Execution Database"; "State by State: Maryland," *Deadline the Movie*, 2010, http://deadlinethemovie.com/state/MD/index.php.

77 "Searchable Execution Database."

78 Lisa Rein, "Anticipated Death Penalty Protests Prompted Spying; Md. Police Chief Says Surveillance Showed Poor Judgment," *Washington Post*, 26 July 2008 (www.washingtonpost.com/wp-dyn/content/article/2008/07/25/AR 2008072502163.html).

79 John Wagner and Eric Rich, "Ire over O'Malley's Inaction on Executions," *Washington Post*, 8 July 2007 (www.washingtonpost.com/wp-dyn/content/ article/2007/07/07/AR2007070701056.html).

80 Julie Bykowicz, "Narrow Majority of Md. Senators Oppose Repeal of Death Penalty, Survey Reveals," *Baltimore Sun*, 17 February 2009 (www.baltimore sun.com/news/maryland/bal-te.md.penalty17feb17,0,6382529.story).

81 "Thank the General Assembly for Passing Death Penalty Commission," Maryland Citizens against State Executions, 2010, www.mdcase.org/node/97.

82 Maryland Commission on Capital Punishment, "Final Report to the General Assembly," 12 December 2008, www.goccp.maryland.gov/capital-punishment/ documents/death-penalty-commission-final-report.pdf, 10.

83 Ibid., 3.

84 Ibid., 22.

85 Ibid., 44.

86 John Roman et al., "The Cost of the Death Penalty in Maryland," Urban Institute Justice Policy Center, March 2008, www.urban.org/UploadedPDF/ 411625_md_death_penalty.pdf.

87 Maryland Commission on Capital Punishment, "Final Report to the General Assembly," 23.

88 "Death Penalty Review," *Baltimore Sun*, 1 August 2008.

89 "Capital Punishment, Fatally Flawed," *Baltimore Sun*, 25 September 2008.

90 "Testimony before the Senate Judicial Proceedings Committee on the Repeal of Capital Punishment in Maryland," Office of Governor Martin O'Malley, 18 February 2009, www.governor.maryland.gov/speeches/090218c .asp; "O'Malley Testifies against Death Penalty," wbaltv.com, 18 February 2009 (www.wbaltv.com/r/18743978/detail.html).

91 Quoted in Ian Urbina, "Citing Cost, States Consider End to Death Penalty," *New York Times*, 24 February 2009 (www.nytimes.com/2009/02/25/us/ 25death.html).

92 Bykowicz, "Narrow Majority of Md. Senators Oppose Repeal of Death Penalty."

93 Julie Bykowicz, "O'Malley Vows to Work to End Death Penalty," *Baltimore Sun*, 16 January 2009 (www.baltimoresun.com/news/maryland/politics/bal-session0116,0,5845658.story).

94 Michael Frost, "O'Malley Calls for Tighter Restrictions on Death Penalty," *Southern Maryland Online*, 18 March 2009 (http://somd.com/news/headlines/2009/9642.shtml); Bykowicz, "Narrow Majority of Md. Senators Oppose Repeal of Death Penalty."

95 Julie Bykowicz, "Vote Urged on Death Penalty" *Baltimore Sun*, 19 February 2009 (http://articles.baltimoresun.com/2009–02–19/news/0902180138_1_repeal-capital-punishment-death-penalty).

96 Criminal Law-Death Penalty-Evidence, Senate Bill 279, Chapter 186, 7 May 2009, http://mlis.state.md.us/2009rs/chapters_noln/Ch_186_sb0279T.pdf; Julie Bykowicz, "Death Penalty Repeal Unlikely, Senate President Says," *Baltimore Sun*, 15 March 2011 (http://weblogs.baltimoresun.com/news/local/politics/2011/03/death_penalty_repeal_unlikely.html).

97 Quoted in Frost, "O'Malley Calls for Tighter Restrictions on Death Penalty."

98 "Maryland Election Results 2010: Martin O'Malley Beats Bob Ehrlich in a Rematch for Governor," *Washington Post*, 2 November 2010 (www.washingtonpost.com/wp-dyn/content/article/2010/11/02/AR2010110203248.html).

99 "Death Row in the Free State," *Baltimore City Paper*, 28 September 2011 (http://citypaper.com/news/death-row-in-the-free-state-1.1209513).

100 Brian Evans, "Maryland Death Penalty Meets Globalization," *Human Rights Now: The Amnesty International USA Web Log*, 18 February 2011 (http://blog.amnestyusa.org/deathpenalty/maryland-death-penalty-meets-globalization/).

101 "Put the General Assembly on Notice!," Maryland Citizens against State Executions, 2011, www.mdcase.org/node/196.

9. DE FACTO ABOLITION STATES

1 Guy Kovner, "Is Death Row Worth the Cost?," *Press Democrat*, 23 October 2009 (www.pressdemocrat.com/article/20091023/ARTICLES/910239890); Steve Mills, "In Many States, Cost Is Slowly Killing Death Penalty," *Chicago Tribune*, 8 March 2009 (http://articles.chicagotribune.com/2009–03–08/news/0903070157_1_death-penalty-death-row-capital-cases); Natasha Minsker, "Need to Trim Corrections Spending, Governor? Stop Wasting Money on the Death Penalty!," *California Progress Report*, 11 January 2010 (www.californiaprogressreport.com/site/?q=node/7325); Donald G. Pellinen, "Reducing Costs," *Contra Costa Times*, 13 January 2010 (www.contracostatimes.com); "Death Penalty Too Costly," *Recordnet.com*, 7 May 2009 (www.recordnet.com/apps/pbcs.dll/article?AID=/20090507/A_OPINION

01/905070313/-1/A_OPINION); Rone Tempest, "Death Row Often Means a Long Life," *Los Angeles Times*, 6 March 6 2005 (http://articles.latimes .com/2005/mar/06/local/me-deathpen6); "California's Death Penalty Needs Substantial Reforms," *Mercury News*, 7 January 2010 (www.mercurynews .com/); Carol J. Williams, "Death Penalty Is Considered a Boon by Some California Inmates," *Los Angeles Times*, 11 November 2009 (http://articles .latimes.com/2009/nov/11/local/me-deathrow11); Carol J. Williams, "Death Row Foes Now Fight the Cost of Execution," *Los Angeles Times*, 30 June 2009 (http://articles.latimes.com/2009/jun/30/local/me-executions30).

2 Pellinen, "Reducing Costs."

3 Quoted in Tempest, "Death Row Often Means a Long Life."

4 Quoted in Williams, "Death Row Foes Now Fight the Cost of Execution."

5 Kovner, "Is Death Row Worth the Cost?"

6 Natasha Minsker, "California's Death Penalty: Costly, Inefficient and Need-ing Safeguards," *Capitol Weekly*, 30 December 2009 (www.capitolweekly .net/article.php?xid=yirmgmm5jb5r39); Kovner, "Is Death Row Worth the Cost?"; Minsker, "California's Dysfunctional Death Penalty"; Min-sker, "Need to Trim Corrections Spending"; Jon Streeter, Bill Hing, and Diane Bellas, "Replace Death Penalty with Permanent Imprisonment," SFGate.com, 25 June 2009 (http://articles.sfgate.com/2009–06–25/opinion/ 17209066_1_death-penalty-penalty-cases-wrongful); Williams, "Death Row Foes Now Fight the Cost of Execution."

7 Minsker, "California's Dysfunctional Death Penalty"; Streeter, Hing, and Bellas, "Replace Death Penalty with Permanent Imprisonment."

8 Michael Hersek, former California public defender, telephone interview with John F. Galliher, 27 January 2011.

9 David Anderson, California attorney in private practice, telephone interview with John F. Galliher, 31 January 2011.

10 Hersek interview.

11 R. H. Dann, "Abolition and Reinstatement of the Death Penalty in Ore-gon," in *The Death Penalty in America: Current Controversies*, ed. Hugo Adam Bedau, 2nd ed. (New York: Oxford University Press, 1977), 343–51.

12 "State by State Database," Death Penalty Information Center, 2011, www .deathpenaltyinfo.org/state_by_state.

13 Associated Press, "Death Row Opponents Call It Quits," *Register-Guard*, 28 February 2002; "Repealing the Death Penalty," *Catholic Sentinel*, 3 Sep-tember 2009 (www.catholicsentinel.org/); Mary Mooney, "Can Oregon Af-ford the Death Penalty?," OregonLive.com, 18 April 2009 (www.oregonlive .com/news/index.ssf/2009/04/can_oregon_afford_the_death_pe.html); "The Economics of the Death Penalty," Oregon Public Broadcasting,

23 November 2009 (www.opb.org/thinkoutloud/shows/high-costs-death-penalty/newest-first); Kathleen Pugh, "Point-Counterpoint: Death Penalty in Oregon; Opposed," OregonLive.com, 22 April 2009 (www.oregonlive.com/opinion/index.ssf/2009/04/pointcounterpoint_death_penalt.html).

14 "Repealing the Death Penalty."

15 Associated Press, "Death Row Opponents Call It Quits"; Mooney, "Can Oregon Afford the Death Penalty?"; James Pitkin, "Killing Time: Dead Men Waiting on Oregon's Death Row," *Willamette Week*, 23 January 2008 (http://wweek.com/editorial/3411/10288/). See also "Repealing the Death Penalty"; Aaron Clark, "Oregon Lawmakers Consider Moratorium on Death Penalty," *Argus Observer*, 18 March 2007 (www.argusobserver.com/articles/2007/03/18/news/news10.txt); "The Economics of the Death Penalty."

16 "Repealing the Death Penalty"; Pitkin, "Killing Time"; Mooney, "Can Oregon Afford the Death Penalty?"

17 Quoted in Mooney, "Can Oregon Afford the Death Penalty?"

18 Pugh, "Point-Counterpoint: Death Penalty in Oregon; Opposed."

19 Pitkin, "Killing Time."

20 Quoted in Mooney, "Can Oregon Afford the Death Penalty?"

21 Ibid.

22 "Repealing the Death Penalty."

23 "The Economics of the Death Penalty."

24 Pitkin, "Killing Time."

25 Quoted in ibid.

26 Ibid.

27 Quoted in ibid.

28 John F. Galliher, Gregory Ray, and Brent Cook, "Abolition and Reinstatement of Capital Punishment during the Progressive Era and Early 20th Century," *Journal of Criminal Law and Criminology* 83, no. 3 (1992): 538–76.

29 "State by State Database."

30 Rober F. Utter, "Washington State Must Abandon the Death Penalty," *Seattle Times*, 11 March 2009 (http://seattletimes.nwsource.com/html/opinion/2008843232_opinb12utter.html).

31 Abigail Goldman, "Debating the Cost of the Death Penalty," *Las Vegas Sun*, 4 March 2009. See also "Assembly Bill No. 190—Assemblymen Anderson, Leslie, Ohrenschall, Segerblom, Buckley, Atkinson, Claborn, Hogan, Horne, McClain, Munford and Pierce," 18 February 2009, http://media.lasvegassun.com/media/pdfs/2009/03/03/AB190.pdf.

32 Goldman, "Debating the Cost of the Death Penalty."

33 Ibid.

34 Cy Ryan, "Death Penalty a Costly Proposition," *Las Vegas Sun*, 9 July 2008 (www.lasvegassun.com/news/2008/jul/09/death-penalty-costly-proposition/).

35 Jane Ann Morrison, "Using Cost Angle Is Just a Backdoor Way to Get What Death Penalty Foes Want," *Law Vegas Review-Journal*, 28 March 2009 (www.lvrj.com/news/42047162.html).

36 Associated Press, "Death Penalty Study Endorsed," 8NewsNow.com, 15 April 2009 (www.8newsnow.com/Global/story.asp?S=10192459).

37 "Death Penalty Cases with Status," Idaho Department of Correction, 2011, www.idoc.idaho.gov/facts/Death_Penalty_Cases.pdf.

38 Quoted in Christopher Smith, "Death Sentences Often Imposed, Seldom Carried Out," *Moscow-Pullman Daily News*, 23–24 July 2005 (http://news.google.com/newspapers?id=S9gyAAAAIBAJ&sjid=_o8FAAAAIBAJ&pg=1039,2285397&dq=death+penalty+idaho+cost&hl=en).

39 Mike Murad, "Idaho Executions Are Expensive," Klewtv.com, 2 November 2009 (www.klewtv.com/news/local/68729272.html). See also Associated Press, "Death Penalty Cases Stagger Idaho Counties," *Moscow Pullman Daily News*, 20–21 September 2003; "Our View: Case Illustrates the High Costs of the Death Penalty," *Idaho Statesman*, 19 December 2008 (www.pfadp.org/index.php?option=com_content&task=view&id=198&Itemid=71); Patrick Orr, "Idaho Prosecutors Opting Not to Seek Death Penalty," Idaho Statesman.com, 3 November 2009 (www.idahostatesman.com/robertman will/story/959060.html); Chuck Oxley, "Senator Introduces Bill to Fix Idaho Death Sentence," *Moscow-Pullman Daily News*, 9 January 2003; Dan Popkey, "Judge Gives Thoughtful Review on the Death Penalty," *Idaho Statesman*, 13 November 2005 (www.idahostatesman.com/downwinders/story/37566.html?storylink=mirelated); Smith, "Death Sentences Often Imposed"; Marty Trillhaase, "Patching the Death Penalty," *Idaho Falls Post Register*, 19 March 2003 (http://idahoptv.org/).

40 Murad, "Idaho Executions Are Expensive."

41 "Our View: Case Illustrates the High Costs of the Death Penalty."

42 Orr, "Idaho Prosecutors Opting Not to Seek Death Penalty."

43 Quoted in Smith, "Death Sentences Often Imposed."

44 Oxley, "Senator Introduces Bill to Fix Idaho Death Sentence."

45 Trillhaase, "Patching the Death Penalty."

46 Quoted in Smith, "Death Sentences Often Imposed."

47 "Death Penalty Cases with Status."

48 LaMont Anderson, Idaho Senior Deputy Attorney General, telephone interview with John F. Galliher, 31 January 2011.

49 Jim Oppedahl, "Montana Can't Afford the Death Penalty," Helenair.com,

2 February 2009 (http://helenair.com/news/opinion/readers_alley/article_c1726b29-d0e5-5f6d-a709-8a110c876ee7.html).

50 John Connor, "Death Penalty Drains Justice System Resources," *Billings Gazette*, 22 March 2009.

51 Quoted in Dan Testa, "Montana Legislature: Montana Senators Consider Abolishing Death Penalty," *New West Politics*, 7 February 2007 (www.newwest .net/index.php/topic/article/montana_senators_consider_abolishing_death_penalty/C70/L37/).

52 Montana Abolition Coalition, "Current and Previous Death Row Inmates: Post-Furman Convictions," 2009, www.mtabolitionco.org/subpage3.html; Death Penalty Information Center, "Death Row Inmates by State and Size of Death Row by Year," 11 January 2011, www.deathpenaltyinfo.org/death-row-inmates-state-and-size-death-row-year; Death Penalty Information Center, "Number of Executions by State and Region Since 1976," 29 September 2011, www.deathpenaltyinfo.org/number-executions-state-and-region-1976.

53 Jennifer McKee, "The Death Penalty in Montana History," *Independent Record*, 9 August 2006 (http://helenair.com/news/state-and-regional/article_4bdb7dc7-c215-5670-9305-be9493b96125.html).

54 Martin Kaste, "Opponents Focus on Cost in Death Penalty Debate," NPR, 1 April 2009 (www.npr.org/templates/story/story.php?storyId=102570588); Montana Legislature, "Look Up bill Information," (http://wwwlaws.leg .mt.gov/laws09/law0203w$.startup).

55 Mike Dennison, "House Panel Votes Down Bill to Abolish the Death Penalty," Helenair.com, 30 March 2009 (http://helenair.com/news/local/govt-and-politics/article_3a94ffe6-7edf-52cd-86fa-030c896a33a1.html).

56 Quoted in Paul Riede, "Costly Penalty: States Turn Against Capital Punishment Because of Its Price," Syracuse.com, 3 March 2009 (http://blog.syracuse .com/opinion/2009/03/costly_penalty_states_turn_aga.html).

57 "Wyoming's Death Row Down to Just One," *Capital Defense Weekly*, 16 February 2008 (www.capitaldefenseweekly.com/blog/?p=2814).

58 Kevin McCullen, "Death Row Costs State Too Much, Says Doomed Man," *Rocky Mountain News*, 21 January 1992.

59 Jessica Lowell, "SF 20 Gives Judges, Juries Alternative to Death Penalty," *Wyoming Tribune-Eagle*, 13 January 2001.

60 Associated Press, "Plan to Eliminate Death Penalty Given Initial OK," *Summit Daily News*, 15 April 2009 (www.summitdaily.com/article/20090415/NEWS/904159975/1078&ParentProfile=1055).

61 Ed Quillen, "The Death Penalty's Costs," DenverPost.com, 1 March 2009 (www.denverpost.com/opinion/ci_11795714).

62 Kirk Johnson, "Death Penalty Repeal Fails in Colorado," *New York Times*, 4 May 2009 (www.nytimes.com/2009/05/05/us/05colorado.html).

63 Jennifer Brown, "Cold-Case Pursuits vs. Death Penalty: Families of the Slain Urge Funding Shift," *Denver Post*, 13 June 2007.

64 Michael J. Carter, "ACLU: Death Penalty 'Tax' Costs California Billions," Finalcall.com, 20 May 2008 (www.finalcall.com/artman/publish/article_4731.shtml).

65 Patrick D. Gallagher, "Who's Confused?," *Denver Post*, 16 July 2002.

66 "Time to Kill the Death Penalty," *Greeley Tribune*, 30 April 2009 (www.greeleytribune.com/article/20090430/OPINION/904309995/1029/NONE&parentprofile=1025).

67 Dean Toda, "Panel Advances Bill to Abolish Death Penalty," *Colorado Springs Gazette*, 30 April 2009.

68 Associated Press, "Plan to Eliminate Death Penalty."

69 Carl Illescas, "Death-Penalty Pursuit Puts DA under Fire," *Denver Post*, 29 February 2008.

70 Quoted in Kyle Henley, "Budget Cuts May Kill Business Tax Rebate," *Colorado Springs Gazette*, 23 January 2003.

71 "Dispensing Justice," *Colorado Springs Gazette*, 26 January 2000.

72 Stephanie Hindson, Hillary Potter, and Michael L. Radelet, "Race, Gender, Region and Death Sentencing in Colorado, 1980–1999," *Colorado Law Review* 77 (2006): 549–94.

73 Ibid., 580.

74 Ibid., 582.

75 John F. Galliher and Linda Basilick, "Utah's Liberal Drug Laws: Structural Foundations and Triggering Events," *Social Problems* 26, no. 3 (1979): 284–97.

76 "State by State Database."

77 Jacob Hancock, "Utah Bucking U.S. Death Penalty Trend," *Deseret News*, 3 May 2009 (www.deseretnews.com/article/705301233/Utah-bucking-US-death-penalty-trend.html).

78 Ibid.

79 Mathew Brown, "Firing Squad Execution," *Pittsburgh Post-Gazette*, 27 January 1996.

80 Quoted in Ashby Jones, "Utah Gearing Up for Its First Firing-Squad Execution Since '96," *Wall Street Journal*, 8 June 2010 (http://blogs.wsj.com/law/2010/06/08/utah-gearing-up-for-its-first-firing-squad-execution-since-96/).

81 Quoted in Peggy Fletcher Stack, "Coalition Seeks Alternatives to Death Penalty," *Salt Lake Tribune*, 24 April 2010 (www.sltrib.com/sltrib/home/49458081–73/death-penalty-gardner-burdell.html.csp).

82 Pamela Manson, "Money Driving Capital Punishment Debate," *Salt Lake Tribune*, 14 June 2010 (www.sltrib.com/sltrib/home/49749546–73/death-costs-capital-penalty.html.csp).

83 Melissa Payne, "Cost of Death Penalty in Turner County Case," KDLT.com, 24 February 2010 (www.kdlt.com/index.php?option=com_content&task=view&id=1035&Itemid=57).

84 "Donald Moeller Shows Death Penalty Costs Too Much," *Madville Times*, 19 January 2010 (http://madvilletimes.blogspot.com/2010/01/donald-moeller-shows-death-penalty.html).

85 Quoted in Dan Jorgensen, "Economics of Executions," KELOLAND.com, 18 January 2010 (www.keloland.com/NewsDetai16162.cfm?ID=95352).

86 "Death Row Diminished," *Philadelphia Inquirer*, 4 January 2010; Bobby Kerlik, "Pennsylvania Maintains Nation's Fourth-Largest Death Row," *Pittsburgh Tribune-Review*, 18 December 2009 (www.pittsburghlive.com/x/pittsburghtrib/news/state/s_658347.html); "Several States Abandon Death Penalty Because of Cost," WGAL.com, 31 March 2009 (www.wgal.com/money/19050326/detail.html). See also Paul Carpenter, "The Death Penalty Can Be Justified," *Morning Call*, 13 January 2010 (www.mcall.com/); "Pa.'s Death Penalty; No Return," *Philadelphia Inquirer*, 16 October 2007 (www.pamoratorium.org/documents/Philadelphia_Inquirer_101607.pdf).

87 "Death Row Diminished; "Pa.'s Death Penalty."

88 Kristen Dalton, "Another View: Pennsylvania Needs a New Look at Death Penalty," *Morning Call*, 8 April 2009 (http://articles.mcall.com/2009–04–08/news/4348113_1_row-inmates-wrongful-executions-death-penalty-information-center); Ben Waxman, "Death Row Dollars," WHYY, 17 April 2008 (www.whyy.org/news/itsourmoney/20080417_death_row_dollar.htm); "Several States Abandon Death Penalty Because of Cost"; Robert Zaller, "Death Penalty Expensive, Unjust," *Triangle*, 13 March 2009 (http://media.www.thetriangle.org/media/storage/paper689/news/2009/03/13/EdOp/Death.Penalty.Expensive.Unjust-3671527.shtml).

89 "Several States Abandon Death Penalty Because of Cost."

90 Zaller, "Death Penalty Expensive."

91 Dalton, "Another View"; "Death Row Diminished."

92 Marshall Dayan, chair of Pennsylvanians for Alternatives to the Death Penalty, telephone interview with John F. Galliher, 27 January 2011.

93 R. G. Dunlop, "Kentucky's Troubled Death-Penalty System Lets Cases Languish for Decades," Courier-Journal.com, 7 November 2009 (www.courier-journal.com/article/20091107/NEWS01/911080316/Kentucky%5C-s-troubled-death-penalty-system-lets-cases-languish-for-decades); Mark R.

Chellgren, "Death Penalty Study in House Budget," *Park City Daily News*, 23 February 2005.

94 Chellgren, "Death Penalty Study in House Budget."

95 Ernie Lewis, "The Death Penalty: A Failed Social Policy," Kypost.com, 7 January 2008 (http://www2.kypost.com/dpp/news/The-Death-Penalty:-A-Failed-Social-Policy).

96 Jane Chiles and Rev. Patrick Delahanty, "Scales Tip against the Death Penalty: Sentiment Growing," *Lexington Herald-Leader*, 13 January 2008.

97 Quoted in Chellgren, "Death Penalty Study in House Budget."

98 R. G. Dunlop, "Killer's Appeals Drag on 29 Years," Courier-Journal.com, 7 November 2009 (www.courier-journal.com/article/20091107/NEWS01/911080317).

99 Dunlop, "Kentucky's Troubled Death-Penalty System Lets Cases Languish for Decades."

100 Quoted in ibid.

101 Ibid.

102 Chellgren, "Death Penalty Study in House Budget."

103 Dunlop, "Kentucky's Troubled Death-Penalty System Lets Cases Languish for Decades."

104 Lewis, "The Death Penalty."

105 Dunlop, "Kentucky's Troubled Death-Penalty System Lets Cases Languish for Decades."

106 Galliher, Ray, and Cook, "Abolition and Reinstatement."

107 "Death Sentences in the United States from 1977 to 2008" (Washington: Death Penalty Information Center, 2010; www.deathpenaltyinfo.org/death-sentences-united-states-1977–2008).

108 "State by State Database."

109 Matt Pulle, "Death, Thou Shalt Die," *Nashville Scene*, 15 January 2004 (www.nashvillescene.com/2004–01–15/stories/death-thou-shalt-die)/.

110 Josh Tinley, "The Price of Death," *Nashville Scene*, 31 October 2002.

111 Quoted in ibid.

112 Quoted in Sarah Kelly, "Dead Again," *Nashville News*, 14 February 2008 (www.nashvillescene.com/nashville/dead-again/Content?oid=1196000).

113 "We Can't Be Too Careful," *Memphis Commercial Appeal*, 25 January 2009 (www.commercialappeal.com/news/2009/jan/25/editorial-we-cant-be-too-careful/).

114 David Spates, "Therefore I Am," *Crossville Chronicle*, 7 January 2008 (www.crossville-chronicle.com/opinion/local_story_007190736.html).

115 Steve Reddick, "Guest Column: Death Penalty Club Is Not One We Need to Join," *Oak Ridger*, 22 March 2000 (www.oakridger.com).

116 "We Can't be Too Careful."

117 Associated Press, "Study Suggests Uniform Rules for Death Penalty Cases," *Elizabethton Star*, 14 July 2004.

118 In the introduction to this chapter, we noted that Mississippi has carried out twelve executions. As noted, this figure was current as of 4 July 2010. However, one prisoner has been executed since then, bringing the total number of executions in the state to thirteen.

119 Charlie Mitchell, "Death Penalty Getting Costly in Mississippi," *Clarion-Ledger*, 6 November 2005 (www.cuadp.org/news/CL-20051108.htm).

120 Ibid.

121 Bill Rankin, "Mississippi County Sues to Get Legal Aid," *Atlanta Journal-Constitution*, 5 May 2003.

122 Ibid.

123 Mitchell, "Death Penalty Getting Costly in Mississippi."

124 Ibid.

125 Miriam Gohara and Sarah Geraghty, "In Mississippi, Two Systems of Justice: One for the Rich and One for the Poor," *New York Amsterdam News*, 19 June 2003.

126 Tim McGlone, "Study Finds High Risk of Executing Innocents," *Virginian-Pilot*, 12 February 2002.

127 Quoted in Williams, "Death Row Foes Now Fight the Cost of Execution."

128 William Yardley, "Oregon Governor Says He Will Block Executions," *New York Times*, 22 November 2011.

10. OPPOSITION IN THE SOUTH AND TEXAS

1 Michael J. Pfeifer, *Rough Justice: Lynching and American Society, 1874–1947* (Urbana: University of Illinois Press, 2004).

2 "Murder Rates Nationally and by State: Regional Murder Rates, 2001–2009" (Washington: Death Penalty Information Center, 2011; www.deathpenaltyinfo.org/murder-rates-nationally-and-state).

3 Quoted in John F. Galliher, Gregory Ray, and Brent Cook, "Abolition and Reinstatement of Capital Punishment during the Progressive Era and Early 20th Century," *Journal of Criminal Law and Criminology* 83, no. 3 (1992): 557.

4 Quoted in ibid., 558.

5 Quoted in ibid., 557.

6 "Searchable Execution Database," Death Penalty Information Center, 2011, www.deathpenaltyinfo.org/executions; "Executions [in] the U.S. 1608–2002: The ESPY File Executions by State," Death Penalty Information Center, 2011, www.deathpenaltyinfo.org/documents/ESPYstate.pdf.

7 Death Penalty Information Center, "Number of Executions by State and Re-

gion Since 1976," 29 September 2011, www.deathpenaltyinfo.org/number-executions-state-and-region-1976.

8 "Death Row Facts," Tennessee Department of Correction, 2011, www.tn.gov/correction/deathfacts.html.

9 "Bill Search," Tennessee General Assembly, http://wapp.capitol.tn.gov/apps/billsearch/billsearchadvancedarchive.aspx?terms=death%20penalty&searchtype=bills&ga=104.

10 Quoted in Associated Press, "Bills Seek to Reform Tenn.'s Death Penalty Process," Knoxnews.com, 20 February 2009, www.knoxnews.com/news/2009/feb/20/bills-seek-reform-tenns-death-penalty-process/.

11 William Redick, "Is Tennessee Going to Fix [the] Death Penalty?," Tennessee Bar Association, 2009, (www.tba.org/journal_new/index.php/component/content/article/333?ed=22), 5–6.

12 Ibid., 8.

13 Orben J. Casey, "Governor Lee Cruce, White Supremacy and Capital Punishment, 1911–1915," *Chronicles of Oklahoma* 52 (Winter 1974–75), 456–75; Gilbert Geis, "The Death Penalty in Oklahoma," *Proceedings of the Oklahoma Academy of Science* 34 (1953): 191–93 (http://digital.library.okstate.edu/oas/oas_pdf/v34/p191_193.pdf).

14 Casey, "Governor Lee Cruce," 462.

15 Ibid., 473.

16 Ibid., 474.

17 Robert Sobel and John Raimo, eds., *Biographical Directory of the Governors of the United States, 1789–1978* (Westport, CT: Meckler, 1978), 3:1242.

18 Quoted in Bobby Dean Smith, "Lee Cruce: Governor of Oklahoma, 1911–1915," in *Oklahoma's Governors, 1907–1929: Turbulent Politics*, ed. LeRoy H. Fischer (Oklahoma City: Oklahoma State Historical Society, 1981) 58.

19 "State Execution Rates," Death Penalty Information Center, 2011, www.deathpenaltyinfo.org/state-execution-rates.

20 "Death Row: Execution Statistics," Oklahoma Department of Corrections, 2011, www.doc.state.ok.us/offenders/death%20penalty.xls; "Searchable Execution Database."

21 "Searchable Execution Database."

22 "Executions in the U.S. 1608–2002."

23 "Our Opinion: Death Penalty Unfair, Must be Abolished," *Atlanta Journal-Constitution*, 27 September 2007.

24 "A Death Penalty Conversion," *Birmingham News*, 6 November 2005.

25 Nick Cenegy, "Sam Monk, Nearing Retirement, Sees Complexities of Death Penalty," *Anniston Star*, 17 December 2006.

26 Sister Helen Prejean, *Dead Man Walking* (New York: Vintage, 1992).

27 Sobel and Raimo, *Biographical Directory of the Governors of the United States*, 4:1442–43.

28 South Carolina, Office of the Governor, "Veto Message for S270, Governor John C. West," 1 July 1974.

29 Hugh E. Gibson, "Governor Vetoes Death Penalty Measure," *Charleston News and Courier*, 2 July 1974 (http://news.google.com/newspapers?id=15h JAAAAIBAJ&sjid=eAwNAAAAIBAJ&pg=1457%2C131628).

30 "House Restores Death Penalty," *Charleston News and Courier*, 3 July 1974 (http://news.google.com/newspapers?id=2JhJAAAAIBAJ&sjid=eAwNAAA AIBAJ&pg=4854%2C289223).

31 "Executions in the U.S. 1608–2002."

32 Quoted in Associated Press, "Reaction Mixed on West's Veto of Death Bill," *Charleston News and Courier*, 2 July 1974 (http://news.google.com/newspapers ?nid=00eUc68sgesC&dat=19740702&printsec=frontpage&hl=en).

33 Quoted in ibid.

34 Quoted in "House Restores Death Penalty,"1.

35 Quoted in ibid.

36 Quoted in United Press International, "Edwards: Shorten Sessions," *Charleston News and Courier*, 5 June 1974 (http://news.google.com/newspapers?id =pZRJAAAAIBAJ&sjid=ZwwNAAAAIBAJ&dq=william%20westmoreland %20law-and-order&pg=4493%2C937652).

37 "Death Row/Capital Punishment: Executions in South Carolina," South Carolina Department of Corrections, 2011, www.doc.sc.gov/news/deathrow .jsp; "Executions [in] the U.S. 1608–2002"; "Searchable Execution Database."

38 Death Penalty Information Center, "Number of Executions by State and Region Since 1976."

39 Matthew Isley, "Senate Supports Death Penalty Pause," *News & Observer*, 1 May 2003.

40 "Death Penalty Doubts," *News & Observer*, 1 May 2003.

41 Matthew Isley, "Bar Will Back Execution Moratorium," *News & Observer*, 1 July 2003.

42 "Legislators Influenced by Tragedies," *News & Observer*, 5 May 2003.

43 Paul Woolverton, "Execution Objections on Rise," *Fayetteville Observer*, 26 February 2006.

44 General Assembly of North Carolina, Session 2009, Session Law 2009–464, Senate Bill 461 (www.ncleg.net/EnactedLegislation/SessionLaws/PDF/2009-2010/SL2009-464.pdf).

45 "Executions in the U.S. 1608–2002."

46 "Executions Carried Out under Current Death Penalty Statute," North

Carolina Department of Correction, 2010, www.doc.state.nc.us/dop/deathpenalty/executed.htm; "Searchable Execution Database."

47 Death Penalty Information Center, "Number of Executions by State and Region Since 1976."

48 "Persons Removed from Death Row since North Carolina's Death Penalty Was Reinstated in 1977," North Carolina Department of Correction, 2011, www.doc.state.nc.us/DOP/deathpenalty/removed.htm.

49 "Offenders on Death Row," North Carolina Department of Correction, 2011, www.doc.state.nc.us/DOP/deathpenalty/deathrow.htm.

50 Michael L. Radelet and Glenn L. Pierce, "Race and Death Sentencing in North Carolina, 1980–2007," *North Carolina Law Review* 89, no. 6 (2011).

51 "Across Sessions: Bills and Resolutions Searchable Database," Virginia's Legislative Information System, 2011, http://lis.virginia.gov/000/sab.htm.

52 Ibid.

53 Larry O'Dell, "Converted Conservative Fights State Death Penalty," *Free Lance-Star*, 22 January 2001 (http://news.google.com/newspapers?id=Vuwy AAAAIBAJ&sjid=cQgGAAAAIBAJ&pg=5262,5265120&dq=frank+hargrove +death+penalty&hl=en).

54 Virginia State Legislature, 2001, http://legl.state.va.us.

55 Frank Green, "Two Death Penalty Bills Introduced; Jury Instructions, Moratorium Are Targets," *Richmond Times Dispatch*, 29 December 2000.

56 Frank Green, "Votes Kill Bills to Foil Death Penalty," *Richmond Times-Dispatch*, 2 February 2001.

57 Alberta Lindsey, "Stand against Death Penalty Reaffirmed; 'It Degrades Us as a Society,' Episcopalian Contends," *Richmond Times-Dispatch*, 19 February 2001.

58 Alberta Lindsey, "Death Penalty Abolition Urged," *Richmond Times-Dispatch*, 17 January 2001.

59 "2001 Session: HB 1827 Death Penalty," Virginia's Legislative Information System, 2011, http://lis.virginia.gov/cgi-bin/legp604.exe?011+vot+H08V0 196+HB1827. See also Green, "Votes Kill Bills to Foil Death Penalty"; "Virginians for Alternatives to the Death Penalty, Spring 2001 VADP Bi-Annual Meeting, The Next Step," www.vadp.org/nlspring01.html.

60 "Searchable Execution Database"; "Executions [in] the U.S. 1608–2002."

61 "Virginia Death Penalty Information: History of the Death Penalty in Virginia," Virginians for Alternatives to the Death Penalty, 2011, www.vadp .org/virginia-death-penalty-facts.html.

62 "State Execution Rates."

63 "Facts about the Death Penalty: Number of Executions by State since

1976," Death Penalty Information Center, 2011, www.deathpenaltyinfo.org/documents/FactSheet.pdf.

64 "Database: Virginia Executions, 1982-Present," *Washington Post*, www.washingtonpost.com/wp-srv/metro/data/vaexecutionsdb_02142011.html?appSession=300218993848968.

65 "Death Penalty Foes Plan Rally," *Richmond Times-Dispatch*, 17 January 2001.

66 Sarah E. Torian, "Could the Death Penalty Die in Virginia? Opportunities for Activism," *Journal of the Southern Regional Council* 23, no. 1 (2001: 15–16.)

67 Bob Lewis, "Ads in Virginia Gubernatorial Race Invoke Hitler in Death Penalty Dispute," Associated Press, 14 October 2005.

68 Chris L. Jenkins, "Kaine Calls Opponent's Ads 'Egregious Misrepresentation'; Kilgore Defends Accuracy of Death Penalty Claims," *Washington Post*, 14 October 2005.

69 William C. Flook, "Execution Puts Va. Sen. Webb in an Uneasy Political Position," *Washington Examiner*, 28 May 2008 (http://washingtonexaminer.com/local/execution-puts-va-sen-webb-uneasy-political-position).

70 "Bills & Resolutions," Virginia's Legislative Information System, 2011, http://lis.virginia.gov/lis.htm.

71 "2010 General Assembly Death Penalty Vote Tracker," Virginians for Alternatives to the Death Penalty, 2011, www.vadp.org/images/2010%20vote%20tracker%20complete.pdf.

72 Death Penalty Information Center, "Number of Executions by State and Region Since 1976."

73 "State by State Database"; "Executions [in] the U.S. 1608–2002."

74 "Executions [in] the U.S. 1608–2002"; "Searchable Execution Database."

75 "Sentences Imposed: Complete Downloadable List of All Death Sentences Imposed since November 1976 (Excel Spreadsheet)," Mississippi Office of Capital Defense Counsel, 2011, http://capdefcounsel.com/sentences.aspx.

76 "Mississippi and the Death Penalty," Mississippi Department of Corrections, 2011, www.mdoc.state.ms.us/mississippi_and_the_death_penalt.htm.

77 "Sentences Imposed."

78 John Mayo, Mississippi State Representative, telephone interview with Larry W. Koch, 23 March 2011.

79 "Clergy, Others Speak against Death Penalty," *Jackson Clarion-Ledger*, 17 January 2001.

80 Mayo interview.

81 Louwlynn Williams, attorney with the Mississippi Office of Capital Post-Conviction Counsel, telephone interview with Larry W. Koch, 23 March 2011.

82 Valena Beety, "[Beety] the Cost of Death," *Jackson Free Press*, 14 July 2010

(www.jacksonfreepress.com/index.php/site/comments/beety_the_cost_of_death_071410/).

83 Anthony Doss v. State of Mississippi, 2008 WL 5174209 (Miss.).

84 929 Quitman County v. State of Mississippi, 910 So.2d 1032, 1052 (Miss. 2005); Stephen Henderson, "Defense Often Inadequate in 4 Death-Penalty States," *McClatchy*, 4 September 2007 (www.mcclatchydc.com/2007/01/16/15394/defense-often-inadequate-in-4.html).

85 Williams interview.

86 "Mississippi Death Penalty Fact Sheet, (10/20/2010)," Mississippi Office of Capital Defense Counsel, 2011, http://capdefcounsel.com/Documents/death%20penalty%20fact%20sheet%2010.10.pdf.

87 James S. Liebman, Jeffrey Fagan, and Valerie West, "A Broken System: Error Rates in Capital Cases, 1973–1995" (New York: Columbia Law School, 12 June 2000; www.jaycesi.com/files/error-rates.pdf.

88 Associated Press, "Judge Finds Mississippi's Death Row Conditions Violate Eighth Amendment," Death Penalty Information Center, 2011, www.deathpenaltyinfo.org/node/826.

89 Larry Binz, "Mayo Dismayed by the Last Killing at Parchman's '32," *Clarksdale Press Register*, 29 July 2007, www.pressregister.com/articles/2007/07/28/import/20070728-archive.txt.

90 Beety, "[Beety] the Cost of Death."

91 Death Penalty Information Center, "Number of Executions by State and Region Since 1976."

92 "Searchable Execution Database."

93 "Executions in the U.S. 1608–2002."

94 "Hudson Seeking Fourth Term for District 33-C Position," *Dallas Morning News*, 6 April 1978.

95 "Chairman to Consider Hudson's Bills," *Dallas Times-Herald*, 14 April 1977.

96 "Hudson Porker No Pig in a Poke," *Austin American-Statesman*, 31 May 1977.

97 "'Fast Sambo' Finally Ends Foodless Protest," *Dallas Morning News*, 31 May 1977.

98 "Rep. Hudson Pre-Files 67 Bills in Texas House," *Dallas Times-Herald*, 20 December 1978.

99 "One of the Poor Folk," *Dallas Morning News*, 12 May 1981.

100 "He Doesn't Mind Letting His Bills Stack Up," *Houston Post*, 8 March 1981.

101 "Hudson Keeps Plugging Despite Setbacks," *Dallas Morning News*, 7 May 1981.

102 "Rep. Hudson to Face Probe," *Dallas Times-Herald*, 4 July 1976.

103 "Suit Seeks to Stop Attorney's Reprimand," *Dallas Times-Herald*, 7 January 1977.

104 "One Hour Late, Hudson Fined, Given a Day in Jail," *Austin American-Statesman*, 25 August 1977.

105 Paul M. Barrett, "On the Defense: Lawyer's Fast Work on Death Cases Raises Doubt about System," *Wall Street Journal*, 7 September 1994.

106 Dotty Griffith, "Hudson Faces $11,000 Debt Total," *Dallas Morning News*, 23 April 1977.

107 "Hudson's Home to Be Auctioned," *Dallas Times-Herald*, 8 June 1978.

108 "Hudson Says Debts Help Him to 'Relate,'" *Dallas Morning News*, 5 April 1980.

109 "Suit Charges Lawmaker Failed to File Tax Return," *Dallas Times-Herald*, 27 June 1984.

110 Paul Burka, Alison Cook, and Kaye Northcott, "The Ten Best and the Ten Worst Legislators," *Texas Monthly*, July 1983 (www.texasmonthly.com/1983–07-01/feature6–7.php); Paul Burka and Alison Cook, "The Ten Best and (Groan) the Ten Worst Legislators," *Texas Monthly*, July 1985 (www.texas monthly.com/1985–07-01/feature4.php).

111 "Texas Lawmakers Praise 'Grumpy, Mean' Moreno," *El Paso Times*, 26 April 1991.

112 "Moreno Relished Maverick, Gadfly Role," *El Paso Times*, 29 March 1987.

113 Quoted in Bruce Hight, "Life without Parole Bill is Rejected," *Austin American-Statesman*, 15 May 2001.

114 Quoted in Nancy San Martin, "Under His Watchful Eye," *Dallas Morning News*, 9 April 2001.

115 Ibid.

116 "After 3 Decades, 3 Public Figures Need Their Report Cards," *El Paso Times*, 5 March 1996; "Power in the House," *El Paso Times*, 2 February 2002.

117 "Moreno Should Focus on City Instead of Calling for Boycott," *El Paso Times*, 3 August 1994.

118 Herbert H. Haines, *Against Capital Punishment: The Anti-Death Penalty Movement in America, 1972–1994* (New York: Oxford University Press, 1996).

119 Quoted in Lee Hockstader, "Texas Shrugs off Debate on Executions," *Washington Post*, 22 September 2002.

120 "Bills to Abolish Death Penalty to Be Heard by Subcommittee March 12 in Texas Legislature," Texas Moratorium Network, March 6, 2009, http://stopexecutions.blogspot.com/2009/03/bills-to-abolish-death-penalty-to-be.html.

121 "Update on Death Penalty Bills Filed in Texas Legislature," Texas Moratorium Network, 31 January 2009, http://stopexecutions.blogspot.com/2009/01/update-on-death-penalty-bills-filed-in.html.

122 "Texas House Bill 819 to Receive Hearing: House Committee Set to Hear

Repeal Bill," Texas Coalition to Abolish the Death Penalty, 25 March 2011, http://tcadp.org/2011/03/25/texas-house-bill-819-to-receive-hearing/.

123 Quoted in Peter Slevin, "More in U.S. Expressing Doubts about Death Penalty," *Washington Post*, 2 December 2005.

124 "Anthony Graves Becomes 12th Death Row Inmate Exonerated in Texas," Death Penalty Information Center, 2011, www.deathpenaltyinfo.org/ anthony-graves-becomes-12th-death-row-inmate-exonerated-texas.

125 Quoted in ibid.

126 "The Death Penalty: It's Time for Capital Punishment to Become Texas History," *Houston Chronicle*, 1 January 2011 (www.chron.com/disp/story.mpl/ editorial/7362050.html); Steven Kreypac, "Judge OKs Hearing on Willingham Execution," *Dallas Morning News*, 28 September 2010 (www.dallasnews .com/news/community-news/tarrant-county/headlines/20100927-Judge-OKs-hearing-on-Willingham-execution-5611.ece); Dave Mann, "DNA Tests Undermine Evidence in Texas Execution," *Texas Observer*, 11 November 2010 (www.texasobserver.org/cover-story/texas-observer-exclusive-dna-tests-undermine-evidence-in-texas-execution).

127 "Perry Move Delays Death Penalty Probe," UPI.com, 30 September 2009 (www.upi.com/Top_News/2009/09/30/Perry-move-delays-death-penalty-probe/UPI-72411254367009/).

128 Chris McGreal, "Texas Accounts for Half of Executions in US But Now Has Doubts over Death Row," Guardian.co.uk, 15 November 2009 (www.guardian .co.uk/world/2009/nov/15/texas-death-penalty-execution-us).

129 Juan A. Lozano, "Prosecution Stands Mute at Death Penalty Hearing," Associated Press, 6 December 2010.

130 "Death Penalty Debate Should Start, Not End," *Fort Worth Star-Telegram*, 15 January 2011 (www.star-telegram.com/2011/01/15/2770547/death-penalty-debate-should-start.html).

131 Ibid.

132 "Gender and Racial Statistics of Death Row Offenders," Texas Department of Criminal Justice, 2011, www.tdcj.state.tx.us/stat/racial.htm.

133 Death Penalty Information Center, "Number of Executions by State and Region Since 1976."

11. SUMMARY AND CONCLUSION

1 "State Execution Rates," Death Penalty Information Center, 2011, www .deathpenaltyinfo.org/state-execution-rates.

2 481 U.S. 279, 107 S.Ct. 1756, 95 L.Ed.2d 262, v.

3 "State & County QuickFacts: New Mexico," Census Bureau, 2009, http:// quickfacts.census.gov/qfd/states/35000.html.

4 David Garland, *Peculiar Institution: America's Death Penalty in an Age of Abolition* (Cambridge: The Belknap Press of Harvard University Press, 2010).

5 Thomas C. Castellano and Edmund F. McGarrell, "The Politics of Law and Order: Case Study Evidence for a Conflict Model of the Criminal Law Formation Process," *Journal of Research in Crime and Delinquency* 28, no. 2 (1991): 304–329; Edmund F. McGarrell and Thomas C. Castellano, "An Integrative Conflict Model of the Criminal Law Formation Process," *Journal of Research in Crime and Delinquency* 28, no. 2 (1991): 174–96; Edmund F. McGarrell and Thomas C. Castellano, "Social Structure, Crime and Politics: A Conflict Model of the Criminal Law Formation Process," in *Making Law: The State, the Law, and Structural Contradictions*, ed. William J. Chambliss and Marjorie S. Zatz (Bloomington: Indiana University Press, 1993), 347–78.

6 Glenn L. Pierce and Michael L. Radelet, "The Role and Consequences of the Death Penalty in American Politics," *New York University Review of Law and Social Change* 18 (1990–91): 722.

7 Robert M. Bohm, "American Death Penalty Opinion, 1936–1986: A Critical Examination of the Gallup Polls," in *The Death Penalty in America: Current Research*, ed. Robert M. Bohm (Cincinnati, OH: Anderson, 1991), 113–45.

8 Herbert H. Haines, *Against Capital Punishment: The Anti-Death Penalty Movement in America, 1972–1994* (New York: Oxford University Press, 1996), 54; Franklin E. Zimring and Gordon Hawkins, *Capital Punishment and the American Agenda* (Cambridge: Cambridge University Press, 1986), 66.

9 Haines, *Against Capital Punishment*, 54.

10 William J. Bowers, "Capital Punishment and Contemporary Values: People's Misgivings and the Court's Misperceptions," *Law and Society Review* 27 (1993):157–75.

11 "In U.S., 64% Support Death Penalty in Cases of Murder," 8 November 2010, www.gallup.com/poll/144284/Support-Death-Penalty-Cases-Murder.aspx; Bowers, "Capital Punishment and Contemporary Values"; Edmund F. McGarrell and Mala Sandys, "The Misperception of Public Opinion toward Capital Punishment," *American Behavioral Scientist* 39 (February 1996): 500–513.

12 John F. Galliher and Linda Basilick, "Utah's Liberal Drug Laws: Structural Foundations and Triggering Events," *Social Problems* 26, no. 3 (1979): 284–97; McGarrell and Castellano, "Social Structure, Crime and Politics"; James W. Marquart, Sheldon Ekland-Olson, and Jonathan R. Sorensen, *The Rope, the Chair, and the Needle: Capital Punishment in Texas, 1923–1990* (Austin: University of Texas Press, 1994).

13 McGarrell and Castellano, "Social Structure, Crime and Politics," 353.

14 Larry W. Koch and John F. Galliher, "Michigan's Continuing Abolition of the Death Penalty and the Conceptual Components of Symbolic Legislation," *Social and Legal Studies* 2 (1993): 323–46.

15 Galliher and Basilick, "Utah's Liberal Drug Laws."

16 McGarrell and Castellano, "Social Structure, Crime and Politics," 349.

17 Ibid.

18 Koch and Galliher, "Michigan's Continuing Abolition of the Death Penalty."

19 United Press International, "Episcopal Church Opens Drive for Abolition of Death Penalty," *New York Times*, 20 March 1961; James M. Galliher and John F. Galliher, "A 'Commonsense' Theory of Deterrence and the 'Ideology' of Science: The New York State Death Penalty Debate," *Journal of Criminal Law and Criminology* 92, no. 2 (2002): 307–33.

20 Hugo Adam Bedau, author of numerous books and articles on the death penalty, interview with John F. Galliher, 2009.

21 Sister Helen Prejean, *The Death of Innocents: An Eyewitness Account of Wrongful Executions* (New York: Random House, 2005), 116.

22 410 U.S. 113 (1973).

23 Timothy A. Byrnes, "How Seamless a Garment? The Catholic Bishops and the Politics of Abortion," *Journal of Church and State* 33, no. 1 (1991): 18–35; James R. Kelly, "Sociology and Public Theology: A Case-Study of Pro-Choice/Pro-Life Common Ground," *Sociology of Religion* 60 (1999): 99–124.

24 Joseph Cardinal Bernardin, "A Consistent Ethic of Life: Continuing the Dialogue," lecture at St. Louis University, St. Louis, MO, 11 March 1984 (www .priestsforlife.org/magisterium/bernardinwade.html).

25 "Catholic Campaign to End Use of the Death Penalty: Statements on the Death Penalty by the Holy Father," United States Conference of Catholic Bishops, 2011, www.usccb.org/sdwp/national/deathpenalty/holyfather.shtml.

26 Thoroddur Bjarnson and Michael R. Welch, "Father Knows Best: Parishes, Priests and American Catholic Parishioners' Attitudes toward Capital Punishment," *Journal for the Scientific Study of Religion* 43, no. 1 (2004): 103–18.

27 Pew Forum on Religion and Public Life, "Public Opinion on the Death Penalty," 23 September 2011, http://pewforum.org/Death-Penalty/Public-Opinion-on-the-Death-Penalty.aspx; Kathleen Maguire and Ann L. Pastore, eds., *Sourcebook of Criminal Justice Statistics* (Washington: Government Printing Office, 2002).

28 State v. William H. Anthony, 121 R.I. 954, 398 A.2d 1157 (1979); State v. Robert Cline, 121 R.I. 299, 397 A.2d 1309 (1979).

29 "Catholic States (1980)," Association of Religious Data Archives, Social Science Research Institute, Pennsylvania State University, www.thearda.com/ QuickLists/QuickList_60.asp.

30 Commonwealth v. Robert E. O'Neal, 369 Mass 242, 339 N.E.2d 676 (1975); District Attorney for the Suffolk District v. James Watson and others, 381 Mass 648, 411 N.E.2d 1274 (1980); Commonwealth v. Abimael Colon-Cruz, 393 Mass 150, 470 N.E.2d 116 (1984).

31 "Catholic States (1980)."

32 People v. Stephen S. Lavalle, 3 N.Y. 3d 88, 817 N.E. 2d 341, 783 N.Y.S. 2d 485 (2004); Galliher and Galliher, "A 'Commonsense' Theory of Deterrence."

33 Barry A. Kosmin and Ariela Keysar, "American Religious Identification Survey: [Aris 2008]: Summary Report" (Hartford, CT: Trinity College, March 2009; www.americanreligionsurvey-aris.org/reports/ARIS_Report_2008 .pdf).

34 "State by State Database," Death Penalty Information Center, 2011, www .deathpenaltyinfo.org/state_by_state.

35 "Catholic States (2000)," Association of Religious Data Archives, Social Science Research Institute, Pennsylvania State University, www.thearda.com/ QuickLists/QuickList_58.asp.

36 Marquart, Ekland-Olson, and Sorenson, *The Rope, the Chair, and the Needle.*

37 Zimring and Hawkins, *Capital Punishment and the American Agenda*, 144.

38 William J. Bowers, *Legal Homicide: Death as Punishment in America, 1864–1982* (Boston: Northeastern University Press, 1984), 278.

39 Franklin E. Zimring, "The Wages of Ambivalence: On the Context and Prospects of New York's Death Penalty," *Buffalo Law Review* 44 (Spring 1996): 303–23.

40 Ibid., 317.

41 Robert Weisberg, "The New York Statute as Cultural Document: Seeking the Morally Optimal Death Penalty," *Buffalo Law Review* 44 (Spring 1996): 283–302.

42 Zimring, "The Wages of Ambivalence," 318.

43 Joseph R. Gusfield, *Symbolic Crusade: Status Politics and the American Temperance Movement* (Urbana: University of Illinois Press, 1963).

44 John F. Galliher, Gregory Ray, and Brent Cook, "Abolition and Reinstatement of Capital Punishment during the Progressive Era and Early 20th Century," *Journal of Criminal law and Criminology* 83, no. 3 (1992): 538–76.

45 Koch and Galliher, "Michigan's Continuing Abolition of the Death Penalty."

46 John F. Galliher, Larry W. Koch, David Patrick Keys, and Teresa J. Guess, *America without the Death Penalty: States Leading the Way* (Boston: Northeastern University Press, 2002), 1–280.

47 Patrick T. Conley, "Death Knell for the Death Penalty: The Gordon Murder Trial and Rhode Island's Abolition of Capital Punishment," *Rhode Island Bar Journal* 34 (May 1986): 11–15.

48 Richard Acton, "The Magic of Undiscouraged Effort: The Death Penalty in Iowa," *Annals of Iowa* 50 (Winter 1991): 721–50.

49 Edward Schriver, "The Reluctant Hangman: The State of Maine and Capital Punishment," *New England Quarterly* 63 (1990): 271–87.

50 Koch and Galliher, "Michigan's Continuing Abolition of the Death Penalty."

51 "Facts about the Death Penalty," Death Penalty Information Center, 2011, www.deathpenaltyinfo.org/documents/FactSheet.pdf.

52 Hugo Adam Bedau, *The Death Penalty in America*, 3rd ed. (Chicago: Aldine, 1982), 69.

53 Weisberg, "The New York Statute as Cultural Document."

54 Garland, *Peculiar Institution*.

55 Gregg v. Georgia, 428 U.S. 153 (1976).

56 Bohm, "American Death Penalty Opinion."

57 Hugo Adam Bedau, "Challenging the Death Penalty," *Harvard Civil Rights-Civil Liberties Law Review* 9 (May 1974): 643.

58 William J. Bowers, *Executions in America* (Lexington, MA: Lexington Books, 1974), 29.

59 Zimring and Hawkins, *Capital Punishment and the American Agenda*, 157.

60 Emile Durkheim, *The Division of Labor in Society* (New York: Free Press, 1984).

61 "Executions by Year since 1976," Death Penalty Information Center, 2011, www.deathpenaltyinfo.org/executions-year.

62 Bedau, *The Death Penalty in America*, 22.

63 Garland, *Peculiar Institution*, 288–89.

64 David Atwood, president of the Texas Coalition to Abolish the Death Penalty, e-mail message to Larry Koch, 1 February 2004.

65 Garland, *Peculiar Institution*, 253.

66 "Catholic States (2000)."

67 Michael B. Farrell, "As Latinos Tilt Democratic, Can Texas Stay Red?," *Christian Science Monitor*, 25 November 2008 (www.csmonitor.com/USA/Politics/2008/1125/as-latinos-tilt-democratic-can-texas-stay-red).

68 Franklin E. Zimring, *The Contradictions of Capital Punishment* (New York: Oxford University Press, 2003), x.

Index